Frank Sutcliffe
Photographer of Whitby

Frank Sutcliffe in his seventies.

Frank Sutcliffe

Photographer of Whitby

MICHAEL HILEY

 Phillimore

First published in 1974 by the Gordon Fraser Gallery Ltd
Second edition published 2005 by Phillimore
This paperback edition published 2022

The History Press
97 St George's Place, Cheltenham,
Gloucestershire, GL50 3QB
www.thehistorypress.co.uk

British Library Cataloguing in Publication Data.
A catalogue record for this book is available from the British Library.

ISBN 978 1 8039 9003 3

Printed and bound in Great Britain by TJ Books Limited, Padstow, Cornwall.

Trees for Life

dedication

This one's for Robin

Contents

List of Illustrations and Acknowledgements

Acknowledgements

I would like to record my thanks to various members of the Sutcliffe family for their help, in particular the late Miss Kathleen Corner, whose hospitality made each visit to Whitby a pleasure and whose information about the Sutcliffe family was invaluable. I also received help from the late Marquis of Normanby, the late Mr H. A. Lambert Smith, the late Mr Lionel Horne of the Whitby Gazette, and various officials of the Whitby Literary and Philosophical Society. The staff of Birmingham Central Library, the British Library Newspaper Library, Colindale, London, and Leicester University Library made the task of research easier by their helpfulness and efficiency.

In particular, my thanks go to the late Bill Eglon Shaw of the Sutcliffe Gallery, Whitby, without whose help this book could not have been written. His knowledge of the collection of the Sutcliffe negatives at Whitby was unrivalled, and his own experience as a professional photographer provided me with many insights into Sutcliffe's photographs and his methods of working; in addition, his very extensive knowledge of the Whitby area proved invaluable. Sutcliffe's photographs made Whitby at the beginning of the 20th century 'The Photographer's Mecca'. I hope that if this book stimulates readers to see Whitby and Eskdale today, they will make a modern pilgrimage to the Sutcliffe Gallery in Flowergate. Sutcliffe would be proud of this gallery established by Bill Eglon Shaw, where, under the guidance of his son Mike Shaw the Gallery still produces superb modern prints from Sutcliffe's original negatives—including those from which the plates for this book were made. These photographs are reproduced by courtesy of the Sutcliffe Gallery, Whitby, by agreement with the Whitby Literary and Philosophical Society.

Michael Hiley
Leicester
April 2022

Introduction

Frank Sutcliffe was one of the first men to devote his whole life and creative energy to photography. His father was a painter but Frank made the decision to move away from traditional picture-making skills and to explore the new technology. Sutcliffe's working life as a photographer spans from the 19th century to the 20th, and to trace his career is not only to view a prospect of Whitby as it was in his lifetime, but also to follow photography from the days of the wet-plate process and portable developing tent, when exposure times were anything from a few seconds to a few minutes, to the Kodak era of the instantaneous snapshot.

Sutcliffe built up a very successful photographic business in Whitby. He took portraits of holidaymakers who had come to visit the town, but he also produced photographs which were exhibited around the world. In the 1890s and early 1900s if you were to pick up any photographic journal—many of them encouraged a creative approach to photography—you would be likely to find an article or a photograph by Sutcliffe.

So it was Whitby's good fortune that so much of Sutcliffe's energy went into photographing the town which he knew for over eighty years. It is through his camera that we can see his vision of an area which he loved to photograph a century ago. His perceptive observations of people in their community and his sensitive renderings of the delicate light effects which transformed 'ordinary' scenes still give pleasure today and provide an extraordinary blend of record and of personal interpretation. This is Sutcliffe's view of Whitby, and the everyday heroes and heroines he shows are the people of the town.

A brochure on sea-fishing published at the time when Sutcliffe was working stated: 'Those visitors who fish off Whitby in September will, if unaccustomed to such a spectacle, be interested by the sight of fine salmon, up to 12 and 15lb., leaping in the sea close to their boat as it approaches the harbour after a day's fishing.' To someone like myself who has lived in a city all his life Whitby has always seemed a magical place full of surprises and full of history. To Sutcliffe it held endless fascination. His photographic skills enabled him to convert what he felt about Whitby and the countryside around—the feelings he carried inside himself from the time he came from smoky Leeds as a child to first see the coast—into a visual tribute which goes far beyond mere documentary recording.

chapter 1

Childhood

'FRANK MEADOW SUTCLIFFE was born of one humble and one proud parent at Headingley on the sixth of October, Anno Domini 1853. The greater part of his youth was spent in his father's studio, and on the wilds of Yorkshire, which accounts for the savageness of his nature, and the small size of his feet.'[1]

So begins an autobiographical note which Frank Sutcliffe contributed to a book published in his old age. The wry touch of humour gives a glimpse of a character which was both forceful and unhampered by the inflexibility of a conventional outlook upon life. He was no rebel—in fact 'savageness' was completely alien to his nature—but his approach to life and to photography was governed by a personality which both refused to take things too seriously, and yet at the same time concealed an ambitious, perfectionist streak which saw him through early family tragedy and personal disaster, and lifted him to the heights of success in his chosen field—photography.

The Sutcliffe family was an exceptional one. Frank's grandfather, Joshua Sutcliffe, was born in Bradford in 1786 and was brought up to live the life of a leisured gentleman; but although he 'hadn't been brought up to work', he ran away from home when he was a youth and got himself a job with a wine merchant, which involved him in the buying of wines. He became expert at this and could sample his sherries merely by smelling at them. Striking out on his own, he bought the *Leeds Arms* in West Street, just off Leeds city centre, and the three owlets on the inn sign which showed the Leeds coat of arms earned him the family nickname 'Jossy Hullarts'. He was a cut above most public house keepers, and the city directories from 1826 on list him as a victualler and wine and spirit dealer. He was friendly with Joshua Tetley and his family, who had just taken over the brewery in Salem Place, Hunslet Lane. His social status was further enhanced by his marriage to a relation of the Marquis of Ripon— Elizabeth Robinson, daughter of a former Lord Mayor of York. This could be called a marriage of convenience, as it was rumoured that she 'drank like a fish'.

Out of Joshua Sutcliffe's family of ten children, only four survived childhood, and the youngest of them, named Thomas, was born on 5 April 1828. What prompted him to take up a career as a painter is not known, though it seems that Thomas was not the first artist in the family. As he said himself: 'Painting and preaching have run on in our family for several hundred years; if you don't believe it ask the Moravians.' This link with the Moravian Church—or United Brethren—is obscure. Thomas and his family seem to have been Anglicans, though shades of one of the doctrines of the Moravians—that of the universal depravity of man—are occasionally seen in Thomas's sketching notebooks. On one visit to Hull he observed that 'as a rule these little public houses are an unspeakable evil and the hot beds of all that is wrong.' What his father thought of these views is not recorded.

Joshua must have been both an understanding father and well-to-do, as he not only let Thomas take up painting, but also was able to send him to study at the Royal Academy Schools in London. He returned to Leeds and in 1852 married Sarah Lorentia Button, whose father was a dispenser of medicines. They moved out of the centre of the city—which was rapidly expanding during this period— and set up house at Far Headingley, which at that time was in the countryside. There Sarah gave birth to a son on 6 October 1853, who was christened Francis

Meadow Sutcliffe; but everyone called him Frank, and never Francis. After him came two brothers and five sisters, and the rural theme, touched on when Frank was given the unusual middle name Meadow, was sounded again in several of their names—Kate Harebell, Lily, Annie Heather, Glen and Jessamine (Jasmine).

Frank's father Thomas was to have a very strong influence upon his eldest son; indeed many of Frank's characteristics—his boundless enthusiasm, his dogged perseverance and his sense of humour—can be traced back to his father. After Thomas's death, a friend described him as

> a man of very extraordinary attainments, indeed, he was one of those men of whom it might truly be said 'Nihil tetigit quod non ornavit,'—his artworking was not confined to painting in oil and water colour, in both of which mediums he was an expert, but he was equally at home in lithography, in etching, when etching was not the fashion that it now is, in practical printing of both lithographs and etchings, for each of which he had complete apparatus in his studio, in photography, the great future of which he foresaw, and to the artistic development of which he gave much time and thought; but perhaps his greatest power was as an artistic analyst, and those who had the privilege of hearing his lectures … left the lecture room after an evening spent in laughter, with their store of Art knowledge incredibly increased—they hardly knew how—it had been so humourously but incisively poured into them.[2]

From his birth Frank lived in the midst of his father's artistic activities. He slept in a little bed in his father's studio, and surrounding him, instead of nursery animals, were plaster casts of pieces of classical sculpture. His father had bought one hundred pounds-worth of plaster casts at Brucciani's—who shipped them from Italy—of all the most famous Venuses and Apollos, and there was nowhere else in the house to put them. The studio was a place of unending fascination to the young boy.

For the entertainment of his children and friends, Thomas built a diorama—a form of miniature theatre with dramatic lighting effects—in one corner of his studio, painting all the scenery himself. This first effort, which was about four feet square, was soon supplanted by a much bigger one, which stretched right across one end of the studio, some ten or twelve feet from wing to wing. To Frank, these were a delight:

> Across the stage of these dioramas, figures of all kinds passed to say nothing of snowstorms, and shipwrecks, accompanied by thunder and lightening [sic]. The proudest moment in my life was when I was allowed behind the scenes to shake the sheets of tin which made the thunder, while my father turned the gas on and off quickly to make the lightning, while an artist friend passed the tempest-rocked ships slowly and fitfully across the stage between painted seas which lifted. These ships, though only built in profile, were wonderfully rigged, and their ropes and stays and halyards all correctly done in black thread. One scene, of which I never tired, represented the fable of the old man and the ass, and when the old man and his sons allowed their burden to fall into the river as they carried it over a cardboard bridge, I always screamed with delight when I heard a piece of wood, substituted for the cardboard ass, fall into a pail of water placed under the stage for the purpose.[3]

Thomas encouraged his children to use his studio printing apparatus. The letter heading of Frank's letter to his brother Horace illustrated here was printed on the lithographic press. More ambitious were small books of stories written by Thomas under the pseudonym 'Jossy Hullarts' and illustrated by him and the children. The whole of the printing of these was done by the children—the typesetting, printing of illustrations and binding. One of them was called *The Little Boy and the Big Bottle* and, in professional fashion, carries the imprint on the title page: 'Published by Harebell and Horace Sutcliffe, Headingley, 1869,' and on the reverse, 'Printed at the Studio Press, by F. M. Sutcliffe'. Also included is a note received by the publishers: 'Please, father didn't do *all* the pictures, *I* did some. from—ME. Little ANNIE.' Annie was six at the time, and after such a stimulating childhood it is not surprising that she took up painting and was to exhibit at the Royal Academy thirty years later.

Frank looked back to his childhood as a very happy and creative period:

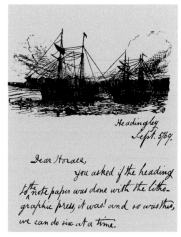

Letter heading printed on their father's lithographic press by the Sutcliffe children.

> Half my childhood was spent in running up or down narrow lanes only wide enough for one carriage … Yes, it was a delightful existence … The boy who has lived a country life and whose eyes and ears are open to every movement in hedge or bank or tree, is much more likely to have his eyes all round him than one who has lived among tramcars and smoke.[4]

His formal education was not extensive. He started at a dame's school kept by a Miss Riley, who combined teaching with her household cooking, with the result that the pots and pans were constantly boiling over, producing a penetrating odour which became known as 'Miss Riley's Smell'. From here he went to a school run by a Dr Brewer, but this made little impression on him. His informal education was more practical and inventive than anything the rigidly disciplined schools of his time could have provided. He made a collection of different varieties of seeds. He was fond of geometry, but for practical reasons:

> When not out of doors my childhood was spent with tiles and bricks. This I believe was a capital education. Give a child a heap of squares and triangles, and let him puzzle with them till he makes a picture or at least an ornamental design. He will not be at a loss to know how to place a group of figures afterwards.[5]

This is not the only instance of an early interest in visual problems which would confront him later as a photographer. One piece of the magic world of the child which stayed with him throughout his life and made an obvious impact upon his work as a photographer was his love of fog, which embraces and transforms familiar scenes and commonplace objects:

> I shall never forget the delight which we used to feel, as children, when the yellow fog crept up towards the house we lived in, from the manufacturing town below, on a winter's afternoon, hiding one house after another, and one lamppost and then another, till only those close to us could be seen; how unreal too did the people seem as they suddenly appeared and disappeared again. How we used to run round familiar squares and by-streets, which seemed, when enveloped in the fog, like fairy land to us. Then we were never

tired of making pictures of the fog. A sheet of tissue paper was invariably turned into a foggy landscape; on a piece of white paper we would paint, in the blackest Indian ink we could find, houses and churches; then over this we would stick a piece of tissue paper, then paint on this nearer houses and lampposts, then another piece of tissue paper, and so on till the drawings on the first ground were almost lost in the fog.[6]

These Leeds fogs must have been laden with smoke from factory chimneys, for they were yellow and affected everyone's eyes and noses. The Whitby fogs which he was to photograph came rolling in from the North Sea and were not yellow, but full of delicate blues, and greens and pinks. But the children's game in copying the effects of the Leeds fog foreshadows many of the later Whitby photographs. Many of the characteristic elements are already there; one only has to replace the Indian ink outline with the outline of Whitby houses, or the Abbey above Old Whitby silhouetted against the sky, and make the lampposts into the masts of boats riding at anchor, and a familiar picture begins to emerge. None of these tracing paper pictures has survived, as Frank and the others were not allowed to keep any of them, and were told that one artist in the family was quite enough.

Thomas's reputation as an artist grew rapidly, and he seems to have been able to find a market for his works both among the newly-rich industrialists of Leeds and in London. In 1856 he exhibited an oil painting—*Study in Harewood Park, Yorkshire*—at the Royal Academy Exhibition, but his first love was for water-colour painting, and in 1857 he was elected an Associate of the New Society of Painters in Water-Colours.* Over the next few years he exhibited 109 works at their exhibitions. One of his paintings caught the eye of John Ruskin at the 1857 exhibition, and another was singled out for critical attention in the following year. This was *A Study in Winter, Adel Moor* (which was close to the Sutcliffes' house at Headingley), and of it Ruskin said: 'The furze in this drawing is admirable, and the whole thing got straight from Nature.'[7] Most of Thomas's work was, indeed, 'got straight from Nature', and he accepted commissions for paintings which meant that he was often away from home on painting trips. He never failed to write to his wife, telling her how his work was progressing. These letters are full of tenderness and family feeling. One journey took him to the Lake District, and after a train journey to Penrith and a long ride over country roads in a wagon, he wrote to her in pencil: 'My dear Sarry, … I have been a long stroll in search of subjects. I am all alone in a room now writing this by candle light. Bless you all a thousand times tell both the boys and the girls that I want them to try and be very good and do all they can to please you. Thomas.' These frequent absences from home were a source of distress to Frank, who decided that as soon as he was old enough he would go with his father on his painting expeditions. Whenever possible, Thomas took his eldest son with him in search of landscape subjects. Frank found these trips idyllic: 'I used to roam about hill and dale with him, eating blackberries, climbing trees, tickling trout, catching butterflies, bird-nesting, gathering wild flowers.'[8] But on his final painting tour, Frank did not accompany him.

Thomas had visited and painted the Yorkshire coast north of Flamborough Head, and decided to explore the possibilities of the southern part down to the Humber. A friend offered to purchase the complete set of coastal studies, and he

* This changed its title to The Institute of Painters in Water-Colours in 1863, and in 1884, after Thomas's death, became the Royal Institute. The changes in title explain some confusing references to, for example, Thomas Sutcliffe, R.I.

set out on 2 March 1865. The weather was still wintry, and accommodation was hard to find. On Spurn Point the rising tide came under the door of the house in which he was staying and put the fire out. Great waves broke over the house. The worst place of all was Hornsea, and his sketching notebook chronicles the wretched conditions he had to endure:

Thomas Sutcliffe with his son Frank.

> arrived at Hornsea about 6 o clock town a long way from the sea, I set off at once to find lodgings near the beach found one Inn and a very few houses but none of them could let me stay some said they had no beds aired others that it was their resting time [it was out of season for holidaymakers] others that they could only let the whole house as it stood after trying and looking and asking at all the places about I was obliged to grope my way back in the dark with my knapsack to the Inn at Hornsea where my traps were—after sweating very much with my quick walk and my load I now began to feel chilly and was horrified when I found my tea set out in a long, narrow, dark, damp, place where the liquors were kept with no fire, a stinking naptha lamp hung [from] a beam above covered with spiders webs. the floor under my feet saturated with damp from the ground and the droppings from the dirty beer barrels which were placed on the floor having swallowed my tea I asked if they had no place with a fire was shewn into what they called the taproom which was a huge fire *place* with very little fire though closed in with high backed longsettles and dirty cloths for curtains round the fire were three men smoking one a traveling tinker the other a traveling mason and the other an old chap, a relation to the family who I think was trying to make himself as agreeable as possible to the landlady who was a widow. they were all boosy and there was a good deal of talk but all I could catch was. 'big yr pardn' 'I say no' 'another glass here' … wasn't my back cold, wasn't the tobacco smoke nasty didn't the fellows shaky hands upset some beer. in time I rolled through a twistabout turnabout way into a double bedded room … hated Hornsea and everybody in it and everything belonging to it … some consolation in thinking that the sea would sometime pitch Hornsea down cliff.

He plodded on North carrying a big portfolio, a 'Sarey Gamp umbrella', and a knapsack weighing over twenty pounds. He also had with him a special painting tent to shield him from the worst of the weather. The tent consisted of four pieces—a wooden floor, a zinc roof, canvas sides, and a glass window. It was very difficult to erect on the cliff tops in a strong wind, and it was very heavy if he could not find anyone to carry it for him. As he struggled along the coast near Whitby with his heavy load of painting equipment, he was tramping the same ground which his son Frank was later to travel over similarly weighed down with his photographic equipment.

By the time he was nearing the end of his journey, Thomas was exhausted. A friend who saw him off at Whitby strapped his luggage to the back of his gig and felt he had to add: 'But I'm sure if we'd your missus here we'd keep you in bed; you are not in a fit state to travel.' Thomas brushed this aside with a joke, but he must have realised that he was an ill man: 'I saw them smile as I drove off, but it was almost a last attempt at mirth. It was scarcely possible to be merry with one's heart and chest in a state of violent inflammation. To breathe was a labour, to speak was pain, to lie down was impossible.'[9] 'Sutcliffe's Sketches of the Yorkshire Coast' were shown at a 'Conversazione' of the Leeds Philosophical and Literary Society shortly afterwards. The energy expended in getting them had nearly killed him. For the next four years he was confined as an invalid at home.

The fact that his father was seriously ill was presumably the main factor in deciding that Frank should go out to work. He was 14 and wanted to be a painter like his father, but, with some reason considering his father's state of health, his mother was against this. It was perhaps through friends of his grandfather in the wine and spirit business that Frank was sent to learn to be a clerk at Tetley's brewery. To reach his work he had to travel into the centre of Leeds, which he found disturbingly smoky and noisy after the peaceful existence he had led at Headingley. His weekly wage was three shillings, from which one shilling was deducted for food. Beer was free, but this was no relief to his misery, as he preferred water to beer. He was at the office in Hunslet Lane from early morning to eleven at night, and his health began to give way in the face of long hours toiling away at work which he detested. He stuck it for 18 months, until finally his parents decided that he should leave the job and return home to recuperate. One result of this experience was that he would never again touch a ledger, and his wife and daughters had to keep his books and accounts.

It was during this period of recovery, when Frank and his parents must have been wondering what he was going to do, that Frank found his true vocation in life—photography. He was not completely unfamiliar with photography, as his father was very interested in it, although it seems that Thomas did not take any photographs himself. When he wanted photographs taken, he engaged professional photographers to take them for him. Frank, of course, went along to see what was going on:

> I shall never forget the shock which I got, when a boy, on seeing a photographer, a Mr Wormald, of Leeds, develop a plate in the corner of a quarryman's hut at Weetwood Quarry, without any further protection from day light than the pinning up of a green shawl over the window and shielding the plate from what sunlight came through the chinks by the door with his own body. The photographs were made for my father, who was interested in Geology, some unusual strata having been bared at Weetwood. Mr Wormald kept singing from time to time, 'If I'd as much money as I could tell I wouldn't go crying "Young lambs to sell, young lambs to sell."'… Whether it was, that Mr Wormald found it very tiring lugging a 15 x 12 camera* here and there on a broiling hot day at the beck and call of a geologist, or whether it was that he found photography a non-paying concern, I could not decide; but I remember thinking that if photography made its professors so intensely miserable I would take care not to have anything to do with such a business when I grew up.[10]

It is probable that Frank's interest in photography developed gradually during this period as he met various friends of his father who dabbled in 'the black art'.* If there was one particular moment of decision, the story is that it was

* That is, a camera taking pictures on glass plates measuring 15 by 12 inches.

his discovery of a book at home which had the title '*Photography*—Lake Price' on its spine, and which Frank took down thinking it was about an area of the Lake District which he had not heard of before. In fact this was a book by an artist-turned-photographer called William Lake Price (*c*.1810-96) entitled *A Manual of Photographic Manipulation, treating of the Practice of the Art and its various applications to Nature*, published in London in 1858. This was one of the first books which treated photography as more than a scientific process, and suggested that its artistic potential had, as yet, hardly been tapped. The tone of the book was enthusiastic and stimulating, and Lake Price's attitude to photography was refreshingly straightforward. The book put forward photography as a field of activity which was worthwhile in its own right, and not as some sleight of hand which was to be despised by any creative person with artistic ambitions. 'In a multiplicity of ways,' Lake Price says in his introduction, 'Photography has already added, and will increasingly tend to contribute, to the knowledge and happiness of mankind.' In the light of Sutcliffe's later work, Lake Price's comments on photographs as historical records are particularly interesting: 'Posterity, by the agency of Photography, will view the faithful image of our times; the future student, in turning the page of history may at the same time look on the very skin, into the very eyes, of those, long since mouldered to dust, whose lives and deeds he traces in the text.' The whole field of photography was seen as one which was new, and which was going to undergo rapid development. Lake Price looked forward to technical innovations which would advance photography tremendously, even foreseeing the coming of colour photography. But most important of all, he felt that, in order to realise its full potential, photography should turn

> to the artist, for that judicious selection and arrangement, whatever his materials may be—for everything in nature, even to the smallest weed, has beauties and capabilities—that the pictures we shall see may show marks of reflection and intelligence, and conformity to those rules of art, in the composition of their lines, and effect of their light and shade, which will cause them to be looked upon with the respect and interest the exquisite beauty of Nature's own drawing should inspire, when not marred by the unskilful translation or promiscuous selection of her votaries.[11]

Frank Sutcliffe read the book and his imagination was fired by it. He decided to take up photography.

* A name which photography earned by the fact that its chemicals often blackened the hands and clothes of its early devotees.

chapter 2

Early Ventures in Photography

Frank's newly-found interest in photography was welcomed by both his parents. His mother had, he said, told him from his earliest infancy that she would have him smothered like the Princes in the Tower if he showed any inclination for being an artist. 'She thought', said Frank, 'all artists little better than lunatics', and added, 'that she might as well have married a sailor, for her husband was never at home, but always away at some outlandish spot or other.' His father arranged that half the hayloft should be fitted up as a darkroom, and found him an old camera to work with. It was solidly constructed of mahogany, and was enormous. Built like a square box, it was three feet long when fully extended, and probably had belonged to Thomas's friend Mr Ramsden, who was said to have owned the first camera in Leeds. This first camera with which Frank started photography at the age of 15 took glass plates 24 by 18 inches, but as plates this size were expensive, he worked plates 15 by 12 inches, and then whole plates (that is, 6½ by 8½ inches). The focal length of the huge brass lens was great—24 inches—which meant that his angle of view was very limited, 'but things looked big, which was the main thing'. With this monster camera, he was soon making glass positives of all his friends and neighbours, and set up a portable developing tent under his camera legs. He was using the wet collodion process, which involved sensitising and developing plates on the spot. To take photographs any distance away from a darkroom meant carrying not only the camera and tripod, but also the dark tent, water bottle, silver bath, dipping bath, iron developer, and cyanide fixer. The equipment was cumbersome and heavy, the process messy and yet demanding scrupulous cleanliness on the part of the photographer if the finished negative was to be reasonably free from specks of dust and other flaws. But the process worked, and Frank began a long apprenticeship in mastering the various skills required of the wet-plate photographer.

During this period, one important figure in advising and guiding Frank's progress was John William Ramsden, who combined making collodion with the work of a portrait photographer, and was a founder member of the Leeds Photographic Society. In the late 1860s he moved into a new studio in Park Row, Leeds. Thomas Sutcliffe helped by painting some backgrounds for him—necessary theatrical props for the Victorian portrait photographers—which would be suitable for the crinolines and plaid trousers of Mr Ramsden's sitters. Wandering around the new studio and, incidentally, finding that he liked the smell of collodion, Frank came across a long shelf with neat piles of photographic journals arranged in years. Seeing his interest, Mr Ramsden, whose stutter Frank faithfully transcribed, said: 'You c-can r-r-read these if you like. B-b-but m-m-mind you d-d-don't m-mix them up. K-k-keep each year b-by itself as it is n-n-now.'[1] He was allowed to take some home with him and read them all through from the beginning. This was not a task to be undertaken lightly. The photography periodicals of that time were learned journals dealing mainly with scientific and technical matters, and had little in common with the photographic magazines of today, with their feature articles and journalistic approach. Nevertheless, he not only read all Mr Ramsden's journals, but also wrote out in an indexed book everything which he thought would be useful to him.

As a beginner in photography, one of the problems he encountered was that of choosing the correct aperture for his lens. The lenses he was using had

Carte de visite portrait of Thomas Sutcliffe, by J.W. Ramsden.

Waterhouse stops—small metal plates each with a hole of a different size—which were placed into a slot in the lens tube. The set of stops was kept in a small leather case:

> Sometimes Providence interferes and saves the beginner from all trouble with his stops. It did so with me. I had a dog which took a great interest in my first camera from the very beginning. There is, perhaps, something about morocco leather which reminds a dog of the Elysian fields. It was a lens-cap, morocco bound outside, velvet inside, which Charlie devoured first. A cork out of a pyro bottle fortunately fitted the lens-hood exactly. Then, after eating the cap, while my head was under the focusing cloth, Charlie devoured the leather case, with all the stops in it. This was an insurmountable difficulty. I know I wrote to the maker of the lens to ask what a new set would cost, but as the amount was more than I possessed, I determined to do without. That is why I was saved from under-exposure, which I should surely have been led into with a multitude of stops.[2]

After this minor disaster, Frank said that his camera saw everything as he did, big and broad. It seems that there was what he calls 'a peculiarity' in his eyesight, and that consequently, he could not, for a long time, make his camera see as he saw. He said that he could not see 'the spots and wrinkles on anyone's face, or the darns in their stockings, or the dust on their clothes'.[3] His camera, he said, saw very little else, until Fate, in the form of Charlie, took a hand.

Frank's photography became a part of family life. In a letter to his son Horace, who was to die in 1870 aged 14, and who was apparently staying with friends, Thomas tells him what has been happening: 'Some Keeper shot one of the young herons on Adel dam & the Eddicons sent it to me. Frank made 11 photographs from it and then we sent it to Mr Lee to stuff. We went yesterday to Harewood & Frank got 9 or 10 good photographs there with the new tent. We *all* send our love. … Your affectionate Father, Thomas Sutcliffe.' As his confidence as a photographer grew, Frank attempted much more ambitious shots than still life studies of dead herons. A doctor the family knew in Leeds was interested in the flight of birds and, as Frank described it:

> I foolishly, with the confidence of youth, promised to try to take some birds flying for him. My first attempt was to photograph some swallows flying over a mill pond. Plates then were wet, and slow, and the speed of my shutter, a home-made one, would not be anything like a fiftieth of a second. We were never able to decide whether certain V-shaped marks which appeared in succession over one part of the water were the images of a swallow as it flew, or due to particles of dried collodion which had made bird-like marks as the collodion had been poured over the plate.[4]

Although defeated by the slow speed of his shutter and of the wet-plates, this brave attempt was made at a time when the idea of analysing movement by stop-motion photography was quite new. Sutcliffe was working long before the results of the work of Muybridge in America and Marey in France were common knowledge in photographic circles. The experiment was a failure, but for a boy of seventeen or eighteen even to attempt such a thing reveals an enterprising and imaginative mind at work. In a more directly practical way, he apparently hoped that his work in photography would help his father in his paintings, perhaps by supplying the fine detail which Thomas used in some of his works, and which his ill health may have prevented him getting direct from nature.

His father had, by now, suggested that Frank should make photography his career, but, perhaps with Mr Wormald in mind, Frank objected strongly and pointed out that none of their acquaintances had made pictures or money by photography. To this Thomas replied that it was their fault and not that of photography, 'and that they might make money too if they had better studios, kept them clean and went the right way to work'.[5]

The mention of making 'pictures' by photography touches on an issue which nagged at Frank Sutcliffe all his life, that an artist makes pictures whereas a photographer can only make mechanical imitations of pictures, and that any photographer who could paint well enough would become a painter. He was obviously devoted to his father, and was very much influenced by his opinions. In particular, one remark—probably made quite casually—struck home: 'I never venture to call a photograph a picture', Frank wrote in 1888. 'My father once said to me, "How can the reflection of a gutta-percha world in a brass door-handle be a picture?" This made me ashamed of photography; have never got over it.'[6] This may seem like a throw-away remark, but he returns to the subject again and again. In 1902 he wrote about the influence of his camera:

> Well—it may have strengthened the muscles of my back and arms, but that is all. Was I not in my youth taught to despise all royal roads to success, and was not picture-making by a camera only a lazy way of making pictures which ought to have been done by the sweat of the hand and brain? Were not all photograms held up to ridicule as being but the 'reflections of a gutta-percha world in a brass door-handle'? and were not all photographers looked on as men who thought they could do much when they could do nothing at all? Yes, it is a terrible thing to have been brought up with a feeling of contempt for one's handicraft.[7]

This seems a gloomy view of a field in which the world acclaimed him as a success. Even if one takes a large measure of good-humoured overstatement into account, it must contain at least a grain of truth. Frank himself, because of his feeling of inferiority as a photographer, suggested that his epitaph should be 'Here lies a failure'. But in these surprising statements can probably be found one of the mainsprings which drove him on to produce work which had to be good, because the standards he was measuring it against were the very high ones which he had set himself.

Thomas, after four years of convalescence, seems to have regained his health at least in part, enabling him to lead a more active life. For some years past, he and Sarah had talked about moving to Whitby on the Yorkshire coast, where the family had spent their summer holidays since Frank's childhood. Thomas had friends who lived in and around Whitby, and also among the people who, like himself, were regular visitors. One of these was John Leech, the artist who was on the staff of *Punch* and who had illustrated some of Dickens's works. One of Frank's earliest recollections was of being ducked in the sea by a muscular and over-enthusiastic bathing attendant, much to his discomfort, but to the amusement of his father and John Leech who were watching. This episode was soon immortalised in a *Punch* cartoon by Leech. The cartoon was entitled 'A Judge by Appearance', and the 'bathing guide' is saying: 'Bless 'is 'art! I know'd he'd take to it kindly—by the werry looks on 'im!'[8] Leech, who died in 1864, was the first of a succession of *Punch* artists who came to Whitby and became friendly with Frank.

After some delay, Thomas was able to arrange the lease of Ewe Cote Hall, about a mile outside Whitby.* In October 1870, he wrote to a friend, Mrs Oates:

> I have only just got the key of Ewe Cote Hall. I have been put to very much unnecessary troubles by the agent who had the letting of the place. … I wanted to be satisfied that the house would be put in good order, & repair, and I wanted a proper understanding and personal interview with the landlord, and have only this morning obtained them.

All being settled, the removal was made by road, with the furniture van, and pony and trap loaded high with painting and photographic tents and equipment. The procession looked like a circus on the move. Ewe Cote was a large late 17th-century mansion with its own farm, and surrounded by open country. The Sutcliffes happily settled in, and Thomas had new visiting cards printed which read 'Thos. Sutcliffe's Studio and Fine Art Gallery, Ewe Cote Hall, Whitby. Oil and Water-Colour Pictures, Engravings, Artists' Etchings, &c.'

Thomas had already carried out commissions for the Marquis of Ripon and the Earl of Harewood; and the Rev. the Earl of Mulgrave, who was later to succeed his father as Marquis of Normanby, and who lived near by at Mulgrave Castle became both a patron and a close friend. He bought the cream of Thomas's water-colours and arranged for him to teach art at a small school run by him at the castle. It was through this friendship that Frank met his future wife. The Dowager Marchioness of Normanby asked Thomas to make some paintings in the castle grounds and, as usual, Frank accompanied his father. One morning the old man who delivered the mail to the castle did not arrive, and eventually a girl from Whitby Post Office arrived full of apologies. She had forgotten to give the post for Mulgrave to the carrier, and after trying and failing to overtake him at Sandsend, had brought the mail to the castle herself. Frank was told to take her in to the housekeeper and see that she got a good breakfast. She was a local girl, slightly older than Frank, called Eliza Duck. Frank was attracted by her beauty and her kindness, and was soon a regular visitor to the post office. He also got up at four in the morning to take her on short boat trips out to sea, before the town was awake.

The family was very happy at Ewe Cote. Thomas's youngest daughter, Mary Lorentia, was born there in 1871. His career as a painter was opening out before him, they had settled into their new home, and Frank was busy with his photography. Thomas set out once again on his coastal treks, and, at the beginning of December, was caught by the tide while painting among the rocks on the shore at Cloughton, south of Whitby. He just managed to escape with all his painting equipment, but his flight up the cliff had strained his heart. He returned home to Ewe Cote, and the family must have realised how ill he

Detail from *Punch* cartoon by John Leech.

View of Ewe Cote Hall taken by fms, *c.*1870.

* In July 1870 the family were living, probably temporarily, in a house at Quarry Moor, Ripon.

was from his ghastly looks. The photograph taken by Frank on 7 December shows Thomas looking like the ghost of his former self. He was 43 when he died on 11 December. The cause of death was given as 'severe valvular disease of the heart for some time previously'. Sarah was left with a large family and no assets, as Thomas's work was only just beginning to be widely known. The Earl, together with several influential friends, including Colonel Oates, made a trust fund for her which brought in enough to keep the family going. This alone was a measure of the respect and love which Thomas had engendered during his relatively short lifetime.

Frank was 18 when his father died, and a photograph taken soon after Thomas's death shows the bereaved family on the steps of Ewe Cote, with Sarah in her black widow's dress, and Frank, looking very sad, in his new position as head of the household. During the period after his father's death, Frank took up photography in earnest and began to bring his work up to a standard which would allow him to work as a professional, at the same time attempting to produce pictures which met his own high standards. It was inevitable that he worked in the shadow of his father's achievements. He was bitterly disappointed with his first attempt at a photograph of a scene under snow:

> Instead of the snow showing white, as we fondly imagined it ought to be, it came out in the prints as greys of varying tones. Hanging in our kitchen at home … was a water-colour sketch of my father's of the view from the kitchen window of the backyard in wintertime. The sky was a leaded yellowish grey, against which the snow on the stable roof, trees, etc., stood out white; if the snow in the foreground was lower in tone, it seemed to be nearly white when contrasted with the dark black birds and sparrows which the yard was always full of. In my ignorance I foolishly expected the snow in my first snow picture to be like the snow in this water-colour. I know I nearly wept when I found that the snow on the branches of some elder trees in the foreground was considerably darker than the blue sky above and around them. It was only when I came to compare the tones of snow in shadow with the sky that I could believe that snow could be so dark.[9]

But he kept at it, and produced some beautiful studies. *Ewe Cote—Winter, Back Door*, and the woman with the fish in the basket all belong to this early period.

In 1872 Sutcliffe spent the summer in the Lake District 'photographing for a lot of friends of my father's who had houses at Derwent, Ullswater, and Coniston'. These were his first attempts at landscape photography, and he had to come to terms with the limitations of the equipment and plates at his command:

> One of my first experiences of photography was waiting beside a photographer and his camera till the sun went in. This it did at last. When the photographer had taken the cap off the lens and had put it on again, and had closed up his dark slide, I ventured to ask him if he did not think the view looked much better when the sun was shining on it than it did when he made the exposure. The photographer agreed, but said that if he had taken his picture in sunshine the result would have been very hard; it was to obviate this hardness that he always tried to expose his plates when there was no sunshine. Whether this excessive contrast which he tried to avoid was

Carte portrait of Thomas Sutcliffe taken by fins a few days before his death in December 1871.

The Sutcliffe family on the steps of Ewe Cote shortly after Thomas's death.

Ewe Cote, Winter—early study by fms.

Back Door—early study by fms.

Woman with fish in basket—early study by fms.

due to a too powerful developer or to over development rather than to the brilliancy of the sun I should not like to say.[10]

Photographs taken when the sun was shining often 'came out so hard that they looked like snow scenes'. The public of the time, though, favoured this 'soot and whitewash' school of photography. The photographs they liked they called 'clear'—that is, with the tones of the subjects falsified so that the whites were too white and the shadows much darker than they are in nature. But the transformation of tone in landscape was not caused solely by manipulation to suit the taste of the public; part of the blame must be given to the wet-plate itself, as Sutcliffe found out:

> I remember in the wet-plate days setting up my camera opposite a mountain in Cumberland, one side of which was lit by the rays of the setting sun so that the mountain side seemed itself to shine. The other side of the hill was in shadow, lit only by the light from the sky. When the plate was developed there was not a trace of sunshine on it; the sunlit side of the hill was no brighter than the side in shadow. I might as well have photographed part of a pancake.[11]

The speed of early plates made special demands upon the photographer: 'In the Lake District, the only possible time for photography if still foliage and reflections are wanted, is before sunrise. Unless you want sunshine on your flowers I would advise you to get up with the birds and get your pictures before the sun rises. Expose fully at this early hour.'[12] The wet-plate process might well be called photography with tears, but photographers like Sutcliffe suffered under dreadful conditions, and looked back on them with the nostalgic pride of pioneers. On this trip to the Lakes, Sutcliffe was probably using his umbrella developing tent:

> The tent was like an ordinary umbrella without a handle, with a few pieces of yellow twill let in. There was an opening for the operator's head, and two others for his arms. He knelt on the ground, and the waste developer and washing water ran also onto the ground. It was his look out whether his knees got wet with this or not. If it was summer weather outside the tent it was a very much hotter place inside. Yes, truly, photography was ever so much more enjoyable in those days, mainly because of those discomforts which have been removed bit by bit.[13]

But the stifling heat of an airless developing tent was not the only danger Sutcliffe had to face. He tripped and rolled down a hillside near Keswick—'the camera and I being in turns uppermost'—luckily managing to stop on a ledge of rock overhanging the lake. There was very little of the camera left. On another occasion near Ullswater, a wind which was known locally as the Helm wind suddenly sprang up on a still day and blew his camera and tripod right over a high stone wall; the camera was smashed to pieces though, miraculously, the ground glass survived intact.

In the early 1870s, Francis Frith, a landscape photographer who owned a photographic business at Reigate, was compiling a collection of photographs which he hoped would cover all the cities, villages and 'beauty spots' in the British Isles. These were to be reproduced as 'local views' and sold in thousands through stationers and other outlets. A friend of Sutcliffe who knew Frith got him to give Sutcliffe a commission to take a series of views of Yorkshire abbeys and castles. The price paid for this work was not even enough to cover Sutcliffe's expenses in travelling and waiting for fine weather, but his work for Frith was to prove valuable in other ways. He travelled the 300 miles from Whitby to Reigate to see Mr Frith:

> He was sitting, when I first saw him, at a table lit from below, cutting pieces of fine tracing-paper to fit over the too transparent parts of some negatives one of his operators had sent in from India; he was, in fact, trying to make the negatives right for printing in a light key.[14]

Frith advised Sutcliffe on how to correct tonal rendering in negatives by using masks cut out of tracing paper. He also advised him: 'Never be tempted to include any figures in your landscapes or architectural subjects.' Sutcliffe asked why:

> I was told that no matter how good a photograph might otherwise be, it would not sell if there were any figures in it. Mr Frith went on to tell me that they had scores of negatives which were useless because there were figures in them. 'Just think', he added, 'when anyone buys a photograph of Rievaulx Abbey or any other building; they don't want Tom, Dick, or Harry, people whom they have never seen in their lives, stuck in the foreground. No; it is the view itself they are willing to pay for, and all they want.' If Mr Frith had told me that the inclusion of figures was likely to spoil a photograph, both technically and pictorially, I might have taken his advice more to heart. However, when I was making the negatives of some of our Yorkshire abbeys and castles for him, whenever a polite stranger in top hat, frock coat, and lavender trousers came up and said, 'Oh, I see you are taking photographs; I will pose for you', I let that stranger go and pose on one leg with the other crossed over it while he gazed intently upwards, but I took care not to take the cap off the lens, or, if he could see the camera out of the corner of his eye, I took care not to draw the shutter of the dark slide. Then, after I had thanked the stranger for his help, I would wait until he had got out of range before making the exposure.[15]

Before leaving Reigate, Frith gave him what he called a 'Yorkshireman's gift' as a keepsake; it was a fine mahogany Kinnear camera, which irritated Frith because instead of a rack and pinion focusing arrangement, it had a focusing handle in the centre of the tail-board. It did not take Sutcliffe long to discover the disadvantage of the positioning of this little handle:

> The maker put it there, I believe, for the sole purpose of pulling the hairs out of my beard each time I use this infernal machine. As soon as ever I get my head under the focusing cloth and I begin to wind the handle, out comes a handful of beard; fortunately the friendly cover of the focusing cloth deadens anything which I find it necessary to say to the brute.[16]

Sunset after Rain. Taken above Rievaulx Abbey, *c.*1872.

One of the places Sutcliffe had photographed for Frith—probably in 1872 or 1873—was Rievaulx Abbey, and Sutcliffe travelled to the nearby village of Helmsley with a fellow photographer. But it was raining hard, and his companion packed up and went home. Sutcliffe decided to stay overnight at a cottage near Rievaulx. Late in the afternoon the rain cleared and the sun began to set behind two pines next to the cottage. He decided to take a photograph of the sunset, and prepared his camera and plate, but found that his work would be hampered by the wind. It was hardly more than a breeze, but from time to time it would gently move the branches of the trees, before dying away again. Even this slight movement would have blurred the image of the branches on the plate. Sutcliffe was intending to make a time exposure, not with a shutter, but by removing the cap from the lens by hand. It was possible to remove and replace the cap without shaking the camera on its tripod. He was, therefore, able to expose only when he saw that the branches were still. In fact his exposure of about two minutes was made up of a series of exposures of a few seconds each, with long intervals of waiting for the breeze to die down. The resulting photograph, which was titled *Sunset after Rain*, shows an atmospheric, luminous effect of the setting sun.

Sutcliffe was pleased with this result—especially so perhaps because it had involved seizing an unexpected opportunity which presented itself. He sent a print to one of his father's friends in the Lake District. The lady to whom he sent it lived near Coniston, and John Ruskin, who had recently bought the house called Brantwood, a little way down the lake, happened to pay his neighbour a call and saw the photograph. It is possible that Thomas Sutcliffe's friend hoped that she might further his son Frank's career by arranging a meeting with the great Mr Ruskin. It is also possible that Ruskin was genuinely struck by the quality of the photograph.* Whatever the reason, he asked for Sutcliffe's address and wrote to him saying that he thought the print of the pines and the sky was 'the most successful attempt at cloud photography'[17] which he had ever seen. He invited Sutcliffe to Coniston to take some views of Brantwood for him.

Ruskin was 54 years old and the critical lion of the English art world; Sutcliffe was 19—an unknown young photographer. He had, as he put it, 'been reared on *Modern Painters* and *The Stones of Venice*, to say nothing of *The Elements of Drawing*,'[18] and, of course, eagerly accepted the invitation to meet their author. Travelling by train and coach, he reached Coniston village one fine autumn evening, probably in September 1873. The next morning he loaded all his equipment onto a cart and set out to meet Ruskin. A contemporary writer describes the approach to his house:

> Every tourist who has 'done the lakes' will remember the striking view which is obtained of the 'Old Man' of Coniston as the coach suddenly heads the hill that overlooks the lake on the opposite shore. If, instead of proceeding to the waterhead, the traveller turns to the left, and makes his way for some distance along the road, above parts of which the meeting branches form an almost unbroken bower, he will at length come upon a simple gateway, near which the foliage seems to be specially luxuriant, and all around is singularly tranquil. This is the entrance to Brantwood on the Coniston side. Passing through the gate, a short carriage drive leads to the house, which is then seen to be situated on a terraced portion of the hill, that slopes up from the waterside. Brantwood, or 'steep wood', stands on a small piece of levelled ground almost on the shore of the lake of Coniston. Behind the house, which is entered, as it were, at the back, the hill rises sharply up, and would render this side of Mr Ruskin's residence a little gloomy, if it were not that through the trees the blue water sparkles in the sunshine, and the hills beyond are bright and green.[19]

It was 'with a considerable feeling of nervousness' that Sutcliffe drove up to the door. On his arrival, he was told that Ruskin was working in his study, but would meet him at lunch. He was greeted by Ruskin's cousin, Mrs Arthur Severn, who said that if he would like to unpack his camera, he might find 'a few bits round the house' worth taking. Mr Ruskin, his cousin said, wished to have a good view of the house, but as the ground sloped away sharply towards the lake, it was clearly going to be difficult to get. The camera Sutcliffe was using was the Kinnear he had been given by Mr Frith, and fortunately it had a rising front with a wide range of adjustment, which enabled the house to be photographed from a low vantage point. Sutcliffe took two views of the house with the morning sun on it, and then another of the house behind an avenue of limes, which were beginning to turn yellow. It was a very still day, enabling him to give exposures of between twenty and forty seconds. He was using an old outhouse with a piece of red calico pinned over the window as a make-shift darkroom: 'The gardener wanted very much to sweep it out for me, but I told him that I would rather he did not, as I preferred it as it was.'[20]

He then went in to lunch and met Ruskin who 'evidently out of kindness to my nervousness and boyish blushes, made me feel completely at home'. Sutcliffe

* Surviving prints of the photograph do not seem to do it justice, judging by contemporary descriptions.

John Ruskin at Brantwood, probably in
September 1873.

was struck by his appearance and described him as having 'the heavenly blue
eyes of a dreamer and the strong nose of a warrior'. After Ruskin had been told
what views had been taken, he asked Sutcliffe what he would like to take next.
'Yourself, sir,' was the reply. While Ruskin was being helped into a new grey
frock-coat by his man, Sutcliffe discovered that he would have to do much of
the morning's work over again. His out-house darkroom had no lock, and the
gardener, apparently still worried about the visitor having to use a dirty shed,
'during lunch time took a besom and swept down the cobwebs from the roof
and shelves, and tidied up the place. Fortunately my silver bath was screwed up,
and he had not moved it, but his besom had scratched off part of two or three
negatives which I had left drying on blotting paper, face up.'[21]

Ruskin was by this time ready, and the camera was set up 'near a favourite
old wall, a wall covered with exquisite growth of ivy and periwinkle and grass,
partly hiding lichen-covered stones of uneven shapes and size'. At least two
photographs were taken of Ruskin, who then posed a picture himself—a girl in
a striped print gown, in an alcove of the old wall, pretending to read a book.
After this had been taken, he said that he would like to have some views from
the rough ground above the house. It took a good five minutes to climb up to
the hilltop through the wood, and Ruskin spent some time deciding which view
of a clump of fir trees growing among the rocks satisfied him best. Sutcliffe was
worried about the wet-plates he had prepared: 'These things were spoilt if they
became dry; twenty minutes was about as long as they would keep wet, and not
so long as that in hot weather, even when the dark slide had been damped with
glycerine and a pad of wet blotting paper placed at the back of the plate.'[22] The
plate was finally exposed, but Sutcliffe

was afraid the plate would be drying and showing the usual oyster-shell markings, so leaving John Ruskin to bring the camera down, I rushed off helter skelter downhill to develop it. Later on in the day, Mr Ruskin said he wished to compliment me on the way I had run down the hill with the plate, and added he was often amused at the nervous way his London friends walked down-hill, with toes foremost instead of trusting to their heels and throwing their shoulders well backwards.

This concluded the first day's work, and Sutcliffe rowed home over the lake to his lodgings.

The next day dawned even finer than the previous one, and after breakfast Ruskin said that the day should be given up to photography. More photographs were taken around the house, of groups by the lakeside harbour, and several plates were exposed on Mrs Severn and her baby. Ruskin was particularly pleased with a portrait of the baby. After lunch he said that he would like to have a photograph of a wild strawberry plant growing on a rock by the lakeside. He was making a detailed pencil drawing of this, but was afraid that it would not last until the drawing was finished.*

Sutcliffe sensitised a plate and they set out for the lake. The boat they were to use lay alongside the pier and was deeply waterlogged. He tried to bale it out with his hat, but it soon filled with water again, and he 'thought that at each stroke John Ruskin, who was rowing, made, the boat would be sure to go to the bottom,' but he consoled himself with the thought that 'it would be a grand advertisement to be drowned in such company'.[23] Having survived the excursion along the lake, Ruskin showed Sutcliffe over the house and its treasures—Greek antiquities, works by Luca della Robbia and Titian, drawings by Mantegna and Botticelli.

Frank Sutcliffe, aged 21.

> I remember he showed me some of his treasures in his turret bedroom, minerals more beautiful than I had ever dreamed of, and water colours, which I could not understand or appreciate, by Turner. These paintings were covered over with loose frames covered with green calico, to prevent the light from injuring the colours, and were replaced when the visitor had seen his see. I remember feeling very much ashamed for being at a loss for words to say anything about these pictures, but what boy could honestly say anything about a Turner in five minutes?[24]

During his visit to Brantwood, Sutcliffe had talked about photography to Ruskin, whose experience was, he understood, restricted to the daguerreotype process. Ruskin said that he found great difficulty in getting the complete range of half-tones from the deepest shadows to the brilliant highlights of distant sunlit mountains. He told Sutcliffe

> that when he heard rumours that photography in colours was on its way, he trembled for fear this might be so. For, said he, photographs in monochrome are bad enough, but they will be ten thousand times worse if colour has to be handled as well. Mr Ruskin also said that he thought all photographers overexposed their plates. I think he meant they over-developed them, for at that time the gelatine dry plate had not appeared, and photographers were in

* This might suggest that the wild strawberry was in blossom, of which a Ruskin drawing exists, dated June 1873. But conflicts in various accounts which Sutcliffe wrote of this visit make it difficult to be certain of some of the details. An entry in Ruskin's Diary for Sunday, 28 September 1873 reads 'Y(esterday) drawing at strawberry rock. Then in afternoon, upsetting boat, with Arfie's help ...'

Carte portrait of fms with his daughter Kathy.

Detail from whole-plate print by fms inscribed
by Thomas: 'T. Sutcliffe at Ewe Cote'.

the habit of adding nitrate of silver to their developer to add strength to their
negatives, and mighty strong they were.[25]

It was this upsetting of tonal rendering to which Ruskin particularly objected.
They also talked about Ruskin's writings on art, and Sutcliffe, 'with the impudence
of youth', asked him, if he was to have his time over again, whether he would
alter any of the things he had written with such certainty earlier in his career:

> After a pause the sage replied, 'Too late, too late, I should like to alter nearly
> everything I have written.' Then when I ventured to add, 'Then why not
> alter some of the more important while there is time', Mr Ruskin said, 'What
> I have written, I have written, and it will have to stand.'[26]

So ended his visit to Brantwood. Sutcliffe returned to Whitby, stimulated by a meeting which had impressed him deeply.

On his return to Ewe Cote, the lofty problems of art which concerned Ruskin were soon supplanted by the more down-to-earth problem of what Sutcliffe was going to do to make a living. His search for a career was given urgency by the fact that he now wanted to marry Eliza Duck. His mother was strongly against his choice of a wife. Not only was she five years older than Frank, Eliza Duck was the daughter of a bootmaker—she wasn't good enough for him. Frank's pleas were, however, supported by the Rev. the Earl of Mulgrave, who offered to perform the marriage ceremony. Sarah seems to have given way, and, as it turned out, Frank's marriage to Eliza proved to be a very happy one. Frank was 21 when he married in 1874. In due course the Earl was to become godfather to their first child, a daughter they named Kathleen.

Frank knew that, if he was to make a living as a photographer, he would have to work as a portrait photographer either as a photographer's assistant or running a photographic business of his own. Unfortunately for Sutcliffe, Whitby in the early 1870s was well provided with photographers. Four photographers served the small town with its seasonal holiday trade—two in the town itself, and two down by the pier to catch the passing trade. He looked for premises in Whitby which would be suitable as a photographer's studio, but was unsuccessful. Now, when he may have been determined to prove his independence both to his mother and to Eliza, and needed to weigh every decision carefully before making what might be a false step, he desperately needed advice on how and where to set up in business. Either he did not ask for or receive advice from friends—his father who certainly would have discussed his ideas with him was dead—or he chose not to take any advice which was given. He decided to build for himself a studio in Tunbridge Wells, a town 300 miles away of which he can have known little. It was to prove a disastrous decision.

chapter 3

The Failure of a Society Photographer

A Victorian Guidebook to Tunbridge Wells declared that, as an inland watering place, its fame was only exceeded by that of Bath: 'the chalybeate springs, known as Tunbridge Wells, have from the first enjoyed a high reputation, and have never failed to attract to the neighbourhood, with every returning summer, a large influx of visitors in search of health, society, or amusement.'[1] The town was easily accessible by rail from London, and its popularity and wealth was growing during the 1860s and '70s:

> During the last fifty years, especially during the latter half of that period, the town has become a very favourite place of residence, and many families of wealth and leisure, with no strong local attachments elsewhere have selected it as their abode. Unbeneficed clergymen, gentlemen who have served their country in the army, in the navy, or in colonial appointments, and retired merchants, have settled in large numbers in this quiet, healthy, and lovely spot. It is also a favourite residence for widows and maiden ladies of independent means. The number of summer visitors certainly does not diminish; on the contrary, it is yearly on the increase.[2]

Families of wealth and leisure, gentlemen, retired merchants, widows and maiden ladies of independent means, in addition to summer visitors—this potential clientele must have looked very attractive to any portrait photographer wishing to set himself up in business.

Needless to say, the fact that rich pickings were to be had in Tunbridge Wells had not escaped the notice of other photographers. At least six photographers were well-established by the time Sutcliffe arrived in the town, early in 1875. One of them was H.P. Robinson, one of the foremost professional portrait photographers of the day, who was also a leading exponent of 'art photography' by combination printing.* He had published a book in 1869 which Sutcliffe had very probably read—*Pictorial Effect in Photography: being Hints on Composition and Chiaroscuro for Photographers*—and had apparently made remarks, in articles he had written, about 'charging well for your work'. Years later, Sutcliffe revealed that this had been a major factor in his choice of Tunbridge Wells as the most promising place to build a studio for himself: 'I, in my innocence, thought the photographers there would get better prices than elsewhere. I expected H.P.R. would charge at least four pounds a dozen carte† portraits.'[3] Either he is exaggerating, or he must have pulled this figure out of thin air, because it is absurd. If he really thought that photographers were so well paid, he cannot have talked to any of the professionals in Whitby. One possible reason for Sutcliffe making such an error was that the leading portrait photographer in Scarborough—just south of Whitby—was one of the richest and most successful in the country. This was Oliver François Sarony. People came from all over England to be photographed by him, and his earnings were put at around £10,000 a year—an enormous sum in those days. There were other photographers selling 60 or 70,000 cartes a year, but they were few and far between, and for every success story, there were many failures.

1875 does not seem to have been a particularly good year for photographers in Tunbridge Wells. Messrs. H.P. Robinson and N.K. Cherrill, well established in their studio adjoining the Great Hall of the New Public Rooms, announced

---

* Combination printing was a form of photo-montage involving the arrangement of several negatives which were then printed from to produce composed pictures which often resembled Victorian narrative paintings.

† 'Carte-de-visite' photographs were mounted on cards measuring roughly 4 inches by 2½ inches, and were the standard small size for portrait photographs.

in an advertisement in the *Tunbridge Wells Gazette* that they had been awarded another pair of medals to add to the 44 others they had won in photographic competitions. But, descending briefly from the pedestal of art photography to rustle up a little business, the advertisement continued:

> Messrs. Robinson & Cherrill find that, in consequence of their unprecedented success in the higher branches of the Art of Photography, as again illustrated by the above fact, their charges for the ordinary kind of Photographs have been represented to be much higher than is really the case, they think it necessary therefore to state that their price is for Carte-de-Visite, 10s. 6d. per dozen.[4]

This was low enough compared with the four pounds per dozen Sutcliffe thought he would charge; other photographers in Tunbridge Wells charged as little as 3s. 6d. per dozen. The opposition had weighed the Tunbridge Wells market up carefully and had built up establishments, the size and scope of which, coupled with moderate prices, indicated a great deal of business acumen. To compete with these experienced professionals, Sutcliffe had only his youth, his enthusiasm and six hundred pounds to set himself up in business.

His search for studio premises was hampered by the fact that property owners were far from keen on allowing a tenant to put up 'such an objectionable building as a studio.' To be successful, he must have realised that he had to set up his business in a suitably genteel neighbourhood. He eventually found the place he was looking for a little way out of the centre of the town at 32, St John's Road, opposite the entrance to Culverden Park. The *Tunbridge Wells Gazette* for 19 March 1875 carried his first advertisement:

By Her Majesty's Royal Letters Patent
———
The Ferranti-Turner Method
of
Finishing Photographic Pictures
———
Mr Frank M. Sutcliffe

Has great pleasure in announcing that he has succeeded in securing the exclusive right to produce the above pictures in Tunbridge Wells; further particulars of which will be given next week, and specimens will shortly be on view at his Studio (now building), due notice of the opening of which will be given in this paper.

MR. SUTCLIFFE also intends to introduce, in addition to the usual size of photograph, the BOUDOIR PORTRAIT, a new picture of different dimensions from those usually made, of which the *British Journal of Photography* says:

The BOUDOIR PORTRAIT will certainly commend the suffrages of ladies as it is well adapted for showing off to advantage a charming full length figure and an exquisite parure; for which reason its popularity may be safely predicted. We have seen many specimens, and in appearance they are exceedingly attractive.'
GLENWYNNE STUDIO
March 12th., 1875.

The two innovations he was offering had both been introduced by the photographic trade as a boost to portrait work. The 'boudoir portrait' was nothing more than a larger format of photograph—the mount was about 8 by 5 inches—introduced in the hope that it would stimulate business and replace the flagging sales of carte portraits. The Ferranti-Turner method of finishing prints was more original. Messrs. Ferranti and E.J. Turner, both of Liverpool, had in 1873 obtained a patent for a method of using pulverised 'pastil' or crayons on portrait photographs which produced 'a brilliant effect … as the figure thus treated forms a vivid contrast with the background, and stands in relief therefrom, thereby giving to the figure and face a miniature-like effect of the greatest softness and brilliancy.'[5] The process was not entirely new, and was introduced in the photographic journals as simply a new method of producing what were called Vanderweyde effects, which involved coloured stipple finishes. Nevertheless, pictures finished by this process were said to present 'a charming effect; and an ordinary photograph is transformed into a perfectly harmonious picture, acceptable to the most cultivated eye, and satisfactory alike to the painter and the art-photographer, presenting as it does, all the appearance of a work of art obtained by labour of the most skilful or prolonged character.' When one looks at Sutcliffe's later photographs of tramps on the road and tough fishermen just back from a fishing trip—pictures as honest and straightforward as one could hope for—it is difficult to believe that he began his career by offering 'boudoir portraits' for ladies and phoney imitations of 'works of art'.

He announced the opening of his studio on Monday, 12 April, and changed his advertisement to include all the silver-tongued pretentiousness which he later was to abhor and reject. The Ferranti-Turner (Royal) patent gave him the excuse to head his advertisement with the Royal coat-of-arms, and his studio became 'Mr F.M. Sutcliffe's Photographic Atelier'. Here, the notice continued:

THE HIGHEST CLASS OF PHOTOGRAPHS
are reproduced daily under
ordinary conditions of light, and
CHILDREN'S PORTRAITURE
IS MADE A SPECIALITE.

Every description of enlargements (coloured and plain) to be seen in Reception Rooms. Also a choice collection of WATER COLOUR DRAWINGS, by the late Mr THOMAS SUTCLIFFE, of the Institute of Painters in Water Colours.

Landscapes and all kinds of
Out-door Photographs
at moderate charges.

Wedding Parties, Fêtes, &c., attended on the shortest notice.

But these costly advertisements were to little avail, and he had hardly any sitters— only about fifty in all the time he was there. He thought himself lucky if he got one or two sitters a fortnight. Not all his callers wanted their portrait taken. Years later, a 'venerable old gentleman' went to Sutcliffe's Whitby studio accompanied

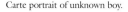

Carte portrait of unknown young lady.	Carte portrait of unknown boy.	Carte portrait of unknown little girl.

by his twin daughters, and said 'You won't remember us.' Sutcliffe couldn't place them, and the man recalled their first meeting:

> I was never so ashamed of myself as I was five-and-thirty years ago, when I knocked you up the night they were born. Don't you remember you had a studio in (St John's) Road, at (Tunbridge Wells) then, and you were too proud to have a shop front like you have now, only a brass plate, with your name and M.P.S.G.B.* on it.

Sutcliffe then remembered the occasion:

> It all came back to me how, one stormy night years ago, an excited, middle-aged man had knocked me up in the middle of the night, and when I went down, expecting to hear that my studio at the back of the house had caught fire, was seized hold of by the visitor, and told to get my hat and coat on at once, as his wife had just been delivered of twins. It took me all my time to shake him off, he was so excited, and to get it drummed into him that he had mistaken my brass plate for that of the doctor, five doors further down the road.[6]

He remembered little else about Tunbridge Wells with amusement, as it was clear that the venture was failing.

On the few occasions Sutcliffe mentions the town and his experiences there, his remarks are tinged with bitterness. Although he was to take many more

* This stood for Member of the Photographic Society of Great Britain, which was later to become the Royal Photographic Society.

photographs of children and babies, he was not happy about having made a 'specialité' of children's portraiture:

> The photographic press has always been keen on advising the photographer to push the photography of infants and children. I am convinced now that such advice must have been inspired by the profitable advertiser. We have been told that the photographer who makes a 'speciality'—rotten word—of children's portraits, worms his way into the hearts of the parents, and so establishes a profitable connection. If, instead of listening to advice of this kind, and buying rocking horses and toys only to be broken by the Young Turks immediately, he had taken the trouble to make a simple calculation or balance-sheet putting on one side all the time and expense, and on the other all the cash received, he would have been startled, and have wondered why he had not found out before that three-quarters of the spoilt plates which he sold to the glass merchants at a few shillings a ton were of young children whose heads wobbled about from one side to the other quicker than his shutter could take them. He would have found, too, that where he could in twenty minutes make three or four good negatives of any one who could sit or stand still, he would be fortunate if he got one good plate in two hours of a fidgetty infant. The wise photographer will make friends with some Chinaman, and ask him to make him the most hideous dragon he can think of. This he will fix at the door of his studio. Only the good children will be brave enough to pass it. All the bad, wobbly ones will die of fright at the sight of it, and will not trouble him.[7]

F. M. SUTCLIFFE   TUNBRIDGE WELLS.

Carte portrait of unknown woman.

In early 1876, he decided to return to Whitby, and sold the business 'to pay increasing debts'. On 24 March 1876, a notice was put in the *Gazette* by Messrs Spencer and Reeve announcing that an auction was to be held at the Glenwynne Studio on the following Tuesday, at one o'clock prompt:

> The Genuine HOUSEHOLD FURNITURE and EFFECTS, comprising birch and iron Arabian bedsteads, palliasses, hair and wool mattresses, bolsters, pillows, marble-topped washstands, inlaid polished pine chest of drawers, toilet glasses, hip bath, walnut drawing room suite in crimson Utrecht velvet, oval loo tables, occasional table, oak dining room chairs in roan, davenport, gilt chimney glasses, nearly-new carpets, floor-cloth, a few volumes of books, photographs in frames, Elizabethan oak chair, deal table, lady's fancy chair in crimson velvet, fenders, fire-irons, glass, earthenware, Windsor chairs, kitchen table, and the usual culinary requisites.

Sutcliffe had lost everything. He took back to Whitby only his camera and lens, some cases full of photographic journals, and his glass negatives in plate boxes. These contained the negatives of all his early work before 1876, and he carefully padded them inside the boxes, which he bound with iron. It must have been a very sad journey back to Yorkshire, and his return marked the low point of his career. But worse was still to come. When he arrived home in Whitby, he opened his plate boxes to find that nearly all his negatives had been shattered.*

The Tunbridge Wells experience must have been disheartening, to say the least, but it had a very strong influence on Sutcliffe's later success. If his venture had succeeded, he might have become a society photographer, pandering to the

* This would seem to explain why much of his early work survives only as contemporary prints or copy negatives made from prints.

whims and fancies of wealthy sitters. His rejection by the upper-crust society of Tunbridge Wells—one can only speculate on such details as the impact of Eliza's Yorkshire accent on the ladies of the town—was followed by his fierce and faithful attachment to the more lowly working town of Whitby. There were to be no more ateliers, no more boudoir portraits, no more carte mounts printed specially in Paris, no brass plate by the big front door, and no more dreams of the riches to be made by photography.

Whitby was in some ways similar to Tunbridge Wells. The town was benefiting from the growing Victorian habit of taking summer holidays away from home. There was a seasonal influx of visitors who came for recreation and not primarily for health reasons—although English resorts continued to stress this aspect of holidays and were fond of using the delightfully ambiguous adjective 'bracing', which conjures up in the mind both the whiff of ozone and a howling gale along the promenade. Ozone, too, might not be what it at first seemed; Sutcliffe recalled the 'powerful smell' of the harbour 'which strangers called ozone'. Many came to Whitby for relaxation from the smoke and bustle of the northern manufacturing towns. The town offered its visitors miles of open sands, and a superb natural setting. The mouth of the river Esk, where it joins the North Sea at Whitby, forms the best natural harbour on the Yorkshire coast between the Humber and the Tees, and the community which had grown up there had for centuries made its living from, and moulded its way of life around, the sea. Although the resident population of Whitby has changed relatively little over the past one hundred and fifty years, the old town had packed the same number of people into a much smaller area. The cottages of the fishing community jostled each other for every inch of space to be had between the river and the steeply rising cliff, below the squat, wind-buffeted parish church, and the stark outline of the Abbey ruins rising behind it. This was the east side, generally known as the old town, and containing the market square. Across the river lay the main street with its business community, and another warren of alleys and yards climbing up the west cliff and sheltering under Burtree Cragg. Whitby had the feeling of age about it, and a history going back over a thousand years to the time of St Hilda, the first Abbess of Whitby, and Caedmon the poet.

Over the centuries, Whitby and the farming communities nearby in Eskdale had developed in relative isolation. As the only market town in the area, Whitby drew to itself the trade of the district, and people from villages and the countryside for miles around came to sell their produce and to buy the goods they required. Sutcliffe remembered the busy market: 'the stalls of which were on both sides of Church Street, from the Wesley Chapel to St Michael's, as well as in the Town Hall Square. All the Inn Yards, too, were crammed full of farmers' gigs; there were carriers' carts and stalls also along St Ann's Staith on Saturdays.'[8] Before the arrival of the railway, access to Whitby was over bleak moorland roads with the traveller at the mercy of the weather. There was no easy route of access from any direction, and, with the moors at its back, the town looked out across the North Sea through the gateway of its two stonebuilt piers. The sea was the natural highway, and in the early 19th century the easiest way to reach Whitby from London would have been to take the steam packet *Tourist*, which called at the port each Thursday during the summer. The coming of the railway

Paddle-tug *Nunthorpe* towing a ship through the old Whitby bridge.

brought more visitors who found a community which seemed untouched by the upheavals of the developing industrial towns.

The local people claimed an ancestry which stretched back to the Vikings. Their fishing boats, which they called cobles, were modelled on the lines of the old longships, with high bows to ride easily over the choppy seas, and to face the rolling breakers both in putting to sea, and in 'backing in' stern first in heavy weather. Also, their dialect contained words and phrases in use in Scandinavian languages. The men who spoke this dialect had thrived in their relative isolation. They built fine sailing ships, and the sturdy Whitby collier brigs were chosen by Captain Cook and the Admiralty for the exploration of uncharted waters in 1768. In the 19th century, Whitby ships were sailing all over the world—on the Australia run, to China, and to South America. Whitby shipyards built emigrant ships bound for Canada, and whalers, which had to withstand the crushing power of the Greenland ice. The Whitby whaling trade had ended in 1838, well before Sutcliffe came to the town, but memories of it lingered on. The whale blubber was boiled down into oil on the river banks above the harbour, and very evil-smelling stuff it was. Sutcliffe met people who remembered this boiling process and who said 'that the smell of it has never left the place yet, and one old lady who allowed her maid to go to Ruswarp fair one day, when one of these whaling ships came home, told us that when the maid came back at night after the dance which crowned the fair, she knew that the girl had been dancing with a whaler by the perfume which hung about her when she brought in the supper.'⁹

When Sutcliffe returned from Tunbridge Wells, Whitby was beginning to lose the astonishing pre-eminence which it once had. In 1828 Whitby ranked in its registered tonnage of ships as the seventh port in England, though its

View across the harbour towards Whitby West Cliff, c.1900.

population was tiny—hardly more than 10,000 people. In 1866 Whitby owned 414 trading vessels, in addition to its fishing fleet; after this the number declined. But the Whitby yards enjoyed a period of prosperity in the last quarter of the 19th century, having turned from building the wooden sailing ships, for which they were famous, to building iron screw steamers. 1871 saw the building of the last Whitby sailing ship, the barque *Monkshaven*, and the first steamship, the SS *Whitehall*. It was the clearance of the old bridge which restricted the size of the ships which could pass through it from the shipyards to the open sea, and so contributed to the decline of shipbuilding in Whitby.

Sutcliffe lived to see the town become dependent on its visitors and the tourist trade, but, before the turn of the 20th century, Whitby was a working harbour, and the harbour, then as now, was at the very heart of the town. One of the busiest days of the year was the first of March,

> when the collier fleet, having received their complete overhaul by shipwright and sailmaker, by rigger and painter, left harbour to begin their year's work. From early tide to late the bridge was open; those who wished to cross the water must do so by the help of cobles, used as ferryboats, and there were the hoarse cries of the watermen, 'Who's for over? Who's for over?' Sometimes the wind flew round and the vessels came crowding back; driving into one another; getting athwart the bridge; pushing their bowsprits into some of the houses then standing near, and occasionally bringing out a table or a chair; then there was shouting of seamen, of pilots, and of harbour-master, rattling of chains and splintering of bulwarks—confusion, excitement and general hullabaloo.[10]

F. M. SUTCLIFFE   TUNBRIDGE WELLS.

Carte portrait of fms, c.1875.

All the trades which went with the repair and equipping of ships were to be found in Whitby. There were dry docks, mast or 'raff yards', canvas factories, 'sail lofts' and roperies housed in 'rope walks' with quarter-mile-long red-tiled roofs. These craftsmen also served Whitby's fishing industry. The scale of the industry can be judged by the fact that, in the 1880s, an average of 30,000 tons of fish were despatched from Whitby by rail during July, August and September. During the summer the fishing was mainly for herring. The herring shoals were followed around the coast of Britain by boats from Scotland, from the Yorkshire ports, from East Anglia and from Cornwall. The Cornish and Scots crews came to Whitby, living on their boats, and, when the shoals left the local fishing grounds, the Yorkshire boats followed the herring to Cornwall. When the fleet was in, the harbour was filled with different types of fishing vessels from many different ports. On summer evenings, the fishing fleet, including the Yorkshire cobles and 'ploshers' (larger open boats), set out for the fishing grounds which could be ten or fifteen miles away. All hands watched for the flashes of phosphorescence in the water which indicated that they had found a shoal, and then the nets were shot, and the crew waited until dawn. When morning came the nets with the night's catch were hauled in, and they set sail for Whitby, or, if the wind dropped, they rowed the boat home. Sutcliffe remembered the days when the harbour was crammed with sailing vessels and fishing boats so that 'the upper harbour looked more like a forest of trees than the muddy flat it appears today'. He also remembered 'the brown sails of the hundreds of fishing boats from Lowestoft, Penzance, and Scotland, bringing in tons of herring and emptying them on to the New Quay for sending away in barrels by rail' and 'the carts laden with herring nets on their way to dry on the fields at Gallows Close.'[11] Throughout the year fishing was carried on from cobles using long lines, with their hooks baited with mussels for catching cod and plaice, or with 'flithers'—the local name for limpets—for haddock. During the season, salmon and trout were fished for with nets. The cleaning and baiting of lines, and the mending of nets involved whole families in the business of making a living by fishing, and the skills were passed on down the family from generation to generation.

Contrasting with the working town of the fishing community was the West Cliff, which was built up to attract wealthy visitors to the town, and which stood above the rest of Whitby both physically and socially. A contemporary writer noted that: 'On the aristocratic West Cliff there is a railed-in enclosure containing a "Saloon", where a band plays daily, and where operatic and dramatic entertainments are given.'[12] However, although it catered for people of class, Whitby was considered to be a place 'where, if so disposed, we may snap our fingers at fashion and Mrs Grundy's proprieties. We may wear wideawakes, and, if so minded, dine in our flannels.'[13] But, dammit, things weren't allowed to go completely to the dogs, and the reader was assured that 'Whitby is not a cheap or common seaside place; the regular 'Arry is not in his element here.'[14] In fact, compared with many other resorts, Whitby had a relaxed atmosphere, which tended to blur the divisions between the various social groupings. The harbourside and pier were shared between the visitors and the fishermen:

I hardly know what Whitby would do without its pier! You meet everybody

F. M. SUTCLIFFE   TUNBRIDGE WELLS.

Carte portrait of Frank's sister Kate Harebell.*

* Because of the few sitters he had, Sutcliffe seems to have had a good many mounts printed 'Tunbridge Wells' left over when he returned to Whitby. These he seems to have used up on photographs of members of his family, after his return from the South.

there at some hour of the day ... The elderly and middle-aged are generally there in the morning and afternoon, if the weather prove fine, while the evening is for the most part given up to youth and millinery! But the fisherman's favourite promenade is also on the pier. They seem to cover the whole distance from Baxtergate end to the lighthouse. The manners and customs of these Vikings of Whitby, as Du Maurier dubbed them, are instructive, not to say amusing. They either stand with their backs to the protective rails at the edge of the sea wall, or march up and down in gloomy quartettes. A most lugubrious set of men, these seafarers; slow-paced and silent, all with their hands buried deep in their pockets, and always seeming to brood over the prospects of the weather. The majority of them are attired in a recognised 'uniform'—slouch hat, that reminds you of the good old days of piracy, blue jersey, blue pilot-cloth trowsers, and heavy sea-boots. And this noble army of fishermen, living partly on *terra firma* and partly at sea, is *en evidence* from early morning to the curfew hour, when it betakes itself instinctively to quarters or indoor recreation.* ... With the social barometer never very high or very low; with pastoral and romantic scenery as a set-off to a vast expanse of sea; with fairly good society, attractive entertainments, facilities for boating, bathing, fishing, and equestrian exercises—I suppose the lachrymose-looking donkeys come under this head?—Whitby is altogether a desirable spot. Walk out any hour of the day, and you will find something round the harbour or elsewhere to beguile the hour.[15]

It was to this interesting and busy town, which managed to combine its rôle of a resort with that of a working port, that Sutcliffe returned from Tunbridge Wells. He was to live in Whitby, or just outside it, for the next 65 years.

F. M. SUTCLIFFE   TUNBRIDGE WELLS.

Carte portrait of Frank's sister Jessamine.

* Evidently, the writer did not realise that they spent the night at sea, and not indulging in 'indoor recreation'.

chapter 4

The Trials of a Portrait Photographer

Frank Sutcliffe was in love—love runs in the family, and his bringing up all went that way—but the course of his love, as usual, has not run smoothly. Nature intended to have Frank Sutcliffe as her companion always; but Fate lets him go to his mistress on rare occasions only. Fate made a photographer of him, and told Nature that she was doing so, and that he and she would then live together always. But that was only one of Fate's tricks, for gradually she kept the lovers from meeting one another, and now, although Frank, whenever he has a chance, escapes from the fetters Fate has rivetted on him, and goes to see Nature, then his mistress withholds her smiles and kisses she used to lavish on him. Yet Fate has not been altogether unkind, but has made his prison beautiful, and, after all, it is possible the work she forces him to do in making portraits of people who live in or come to his beloved Whitby is really more useful than the work he would have chosen for himself, making photographs or painting autumn mists and sunsets.[1]

This was the allegorical account of Sutcliffe's work as a portrait photographer given by him to his friend W.J. Warren, who was writing an article on Sutcliffe for *The Amateur Photographer*. Sutcliffe is remembered for his photographs of life in and around Whitby, but although he sold copies of these photographs both from his shop and through dealers, he could not possibly have made a living from their sale alone. His income came from his work as a portrait photographer, and, although he may often have wished to escape from these shackles, financial necessity kept him hard at work at his portrait business. The photographs which he took for himself, and which he judged by his own standards and not those of a sitter in his studio or a client supervising a commission, had to be fitted in around his work as a professional photographer. The two went closely together, and the enormous amount of skill he acquired working daily as a photographer and as his own darkroom assistant, processor and printer, gave him a flying start in the form of a very deep understanding of photographic processes, and an expertise to know the boundaries of what was possible in photography—how a problem could be got round, or what corners could be cut when photographing difficult subjects. Because he knew what his equipment and plates could and could not do, he was able to push them to their limits, achieving results many of which were technically outstanding, apart from any other merits they had.

When Sutcliffe arrived back in Whitby, he went to live at a cottage in Stakesby, which was near his mother and family at Ewe Cote. His financial situation must have been pretty poor, and his family were in no position to offer help. Before he could bring home any money earned by his photography, he had once again to find a suitable building to use as a studio. In 1876 the Whitby jet industry was in decline. In 1870-2 it had reached its peak, employing the astonishing number of 1,400 men and boys to produce ornaments and jewellery to be worn by ladies of fashion. The number of jet workers was to decline to less than 300 by 1884. Like the fishermen, they too had a distinctive outfit, wearing blue smocks like French labourers of the period. They were made even more distinctive by the stains from brown jet-dust and the rouge used for polishing the finished jet. Plate 47 shows the interior of a jet works, with the men at the central bench trimming rough jet, and those on the outer benches working at grindstones and polishing wheels driven by bands from the overhead flywheels. Sutcliffe found a more humble jet shop in Waterloo Old Yard, which was down an alley near the top of Flowergate. A Mr Barber had his works there and, perhaps because of dwindling trade, was prepared to let half the premises to Sutcliffe. It was far from an ideal place for a studio, and must have made a striking contrast with his Tunbridge Wells premises. But it was better than nothing, and Sutcliffe cleared out the wheels and grindstones, and enlarged the jet shop's skylights. The big drawback was that Mr Barber still had a dozen wheels working away in the other half of the premises, and the noise in the studio was tremendous:

> As these upper storeys had been in many cases run up on nine-inch walls of brick, and as the wheels were in frameworks fastened to a wooden beam about three feet from the floor, it is not surprising that when a dozen or eighteen wheels were all busily humming at the same time, to say nothing of the grindstone on which the tools were sharpened, the vibration was pretty bad.

The place shook so much that some of the more delicate work, such as copying, had to be done between twelve and one, which was the workmen's dinner hour. The racket upset the sitters, but not Sutcliffe: 'The noise from the wheels was deafening, yet I got so used to it that I never heard it, unless a stranger sitting for his portrait asked, "What is that infernal din in the next building?"'[2] Noise was not the only hazard to be braved by his customers. During what he referred to as 'the three hot days which form the English summer' the sun beat down on the glass of the studio roof, and the temperature often soared to 90 degrees. Sutcliffe said:

> Though I revelled in the genial warmth, I lost many sitters from that cause. Stout aldermen would come blowing up my lead-covered stairs, sink into the sitter's chair for a few seconds, and then go out again, saying 'You must be a salamander to stand this; I cannot'. Other sitters of the fairer sex would put a brave face on it, and at times faint, while supported only by the head-rest.[3]

The converted jet shop was up a smelly back alley and the studio windows opened over a spot where the neighbours threw out 'all their over-ripe pears, herrings, and the like'. As a result, the studio and the sitters were plagued by flies. Sutcliffe remembered:

> Many a time have I seen half-a-dozen flies crawling over my sitter's coat, to say nothing of an occasional fly inside my camera, making strange marks as it walked across the plate at the time of exposure. How to get rid of these flies bothered me for years. I made friends with the spiders, as I did with a mouse who used to sit near my sink edge as I developed on a night; but there must be a limit even to the appetite of spiders, for my flies never seemed to decrease, though the spiders increased so that I have seen more than one spider's web inside my camera.[4]

His problem was eventually solved by the purchase of an auralia, a plant which, by some strange process, banished flies from his studio.

With his customers having to run the gauntlet of flies and heatstroke, Sutcliffe needed all the support for his business he could get, and, as Ruskin had suggested on his visit to Brantwood, he began to put on his photograph mounts the proud title 'Photographer to Mr Ruskin'. At the entrance to the alley leading to his studio, there was a showcase of specimens of his work, and on this he announced himself as 'Photographer to John Ruskin'. Unfortunately, not everyone in Whitby had heard of John Ruskin, and the kindly but ignorant 'Mayor' of the town took Sutcliffe on one side and said: 'Look here, young man, if you take my advice you'll put on that board of yours, "Photographer to the clergy, nobility and gentry"; they'll put more brass into your pockets than John rustic the countryman ever will.'[5] He apparently thought 'Ruskin' was a combination of 'rustic' and 'bumpkin', and that Sutcliffe was making a bid for the patronage of the local farm labourers.

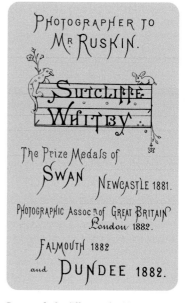

Reverse of a Sutcliffe carte-de-visite mount, *c*.1883.

The Waterloo Yard studio had nothing but the bare essentials for portrait photography, or as Sutcliffe wryly told a friend, 'it did not suffer from any vulgar attributes of elegant sumptuousness or overequipment either in apparatus or decoration'. The studio itself was tiny, and there was no room for such luxuries as a reception room. During the season, when business was brisk, sitters had to wait their turn behind the 'background', whilst the business of arranging the previous sitter and exposing the plate went on in the studio. The darkroom was below the studio and, as he was using the wet-plate process, but had no assistant, Sutcliffe had to run up and down the stairs once or twice for each sitter. His main business was in taking carte portraits, which he took two on a plate, and charged 10s. per dozen. This would seem to have been a good price, but Sutcliffe worked hard to get it, doing everything himself—acting as receptionist, sensitising the plates, taking the portraits, developing the plates, printing from them, cleaning the old images off plates which had already been printed from, sweeping out the studio and, in winter, lighting the fire and sweeping the snow off the studio roof. Even when his day's work was done at the studio, he took home the day's output of prints to mount. This kept him and Eliza at work until 2 a.m. during the summer season. He had a little garden at Waterloo Yard where he did his printing in frames by sunlight, but this was later built over. The theatre which stood there cut down Sutcliffe's already limited working space and also the amount of light which reached the studio, but it proved helpful in unexpected ways. During one season when he was working late at the studio, he listened for two shots to ring out from the theatre, which meant that the villain was dead, the performance over, and that it was 11 p.m.—time for Sutcliffe to walk home.

Despite its unsavoury situation, the little studio attracted distinguished visitors. George Du Maurier, the illustrator and writer, often came to chat with Sutcliffe, but would never sit for his portrait on his own, though he promised to do so 'in the event of finding himself sufficiently good-looking'. On other occasions, Sutcliffe photographed members of the Du Maurier family, and also the American poet and diplomat James Russell Lowell. Sometimes these distinguished sitters made their way up the alley unannounced:

> When I was in the dark room preparing plates for or developing those
> exposed on a sitter in the studio I could hear anyone go up the stairs over my
> head. If the person who went up came down before I could leave my plate, I
> used to shout, 'Hullo! Who's there?' If the reply was only, 'The gas account,
> please,' then the gas would wait at the foot of the stairs till I came out. …
> Nervous old ladies have been said to have jumped from the top of the stairs

to the bottom on hearing my answer from below them to their knock on the door above, but as I was in the darkroom I never saw these jumps. … One day, however, in reply to my 'Hullo! Who's there?' came the reply, 'The Archbishop of York,' and in reply to my question, 'What can I do for his Grace?' came the answer 'He would like to have his portrait taken'. Then I came out, and said that I should be most pleased to do so after I had got rid of the baby who was then raising Cain in the studio.[6]

'Get on with the baby,' he said to Sutcliffe, 'babies are more important than archbishops.' Unfortunately, the baby proved temperamental, and by the time Sutcliffe had been able to get its portrait, Archbishop Thomson had gone.

At this time, Sutcliffe was using albumenized paper to make his prints. One of his favourite anecdotes, written in his own inimitable style, was as follows:

It took I forget how many whites of eggs to albumenize a ream of paper, a paper, by the way, which either bore the water-mark of Rive in France, or of Saxe in Germany. There were too many shirt buttons ground up in the pulp of English-made papers to make them suitable for photographic use. Each particle of shirt button made a black spot on the paper when it came to be printed. If this black spot appeared on the nose of a portrait, the sitter felt annoyed, and even when the photographer undertook to fork out the spot with the point of a needle it was easy to see that the sitter was still unhappy.

It took a good many pounds of silver to make a bath which would float a sheet of paper [to sensitise it], and it also took a lot of a saturated solution of silver to keep the bath up to the mark each day. Besides which it had to be kept free from any dust or impurities, and was filtered every day after use. The charlady came on a Friday, according to custom: on turning the tap over the sink no water came. Very likely the Waterworks Company had cut it off because we had not been able to pay the water rate.

Seeing a big jar full of what she took for water she naturally emptied it into her pail and set to with soap and scrubbing brush on her knees to make the darkroom and sensitising room as clean as a new pin.

It was my custom to leave the studio to Providence on a Friday morning. No one ever came to be photographed on a Friday, such a thing would have been too unlucky for words, and as Fridays, like Sundays, were invariably finer than the other five days of the week I tried to make hay on the beach or in the country.

Well, when I looked in about noon the charlady met me at the door with hands outstretched, hands and arms becoming blacker and blacker every minute she stood in the sun. Her face, too, was black in places where she had wiped the sweat from her brow or had pushed back a stray lock of hair. I saw at a glance what had happened, for were not my own fingers, and often my trousers, black from the same cause. In spite of the loss of many pounds worth of silver I could not help smiling at the way the silver had decorated the lady's face.[7]

Sutcliffe was also familiar with the difficult carbon process.* He said that when he was young, there were only two printing processes to choose from—albumenized paper, and the carbon process. 'It was pointed out to me that any duffer could use the former. I had therefore no alternative but to choose the latter.' He had no book or instructions on carbon printing, and learned the hard way from experience and from failures. When he had mastered the process and was producing beautiful carbon prints, he went to London to see if he could sell any prints of photographs which he had taken for himself, and which might enable him to escape from the daily grind of portrait photography:

> I made some prints on sepia tissue, and even went to the trouble of mounting them on drawing-paper, that they might be quite flat. These prints were mostly from whole-plate negatives, but I cut each print down where I thought cutting down would do it good—some prints even had skies printed into them. Then I went into the market-place [i.e. to London] and received a shock from which I never recovered. The dealer in London to whom I showed them told me that they would not sell. He said they looked too much like pictures, and not enough like photographs. He also said that people who wanted pictures went to Mr Agnew for them, and that people who wanted photographs would only buy them if printed on albumenized paper, and that the prints, too, must be cut all exactly to one particular size, and that to add skies and improve the photographs in any way was simply a waste of labour which the customer would not pay for. He would not try to sell my carbon-prints just as they were. No, I must go home and print them on albumen-paper like those he showed me—books full of them—and cut them all as big as the plates would allow. He even went so far as to tell me that if I could make the prints half-an-inch bigger both ways than the largest I had, they would sell all the better, for it seemed that people who bought photographs went by the size more than anything. That it was possible to do anything too well was certainly a terrible shock to a youngster. I remember going the same day into the British Museum and wondering whether the old monks who had written some of the exquisite Books of Hours and Missals I saw under glass cases, had ever been told their printing was 'too much like pictures'.[8]

It was at times like this that Sutcliffe felt 'the depressing drudgery of a photographer's life' hanging heavy about him, which made him wonder if it was all worth it:

> When we consider our work seriously, … we cannot help wondering what attractions photography had for us when young, that we should give the rest of our lives to it. Certainly the prospect of having to stand in front of an evil-smelling sink, with our hands in poisonous chemicals† in a dark-room with a dimmed red light in our eyes, for the best part of every summer's day, did not enter into our youthful calculations.[9]

He came to the conclusion that good photography had little or nothing to do with a successful photographic business: 'Not only has the quality of the work done very little effect on the business, but the photographer soon finds that if he is to get on he must devote his energy to other things besides photography or art.'[10] Many successful portrait photographers, he said, were businessmen who knew very little about photography, but walked about their studios, signing cheques and keeping a keen eye on the accounts. This sort of life had nothing

* He was also expert at printing platinotypes, and tried each new printing process as it was introduced throughout his career.

† Sutcliffe was careful with the dangerous chemicals which he used in the darkroom. Nevertheless, he almost asphyxiated himself when he accidentally dropped a Winchester full of ammonia which, at that time, was used as a developing agent (it was mixed with pyro, and was later replaced by soda). Night after night he was kept awake by fingers made painful through contact with his photographic chemicals. It is little wonder that, at his worst moments, he thought of his darkroom as a dangerous prison.

to do with photography as Sutcliffe understood it, but as it was his 'bread and butter' work, he had to grin and bear it.

Time and again, Sutcliffe was brought back down to the hard reality of the life of a professional photographer. He must sometimes have hated the work which kept him indoors when he could have been out and about taking photographs round the harbour or in the countryside. He felt that he was stuck in his studio

> taking portraits of babies and twins, and groups of young children, and old maids. Sometimes I get out with my camera before breakfast. If I venture out in the daytime I am sure to meet a fond parent who is bringing little Johnnie to be taken again, as his grandmother (who is nearly blind) thinks he is laughing too much. How I envy that Italian photographer who can afford to refuse to take all sitters but those he thinks will make good pictures.[11]

The frustrating thing was that he believed that, with capital, he could have risen above the unquestioned conventions of the portrait photograph:

> At present few photographers have sufficient capital to develop the artistic side of their businesses. The photographer may lie awake all night planning improvements in his studio and devising tasteful ways of 'setting' his wares, but when daylight comes he seldom finds enough money in his trousers pockets to buy the raw materials with.

He resented the fact that photographers were regarded as just one more variety of shopkeeper, although he saw the value of having a subsidiary line of business—frames, artists' materials or whatever—to help make ends meet and relieve photographers of some of their financial worries. This, Sutcliffe said, would give the photographer more time for thinking about his proper work, but he adds:

> His proper work! What is that? Making pictures of his sitters, of people he has never seen in his life before, and whom he will never see again. In fifteen minutes he and his sitter have to become acquainted; he must make his sitter feel at home, no matter what his or her age may be, no matter whether he or she is all flesh or all nerves; he must take that sitter's portrait when the sitter is not aware of it, and he must arrange the light so that the sitter looks his best. The successful maker of pictorial portraits truly must find it difficult to know where to look for a school which will teach him all this.[12]

One of the difficulties which Sutcliffe had to face was that many people had been photographed by professionals only once or twice before in their lives, and many had been 'so roughly handled by unskilful practitioners that they dread to repeat the operation'. Many looked forward to a visit to the photographer's with as little enthusiasm as a visit to the dentist's. Sutcliffe tried to put his sitters at their ease by chatting to them, and time and again his customers would tell him how nightmarish their last visit to a photographer's had been:

> Generally the sitter is ready to tell the experiences of his last sitting, many years ago. He might probably say that it was a very hot day, chosen by himself, no doubt, because it was so bright and sunny, and therefore suitable for the purpose, and then go on to explain how the young lady at the bottom of the stairs took his name and his money, and how the ascent of

the staircase landed him breathless into the studio, where his misery was increased by the photographer directing him to stand with one hand on a pile of books on a table, and with one leg crossed over the other, while the artist pulled his personal appearance to pieces; then the unfortunate victim gathered, from remarks addressed more to the camera than the sitter, that his eyes were too blue to take, that red hair always came out black, that he would have to be puffed, that the necktie he wore would come out white, and then, after having stood in this most trying position for some time, was perhaps told that a standing position did not suit him; a wonderful accessory would then be brought out, and an uncomfortable seat made of one of its many changes. Though glad of a rest, the unfortunate sitter would be twisted this way and that way till, as he said, he felt no longer a living person, but a kind of vegetable, bathed in a cold sweat. At last, when nature could stand no more, and he was rapidly losing consciousness, he was told to look there, and not to wink till the photographer counted thirty—then, with a splitting headache, and a resolve never to be taken again, the victim was allowed to depart.[13]

Sutcliffe placed the blame largely on the type of men who became portrait photographers between 1860 and 1895. Whereas the first photographers were, most of them, 'men of education, painters, engravers, and the like', the next generation of photographers were 'men, in many cases, of less refinement, who saw there was money in the job. They learnt the rudiments of the work from the men who had cameras and lenses to sell. These were bought on condition the vendor taught the buyer how to use them.'[14] This was a period of unnatural portrait photography, when the inside of many photographic galleries was 'utterly unlike any place to be seen on earth, or dreamed of in dreams'. Gentlemen often were posed leaning on cardboard columns, with one leg crossed over the other, and with their hat in their hand. A hidden iron support held the head in position, and behind the standing figure, a painted background showed parkland sweeping away into the distance. Sutcliffe acknowledged that 'even Sir Joshua Reynolds used to throw in a bit of park and a marble pillar with his portraits; but then Sir Joshua's sitters very likely all owned parks of their own.'[15] A whole industry was geared to make props for a photographic trade which was rooted in artificiality:

Everyone, from the optician to the cabinet-maker, helped to make photographic portraits as inartistic as possible. The optician gave the photographer lenses which showed every link on a man's watch-chain and every lace hole in his boot with microscopic definition; the cabinet-maker 'designed' furniture on purpose for the photographer—furniture never seen anywhere but in photographic galleries.[16]

However, although Sutcliffe saw the absurdity of pretending that sitters in the studio were posed in front of parkland, or beside waterfalls, business demanded that he too should equip himself with posing chairs and all the other paraphernalia required. He had a series of painted backgrounds, which were mounted on a system of rollers so that they could be changed easily. They showed various idealised settings—such as an open landscape, with sky above, trees on the left, a river winding its way into the distance, and with a balustraded terrace providing the foreground. A turn of the handle replaced this with a conservatory full of plants, another turn produced a background of cumulus clouds; another produced

> a stormy sea, with storm-clouds gathering above it. On the right was a rock, with a lighthouse upon it; in the foreground were rocks and a big breaker just about to break. As a seaside photographer, that background and I were seldom far apart; in the day-time I saw it nearly every time I looked on the ground glass of my studio camera, and it made a background for my dreams on a night.[17]

His favourite background was of plain black. This was the first he ever used and, at that time, the only one he had. He had hung two engravings of paintings by Rembrandt in the studio to show his customers how fine black backgrounds were. But people never saw the backgrounds, and instead asked him whatever had made him hang 'such horrid old frights' up there. So it was usually back to the scene of the stormy sea and the lighthouse, with a shovelful of sand, shells, and seaweed scattered to cover the pattern of the oilcloth on the studio floor. The sand and shells were kept in a special box in the studio. The finishing touches were made to the seashore scene by the addition of two stuffed seagulls, one of which had lost an eye and was losing its stuffing. Other props included an artificial rock, a fence, and a home-made stile, with the top rail polished beautifully. When his sitters commented that many people must have sat on the stile to give it such a polish, Sutcliffe had to explain that he had got the rail out of a cow-house, and that an old cow had done the polishing.

Young woman by studio 'rock' with painted background.

When he wasn't saddened by the low level of photography which public taste and financial necessity brought him to, he could see the funny side of life as a portrait photographer. It would make an interesting chronicle of events, he said; one could

> describe the photographer's state of mind when he woke up in the middle of one Saturday night, and remembered, without doubt, that he had locked up the studio at noon with a sitter in it. … What thrilling accounts of shipwrecks on land could be told. How a coming storm had made the creaky old studio roof groan and snap in an appalling way, how all hands had been called to clear the decks, how gallantly attempts had been made to save the roof by making it fast with cord to the table and stove, and how at last it all went at once when a gust of wind more spiteful than the rest tore it off, carried it away, and threw it down in the yard behind in a crumpled heap. How soon we learn that a skylight is but little protection from the weather, how the hail and the rain, the heat and the cold find their way in, how tiresome the flies, how they always seem to settle on the sitter's nose just as the cap is taken off. What a capital model a photographer would be for a 19th-century Job, whom the photographer—tormented by groups and babies, advertisement touts and commercial travellers, book hawkers, background painters and assistants—often envies, for was not old Job allowed to sit down, at least the artists generally make him sitting. When the last perambulator has wheeled its infantile cargo away—now that perambulators have rubber tyres they spring

on the photographer unawares before he has time to rush out of the back door—too often a baby in arms will come and tell him that there is no rest for the weary.[18]

Sutcliffe saw an unending procession of humanity troop through his studio, and he met a great variety of people. He had many stories to tell about his sitters. Whilst taking a portrait of an engaged couple, the fork of the head-rest slipped and lifted off the young man's hair completely, to the utter astonishment of his fiancée. On another occasion a group of five sailors came to the studio, and one asked if he could smoke. Sutcliffe said yes, and went to put the plate in the silver bath. When he returned with it ready for exposure, he found all five smoking and the little studio fog-bound by the smoke—'but there was no appreciation of mist effects in those days, so we opened the window and fanned it out with a sheet of cardboard'. Another customer was a tall countryman who wished to be taken full length, standing. The head-rest had gone to the blacksmith's for repairs, and the young man's head 'followed the plough in imagination in regular beats from right to left'. On developing the plate—a wet-plate—there was, as Sutcliffe had feared, no head to be seen. He showed the developed plate (a wet-plate can be seen as a positive) to the countryman who, to Sutcliffe's astonishment, declared that he was perfectly satisfied: 'Niver mind t'heead, my boots is beautiful.' His new boots were, apparently his most important feature. Sometimes the language of people from the dales was not easily understood. A young couple of farm servants came into the studio, and Sutcliffe listened in amazement as the young lady asked: 'Wilt er be stript, lad?' to which he replied, 'Aye, lass, ah'l be stripped.' She only meant should they take their top coats off or not. Occasionally it was Sutcliffe's language which caused trouble. Once he was photographing a tall lady whom he described as being 'without any suspicion of sauciness'. He wanted to get rid of the photographic stare which she adopted, so that she would appear more natural, and said, unfortunately mixing his words: 'You may *wink* as much as you like, madam.' To this she made the withering reply: 'Sir, I am not in the habit of *winking* at any time; if you mean that I may *blink*, you ought to have said so.'[19] Sutcliffe had one final piece of advice to offer his fellow professionals: 'Whenever you are troubled with a sitter who has fared "not wisely but too well", don't tell him he is drunk, and that he must go away, but pretend to take him, and he will go away at once like a lamb.'[20]

Young boy, probably Frank's son Horace, taken against his studio 'rock'.

Like modern portrait photographers, much of Sutcliffe's studio work was photographing children and babies. He found children much more natural sitters than adults:

Strange to say, the camera has no terrors for children, and it is in the portraits of them that we find the most natural expressions. Even when they have been threatened with the most terrible punishments if they are not good, they soon forget these threats, and appear quite natural. One of the most charming groups of children which ever impressed itself on my camera was made up of five young children. When the sitting was over I told their mother how good they had been and how charming they looked. She replied: 'Yes, I thought they would be good, for I gave them all a good 'skelping' before they came.'[21]

Children, he found, were much less inhibited about saying what they thought about the business of having their photograph taken:

> If our grown-up sitters would only say what they think, as children do, their portraits might be more like them. A head full of unuttered remarks must be a sore trial for any camera. … In entering the studio, if they were to look up at the white blinds on the skylight and say, 'Hulloa, is it washing day, mister?' or down at the white 'continuation' of the white background and say, 'I like your white carpet, but don't you think it wants washing?' or, 'I've come to be photographed', and then, rather nervously, 'Will there be anything left of me afterwards?'—if grown-ups would only pretend that they enjoyed having their likenesses taken, what a much more glorious quarter of an hour they might have.[22]

He had projects for bringing his camera down to the level of his young sitters. One of his ideas was to make the camera in the shape of a pig, with the lens hidden inside the snout, and with ears, eyes and tail added to give life to the deception.

Sutcliffe, over the years, had photographed hundreds of babies.* In one article he writes of them passing before his eyes in a dream:

> The first few were not bad; I was not ashamed of them, for they were babies in wheelbarrows held by some older sister, or of babies in perambulators. … Here followed dozens and dozens of babies in an arm-chair, which I recognized as the substantial, hard, windsor chair which I bought to put my sitters in when I started my first studio. As I looked at the babies in that chair I could hear them cry with pain as they lurched sideways and bumped their poor little skulls against the arms of the chair. Behind many of these pictures, as they flitted past, were ghostly images of anxious faces, and hands clutching at the baby's clothes. Then I remembered that these were no ghosts, but the fragments of nurses and mothers who had tried to hide themselves behind the babes while endeavouring to keep their precious charge from overbalancing and falling headlong out of my chair.[23]

'The New Camera'.

The best place to photograph a baby, he found, was on the floor where it could not fall and hurt itself. The only problem on the floor was when babies became mobile, and Sutcliffe had a solution to this. 'If the baby has learned the gentle art of crawling, we tie it to the table leg, but only as a last resort.'

Chancellor Austen, for many years the Rector of Whitby, often told Sutcliffe that the long arch and alleyway which led to his Waterloo Yard studio was too much like the Biblical bushel—that Sutcliffe's light was too much hidden beneath it—and that he ought to move into better premises. In 1894 he opened a new studio in Skinner Street which was by far the best in Whitby. The *Whitby Gazette* reported:

> The whole is a credit to Mr Sutcliffe, and forms an additional attraction to the too few modern structural beauties of Whitby. Not merely are the dressing-rooms and waiting-rooms, the guest-rooms, and the reception-rooms arranged with all due regard to visitors, but the apartments for developing, printing, toning, and the like—all indeed within the nomenclature of the photographic artist—are in perfect order and sequence.

Photographing the First-Born; illustration by George Du Maurier.

* Sutcliffe had a copy of George Du Maurier's illustration *Photographing the First-Born* hanging in his studio. Although the drawing predates his friendship with Du Maurier, Sutcliffe obviously identified closely with the struggling photographer.

The frontage of Frank Sutcliffe's studio at 25 Skinner Street, Whitby.

The entire building will be warmed in winter by hot-water pipes and cooled in summer by a well-conceived system of ventilation.[24]

Sutcliffe had come a long way from his early days in the rattling, roasting jet shop.

His ideal studio would have been enormous. He once described such a place which, he admitted, would cost a fortune:

A photographer should not be tied to work in one room and one light; he should have many rooms, bright and dull, where he could make such pictures as his mood felt imperative or as the dress or face of his sitter suggested—real rooms, with real seats in the windows, quite unlike the photographer's studio full of shams.[25]

The Skinner Street studio was a step in the right direction:

In my studio I have no painted backgrounds now, but use the walls of the room. For variety's sake I have a few curtains on wires stretched across the room, which can be used as backgrounds. I believe they look more homelike, and certainly do not take up so much room as painted backgrounds; besides, the sitter *feels* more at home when the studio looks like a room, and not like the wings of a stage.[26]

He had designed his studio so that different lighting effects could be attempted. He criticised photographic portraits for their monotonous similarity,* and censured photographers for a lack of boldness in using strong light. Some of Sutcliffe's portraits show a striking use of lighting.

In his new studio, he tried to get away from the artificiality of some of his early work:

Carte portrait of unknown woman.

Carte portrait of Frank's daughter Kathy.

Carte portrait of unknown woman.

Carte portrait of unknown man.

Carte portrait of mother and baby.

Carte portrait of unknown boy.

Carte portrait of fms as a 'ghost'.

Detail of whole-plate print by fms of his daughters Kathy and Lulu.

We laugh when we see the strained attitudes of the people who were taken during the carte mania, between 1860 and 1870—men standing with one leg crossed over the other, and the like; but the photographers of 1930 and 1940 will laugh at us quite as much, unless we try to be more truthful in placing our sitters before we photograph them. Nowadays no photographer who values his reputation does pose his sitters. He lets them pose themselves, and only when they appear natural does he expose. It is often difficult in the short time at the photographer's disposal to know whether his sitters are natural, or whether they are posing themselves. As a rule, all quiet, unrestrained attitudes are natural, while, when the sitter throws his arms and legs about all over the furniture, they are unnatural.[27]

The problem was that the acute observation of the sensitive photographer had to be blunted so as not to offend the vanity of the sitter.

When once the painter has gathered from the remarks his sitters and their friends make how much thinner, stouter, darker, fairer, taller, shorter, etc.,

* One reason for this was retouching, which, Sutcliffe said, 'improves the likeness so much that no-one recognises the portrait'.

etc., the sitter wishes to be, the rest is easy, easy that is for the painter, but often very difficult for the poor photographer. Many people will say, like Oliver Cromwell, when they enter the studio, 'I wish to be taken just as I am, without any flattery of any kind'. It is these people who are the most difficult to please, for they have got an idea in their heads that they know what they are like, and if the photographer fails to hit this idea in his work then the result is a failure. The photographer of experience knows that, as a rule, people under eighteen wish to appear as old as possible, and those over eighteen as young as possible, and that all who weigh over eighteen stones wish to look less heavy, while those who are lean wish to look well fed. With the help of dress, the direction of light, and the tone of the background these problems may be solved to the sitter's delight.

With skill, a stout lady could be made to look slimmer: 'Of course, her friends will say the photograph is not a bit like her, that it is not heavy enough, and other kind things, but it is the sitter who pays, and not her friends.'[28]

Working within the limits set by the wishes of his sitters Sutcliffe tried to avoid any form of artificial posing, looking instead for those positions when the sitter was naturally at rest. He had to accept the compromises which were forced upon the portrait photographer by his sitters, but tried to make his professional work rise above the mundane business of merely taking 'likenesses'.

chapter 5

'The Pictorial Boswell of Whitby'

Frank Sutcliffe's friend, the photographer Harold Hood, called him 'the
pictorial Boswell of Whitby'. The photographs which Sutcliffe took in and
around the town after his return from Tunbridge Wells provide a fond and
faithful record of the changing life of a community over the years before the
turn of the century. But although Sutcliffe often took photographs for what he
considered the best of all reasons—sheer pleasure—and would no doubt have
photographed the beauties of Whitby and the coast in any case, Harold Hood
pointed out that one motive which drove him to produce the body of work
from which the main illustrations of this book are drawn, was 'a sort of reasoned
desperation'.[1] After setting up the Waterloo Yard studio in 1876, Sutcliffe ran
his business single-handed, and with a minimum of overheads. Despite working
himself to the point of exhaustion during the summer season, it soon became
clear that he could not make a living from portrait photography alone. The
reason for this was not that he lacked skill as a studio worker, nor that he was
incompetent as a businessman; it was simply that the annual 'season' for tourists
lasted barely six weeks and, however hard he worked during this brief period, he
could not hope to make enough to live on for the rest of the year. The residents
of Whitby and Eskdale brought just enough business to keep the studio open
throughout the year, but not enough to enable Sutcliffe to look to his portrait
business for a regular income.

There are almost no photographs by Sutcliffe of tourists in Whitby on a
summer's day. The sunshine brought out the visitors and for Sutcliffe meant
a day working hard in the heat of his studio and the gloom of his darkroom.
He had to take photographs out of doors whenever he found the time. It was
probably not visual sensitivity alone which led him to tell his readers that the
best hours for photography in summer in fine weather were in the early morning
and the evening: 'The hours before eight o'clock in the morning, before the sun
has driven off the mist, and late in the evening, when the shadows are long, will
be found to surpass every other part of the day when the sun is high and the
shadows broken and scattered.'[2] These were the times when he could get away
from his studio to take photographs for himself. Fate was keeping him away from
his mistress, Nature, but Sutcliffe still managed to catch glimpses of her:

Woodcut by Irene Sutcliffe of Frank peering
out of his darkroom.

> If the budding photographer is compelled, as I was, to walk home in the
> twilight year after year, rather than travel by train or tram, he will have
> greater opportunities for listening to Nature's sermons. He will, in fact, find
> it at times impossible not to listen as he looks up to the skyline or some
> familiar bit of street or landscape. Nature, in fact, at such times speaks at him
> with no uncertain tones, and says: 'Don't I look grand at this moment, with
> the sky ablaze with light, and all the insignificant paltry little details sunk
> into nothingness. Look at the block of chimneys against the sky. You would
> not think they were such ordinary commonplace things as chimney-pots as
> you see them now. You would say they were part of the battlements of an
> enchanted castle rather. If you cannot see how grand they look just now,
> look at them tomorrow morning over your shoulder as you go to work; they
> will then be chimneys, and nothing more.' ... The twilight is the time for
> finding pictures; not only are the little things the lens sees only too well lost
> in obscurity or 'wropt in mistery', which is the same thing, but the student's

Beggars Bridge, Glaisdale, under snow.

mind is more open to receive impressions after his day's work, when he is able to leave his load of paltry trifles and annoyances behind him in the office or workroom. If the young photographer is foolish enough to think that he can make pictorial photographs and hope to find an insight into Nature's secrets while thinking of his business, or other matters, he is mistaken. Nature demands an open mind, one free from the cares and worries of this restless world. Then, when she finds one full of that peace which passeth understanding, she will pour into that mind her treasures with both hands.[5]

The Sutcliffe family used to spend periods during the summer in Eskdale, sometimes in rented cottages, and sometimes at Hart Hall, Glaisdale. Many of Sutcliffe's country scenes were taken around Glaisdale and Lealholm in Eskdale. These visits to the country can hardly be described as holidays for Sutcliffe. A typical day would involve getting up at 4 a.m. and either photographing or gardening until breakfast. He then walked four miles to the railway junction at Grosmont and caught the early train to Whitby. After a day spent in the studio photographing visitors and babies, he left the studio at 6.30 p.m. or later, caught the train back to Grosmont, walked the four miles to Glaisdale, and then went out taking photographs until it was too dark for the camera to see. Winter was the season in which Sutcliffe had most time on his hands, and he delighted in waking up to find the landscape transformed overnight by frost or snow. He used to rush out with his camera without waiting for his breakfast: 'How many pairs of new boots have we spoiled, how many weeks have we spent in bed, how many plates have we spoiled over snow scenes, no one can tell.'[4] To Sutcliffe's sorrow, the public did not share his love of snow scenes, and by the index number of the negative of Beggar's Bridge Glaisdale under snow he wrote, 'Don't do any more snow scenes: nobody buys them'.

As early as 1875 Sutcliffe had contributed an article 'On Out-Door Photography and on Printing' to *The Year-Book of Photography and Photographic News Almanac*. In it he describes how he approaches photographing figures out of doors:

> When photographing rustic figures out of doors, I think the best plan is to quietly watch your subjects as they are working or playing, or whatever they are doing, and when you see a nice arrangement to say, 'Keep still just as you are a quarter of a minute', and expose, instead of placing an arm here and a foot there, which is sure to make your subject constrained, and consequently stiff. To be able to wait and watch, you will want a plate that will keep moist at least a quarter of an hour. This may easily be done by using old collodion, and in hot weather, also sponging the inside of the dark slide, making it quite wet.[5]

It is obvious that Sutcliffe's portrait work would make him skilful at dealing with many kinds of people and making them swiftly feel at ease, but it is interesting to see, in addition, that his method of approaching figure studies was an extension of his portrait work. In both types of work he only exposed when the subjects were naturally at rest. There was no posing, and the fact that he asked his sitters to keep still was not an idiosyncrasy which tended towards artificiality, but was a necessary request because of the slow speed of the equipment and plates which he was using.

He had begun his landscape and genre work early in his career as a photographer. On his visit to Rievaulx to take photographs for Mr Frith, he noticed that there was a pretty girl at the farm nearby. On another visit he decided to take a photograph of her, if he could. But she was away for the day, and so instead Sutcliffe got the old lady who minded the gate to the Abbey to sit for a full length portrait. 'I believe this old lady sold well', he recalled, 'perhaps better than the pretty girl would have done.' Sutcliffe was very careful not to sell prints of subjects which had originated as portrait commissions, but sometimes his portrait and genre work overlapped. When Sutcliffe was out walking with his camera one day he met a farmer who said he would like him to take a photograph of his mother. Sutcliffe asked when it would be convenient for her to come to the studio but was told: 'Oh, she won't do that; you'll have to take her at her own house. She never goes from home.' So he arranged that he would take the old lady at her own house 'some fine morning':

> The next morning it rained heavily, but the farmer evidently thought the rain was fine for his turnips; at four o'clock he knocked at my door, and when I had dressed we set off over the moors to the old lady's house, three or four miles away. When we got there it still rained heavily, and I was afraid photography would be out of the question, for I was soaking wet,

and my apparatus was also far from dry. The old lady, however, was such a cheerful old soul, and the breakfast she gave us brightened us up so, that I determined to see whether it was possible to work in the rain. The old lady did not mind sitting in the yard, and I could not get any wetter. Placing the sitter's chair in front of an open doorway, she was assisted to it, and the exposure was made.[6]

Sometimes he found subjects among the sitters in his studio. A 'fine specimen of a Yorkshire man', over seventy years old, once walked twenty miles to the studio to have his portrait taken. He had something in an inside pocket which made one side of his coat bulge, but he refused to take it out whilst he had his portrait taken:

As he had a very fine head we made a larger portrait of him for our own use, and told him we would send him one for nothing. This was evidently more than the old gentleman could stand, as with obvious hesitation he pulled out of his offending inside pocket the object we had tried to draw before—a large bottle which he offered us to 'sup at' in return for the extra portrait.[7]*

Apart from his portrait work, Sutcliffe received commissions for work which took him out of the studio. He was employed by a lady who wanted some photographs taken on her estate. She went with Sutcliffe to pick out the subjects before he fixed up the darktent. As she knew a little about photography, including the fact that the image appeared inverted on the ground glass screen, she was not going to let the camera mislead her into choosing unsuitable views: 'Whenever she came to a nice group of trees, or a promising subject, she twisted her skirts round her ankles and looked at the view through her legs with her head touching the ground.'[8] Another commission was from an engineer to take a photograph of a hydraulic press. Sutcliffe luckily escaped serious injury when the planks supporting it suddenly collapsed. He was a great walker, and his commissions sometimes involved hardship and even danger. Once when staying at Lealholm he walked with all his equipment to Grinkle Park over the moor. It was a journey of several miles, and dusk was falling as he set off on the return journey. Deciding to save several miles, he cut across the moor. He had never been on this particular piece of moorland before, but he knew that his course lay due south, and checked his direction by the stars. When he arrived safely back in Lealholm, and the story got around, the locals thought he was mad to have tried it. There was only one narrow track over the moor which could be used with safety. On either side of it were dangerous bogs. By some miracle, he had followed the track.

Sutcliffe's commissions took him all round Eskdale, and he never missed the chance to take a photograph if he came upon a subject under the right conditions:

I remember in the early '80s, when dry-plates made it possible to leave our dark tents and water bottles and baths at home, that I went one day with my tripod, camera, and two single dark slides, to photograph a house which a man had just bought. His man met me at a country station with a trap, and we set off for a drive over the moors. He had not gone very far when I

* The portrait of the old man may be Plate 32.

saw in a 'slack' a most picturesque flock of moor-sheep, still unshorn of their fleeces. The sun, shining through these, looked like silver. So I got the driver to stop, and rigged up my camera and exposed my two plates on the sheep. Then I realised that the work I had come out to do was out of the question that day.

A difficult situation was avoided when he managed to borrow two unexposed plates from the stationmaster who was an amateur photographer, and went on to photograph the house. 'I may add that in the course of years I must have sold thousands of copies of the sheep, for of the two plates one proved to be a really good one, and in those prehistoric days a photograph of a sheep with only one head was somewhat rare.'[9]

Sometimes he was able to get a fisherman or a farmhand to help carry his equipment, otherwise he had to carry it all himself. He once was sent for by the vicar of Fylingdales, who was very distressed to see Sutcliffe, who was not a strong man, arrive weighed down with photographic equipment which he had carried four miles. Modern cameras are so compact and easy to handle that it is difficult to appreciate the bulk and weight of the equipment which a photographer working away from his studio had to take with him:

> After carrying one's apparatus for even the short eight hours of an Autumn day one feels 'dogtired' by evening. Weighed at the scales, the apparatus does not weigh much, only 2 stones 4½ pounds. The apparatus consists of six dark slides carrying twelve plates 8½ by 6½; a camera to expose them in; a tripod to carry the camera, and five lenses of 4, 6, 8, 11, and 14 inches focus; a roller blind shutter; a T level; focusing magnifier, two cases of stops, one camera screw, and a focusing cloth. All the above, except the legs which go uncovered, go into your waterproof cases, the one for the camera being stiffened with thin wood boards to save the focusing glass, which folds outwards, from being broken. ... The reader may think that my wish to reduce the weight of the 2 stones 4 pounds and a half is due to laziness, for the British Infantry soldier has to carry nearly twice that weight; but long experience has taught me that only on Sundays, and at other times when the camera has been left at home, do pictures appear as they should do. To be sure, many amateur photographers in the 'Sixties used to carry double this weight; before dryplates came in we had the darktent, silver bath, developers, fixers, and waterbottle to carry as well. The only wonder is how we managed to carry so much. Once, as I was going through Harrogate, my dark tent was mistaken for Punch's stage,* and the crowd eagerly asked me where I was going to perform, but with four stones of apparatus, disposed about one's person, one has not much breath left to answer stupid questions with. My load was nothing to that of some of my six-foot-six friends, who worked 18-by-12 and 18-by-15 plates in the field. Some of these big men condescended to wheel their apparatus, and had their dark tents made like a scissor-grinder's machine, but most of us were too proud to stoop to wheeling, and carried everything on our backs, or in our hands.[10]

The most important item of equipment, which was also the smallest, was the tripod screw. If this was left behind, the camera could not be fixed firmly to the

* A similar thing had happened to Sutcliffe's father. Once, when Thomas was carrying his sketching tent near a farmhouse on his journey along the Yorkshire coast, the farmer asked if a shilling would induce him to set it up, 'for it's many a long year since I saw Punch'.

tripod. Sutcliffe carried several with him in his jacket pockets. They used to drop through holes in his pockets into the lining, and when he came to give his old jacket away, it was not long before whoever he had given it to came round with a few tripod screws which his wife had found while mending the pockets.

Sutcliffe used many cameras in the course of his career, and was quite unconcerned about the appearance of his equipment provided that it produced the results he wanted. He often said that he could not afford the best lenses and most modern cameras:

> For five and twenty years I have been under the impression that to spend much money on photographic apparatus and lenses was unnecessary if not sinful. I thought that good work could be done with the cheapest lenses and the most home-made cameras. So it can sometimes. But not always. Shaky cameras and poor lenses give way at the most unexpected times.

He said that he had got used to 'using tripods which trembled if you looked too hard at them, cameras which leaked like sieves, and lenses which were imperfectly corrected, which gave indistinct images if one forgot to give the focusing screw a half a turn.'[11] If the camera bellows became cracked, he repaired the hole with sticky tape. Sometimes he almost seemed to be on friendly terms with the temperamental quirks of his equipment:

> To be sure, some of the peculiarities of our apparatus are very troublesome at times. I have a tripod which has come to grief so often that I doubt if there is any of the original one left. As I know its habit of casting a limb or dislocating a joint at any moment, I carry some strong string and some wire with it always. I should carry a hammer too, but a couple of stones off the road serve as well.[12]

He once said that it took a clever man to be a photographer—he had to be an artist, a chemist and a mechanical engineer all rolled into one.

Dry plates had their own individual peculiarities. The speed of the emulsion varied greatly from batch to batch. Emulsion was to be found on the back of the plate, as well as where it should have been on the front, and this had to be scraped off before the plate could be printed from. As Sutcliffe put it: 'There was a glorious uncertainty about the early dry plate which made it exciting.'[13] The phrase 'glorious uncertainty' neatly sums up many aspects of photography in the 1870s and '80s. Sutcliffe said that early photographers had to be adventurous: 'The whole of the contents of the chemist's shop and the housewife's store cupboard as well, were liable to be called on at any minute for some new experiment.'[14] He saved all the bottles from his wife's store cupboard and used them in his darkroom. He knew by the characteristic shape of each jam-jar and bottle what each contained, and thus could identify them by feel in the dark. He identified different dry plates in the dark by smell: 'Swan's plates had the most powerful smell of all, just like a bit of seaweed fresh from the beach.'[15] The mixing of photographic chemicals was very casual: 'we never dreamed of weighing out our chemicals from our developers, just a handful of this and a handful of that, and as much water as there happened to be in the kettle, and there you were. No wonder there was often a lack of half-tones.'[16] Sometimes photography adopted its own half-understood magical rites:

> In the wet-plate days, we sometimes purposely exposed the damp plate to
> weak daylight or gaslight before developing it, in the hope of strengthening
> the image. Whether this happened or not I cannot say; perhaps the slight
> veiling of the shadows made prints from under-exposed plates less hard than
> they otherwise would have been.[17]

Of all photography's glorious uncertainties, exposure was probably the
most uncertain, and the inexperienced photographer was given various magical
chants and photographic proverbs to conjure with—'When the wind is in the
East, increase exposure three times at least' and 'When the light is good it is
better than it seems to be, and when it is bad, it is worse' and 'Expose for
the shadows, and the lights will take care of themselves.'* Sutcliffe said that
exposure was based on guesswork tempered by experience. Wet-plates had many
disadvantages, but one advantage of processing the plate on the spot was that
the photographer was always able to secure a correctly-exposed plate. If, on
development, a plate was seen to be incorrectly exposed, a second, corrected
exposure could be made, which was either longer or shorter than the first. Dry
plates, which were introduced around 1880, were much faster than wet-plates,
but exposure was still a problem. Packets of early dry plates were labelled 'Five
Times' or 'Ten Times', which meant that they were five or ten times the speed
of a wet plate. But as this was largely a matter of conjecture, the speed of the
dry plate was still an unknown quantity, though it was certainly considerably
faster than its predecessor. Sutcliffe found that slow plates were much easier to
work with than the fast plates which were later marketed, because a slow plate
allowed greater latitude for error in exposure. In the end experience counted for
more than anything, and it was only after considerable experience and probably
many failures that Sutcliffe could state with confidence such practical facts as: 'A
sun-burnt fisherman's face will need five or six times the amount of exposure
than that of a townsman whose face is not tanned.'[18]

Despite the limitations of the wet-plate process, Sutcliffe attempted to take
instantaneous photographs on Whitby beach in the 1870s. He was using a huge
18-by-15 camera fitted with a Petzval portrait lens working at f.4; a lens with a
large aperture was needed to bring the exposure down to under a second. He
found that the image fogged because of flare from the sun. To eliminate this he
fitted a bright blue chip bonnet-box with a hole cut in it, to the lens to act as a
lens hood. The hood was even bigger than the monstrous camera, which he used
to carry to the beach on top of its tripod with the blue bonnet-box in position,
to the amazement of all who saw him pass by. In this way he managed, in bright
sunlight, to take photographs of moving objects and people on the beach. It is
possible that Plate 55 was taken with this apparatus. In his chapter on subjects
which could be attempted by the photographer, Lake Price had advised that: 'the
whole of the subjects comprised in the title "Rustic and Picturesque figures,"
gain in character and vigour by being executed in open sunlight, provided that
the shadows are treated with sufficient skill to prevent their degenerating into
heavy black masses without reflexions.' He believed that this class of subjects
provided the photographer with almost untrodden ground and that 'a rich

* Exposure meters and tint meters were not
introduced until the end of the century, when fast
plates were being manufactured in a more controlled
manner, enabling their speed to be predicted with
reasonable accuracy. Early dry plates were given
meaningless speed ratings such as 'rapid', 'ordinary',
and 'instantaneous'.

harvest of admirable material presents itself to the discriminating photographer in every locality'. Lake Price, too, recommended that figures such as these should be taken in natural attitudes, in their natural surroundings, engaged in their everyday activities:

> What is most requisite is, that the figures composing such groups should have an air of natural occupation, as if in their usual vocations or amusements. When, heretofore, they have been attempted by amateurs and others, they have generally been strewn as a stolid half circle of gaping figures, intently staring at the lens. Now it must be evident that such a picture can excite no feeling of satisfaction, even in persons of the most uncultivated tastes in art, who are, however, not slow to appreciate the merits of more tasteful selection and arrangement.[19]

Sutcliffe's figure studies and genre work followed these guidelines very closely.

Sutcliffe's studio work kept him in Whitby for most of the year, and his search for subjects was restricted to the immediate locality or, as Sutcliffe put it, he was 'tethered for the greater part of each year by a chain, at most only a mile or two long'.[20] If one is at all familiar with Sutcliffe's work, it is often difficult to see Whitby without being influenced by his view of the town. Its setting is very dramatic, its appearance varied and full of interest, and its harbour the scene of constant activity. Yet Sutcliffe was able to produce striking photographs from very simple subject-matter—men leaning against a rail, sun streaming through the sail of a boat at the quayside, two women chatting in an alleyway, boys looking over the harbour wall. These scenes were there for all to see, but only Sutcliffe took notice of them and photographed them, and when Whitby became known as 'The Photographer's Mecca',* the vision which drew photographers to the town was as much Sutcliffe's own vision of Whitby as the attractions of the town itself.

He found subjects all around him, and had the time to wait, or return, to photograph them under the most suitable conditions. The harbour provided endless subjects with the comings and goings of trading vessels and of the fishing fleet. Some subjects required both an alert eye to see them and the patience to wait for the best moment to photograph them; for example, a ship which had foundered:

> Years ago, when a ship came ashore she often lay on the sands till the sea broke her up. Meanwhile she became more picturesque every day. When her ribs had lost all their planks and stuck up like the bones of a dead animal, then out came the camera. … A sunset behind the black sodden timbers of a water-logged wreck was far more striking than the same sunset going to bed behind a band stand and a crowd of people walking backwards and forwards.[21]

But subjects did not have to be dramatic to attract Sutcliffe's attention. He observed all the mundane details of ordinary life, and found interest where others might have passed by:

> It is doubtful if anyone has a photograph of any such subject as the lighting of [the town's] street gas lamps, showing the lamp lighter running up his

* A description of Whitby by a writer in *Hurman's Monthly* in November 1905.

ladder, applying his lamp, and then sliding down his ladder and trotting along with it over his shoulder to the next one, to say nothing of the crowd of small boys following the lamp lighter, with their 'Hip, hip, hip', followed by a loud 'Hurrah' as soon as ever the lamp was lit. Plates in those days were not fast enough for photographing in the dusk.[22]

Sutcliffe was also followed by small boys when he took his camera out into the town. They hoped that they might pick up a few coppers for being in a picture. Sutcliffe said they used to address photographers familiarly, shouting: 'Tak' my likeness, Mister.' Sometimes, he added, they even left out the 'Mister' and called them 'Johnny'. All the local lads would have known Mr Sutcliffe by name.

Sutcliffe said that beauty generally appeared when you were not looking for it, and he found beauty in the most unlikely subjects:

> It is a great pity when people are at work that they do not like any one to photograph them, for the positions they take are classical to a degree. I saw a woman washing the paint at the bottom of a door the other day, and as she bent down and rested one hand while the other worked, she reminded one of Discobolus. Laundrymaids hanging out sheets, and carrying heavy baskets of clothes, would make grand subjects if laundrymaids had not such objections to be photographed in anything but their Sunday garments.[23]

If he saw 'a fine grouping of figures', he remembered the arrangement, even if he could not photograph them at the time, and in this way built up a mental index of glimpses of figures which he could draw on whenever required.

The countryside also provided innumerable subjects, and if one merely sat by the roadside, one would be able to see a huge range of characters pass by:

> Haymakers, horsedealers, travelling musicians, scissors grinders, gypsies by the score, sailors tramping home after having spent all their money, fishermen with a cartload of nets, to say nothing of the professional tramp and his followers. The people on the road today are quite as interesting as they were in Chaucer's time. If the camera fails to make them so, that is the fault of the man behind it.[24]

For most people, it was the old story of familiarity breeding contempt. In later life even Sutcliffe regretted not having made the most of his opportunities. Country men and women had characteristic appearances which corresponded with their various occupations:

> Thirty years ago we might have boxed any number of specimens; but having become familiar with them from childhood we had not gumption enough to know that they soon would be rare, if not extinct, species. The old rat-catcher, with his troupe of mongrel dogs; the hedger and ditcher, clothed from head to foot in leather; the old thatchers, the Irish harvest men with knee breeches, blue stockings, red bundle and sickle; even the blue-jerseyed fisherman with his sou'wester and seaboots is passing away.[25]

The fact that it took time to set up the tripod and camera sometimes made figure work difficult. If he met a young man and woman on the road and asked if he could take their picture, the young woman, as often as not was off out of sight before Sutcliffe had all his apparatus ready:

> But the fisherman or the countryman was easier to catch. Instead of telling them how beautiful they were, one had only to point out what glorious weather it was for the hay, or the salmon, and offer one's tobacco pouch— not that one smoked the vile weed oneself, but as a bait for sitters in the country it was indispensable.[26]

Even when Sutcliffe did manage to persuade a less camera-shy country girl to have her picture taken, his troubles were not over, and it took him all his time

> to make the exposure at a time when the hussie's eyes were not on the camera, for … [she] kept blinking at the lens as bold as brass. Now, as we all know, to expose when any one is looking at the lens is to give the show away. It is not done. For a photograph of anyone looking bang into the camera, only looks like a photograph when it is finished.[27]

On other occasions, his difficulties were of a quite different, and surprising nature:

> Among savage tribes, and even in out of the way parts of these islands, it is thought to be unlucky to be drawn or photographed in any way. One finds this objection among old people in outlying moor edge farms, and out of the way fishing villages. Some of the old people will not sit to be painted or pho-tographed on any consideration whatever. The first time I knew anything of this was one day when out on the moors I came across a clearing near a cot-tage, which was being ploughed by a man and two horses, or at least a horse and a pony. Standing above the wall which surrounded the intake I rigged up my camera on its stand and waited till the ploughman turned round and came within range. But the minute the old man caught sight of my camera he bolted, leaving his horses just where he had turned them, and ran into the cottage. I waited some time, but the man did not reappear. I learned after-wards that he had 'a mortal dread of being drawn'.[28]

Happily for Sutcliffe, most people got used to him taking pictures of them. He used to take his camera out to observe the work on the farms as it changed with the seasons:

> An early spring picture which used to plague us so, when our plates were too slow for moving subjects, was the sower, as he walked across the fields, looking neither to the left nor the right as he dipped first one hand and then the other into the basket of grain strapped in front of him, and threw the corn with wonderful rhythm and regularity to this side and to that.[29]

Haymaking provided innumerable subjects (see Plates 41 and 44), and again the main difficulty was the slowness of the plates:

> Perhaps the most attractive subject in the hayfield was the mowing of it, as it was the most musical. The regular swish of the three scythes, as the mowers went forward in unison, was a note to be remembered. But this was a subject which taxed the speed of the early dry plate to the utmost, and the wise

photographer kept back his plates and exposed them when a mower stood up to whet his lye, or in other words to sharpen his scythe. If it were not possible to get pictures of arrested motion, it was possible to ask the mower to 'keep still just as you are' when a happy position was noticed. Here again music, as different from noise, was heard when the scythe was being whetted. Then in those days all the farmer's sons and daughters, and men and girls turned out to turn the hay, with forks and hayrakes. How quickly they moved, far too quickly for the camera on its tripod, which was always missing fine subjects, because they no sooner appeared than they were gone. ... But it was when the hay was dry and the loading began that the photographer's opportunity came. The work of loading a big wagon was such a leisurely thing that the photographer had plenty of time to plant down his camera, focus, and expose before the wagon moved on to the next hay-cock. If the sun was not in the right place as the wagon went up the rows, it might be all right as it came down; if it were not, why, it would be later on in the day. There was no hurry, for it would be dark before all the field was led, even if it were finished then, so the photographer could choose his position and the lighting of his subjects to his own liking.[30]

There was no urgency in taking these pictures. Sutcliffe had no deadlines to meet or quota to reach. Each photograph was carefully set up, and the right moment waited for. He would then ask the figures to keep still for a few seconds while they were photographed:

In many cases this meant that the figure would put down his or her work and stand at attention, looking at the lens. Then the photographer's work would begin, and he would ask the figure to resume his or her work and when the model had forgotten the presence of the camera, and the photographer saw that the restraint which it had produced had disappeared, he would say, when he noticed that the figure was in a pleasing position, 'Now keep still, please, just as you are, without looking up.'[31]

In his figure work, Sutcliffe was always careful to avoid self-consciousness, and his aim was to make his subjects appear as natural as possible: 'if the photographer is not in a hurry the woodenness which affects many people will wear off, and the unconscious gracefulness which is the natural state of strong men and women when at rest take its place.'[32]

chapter 6

Sutcliffe's Style
Water Rats and Other Figure Studies

To modern eyes, there would seem to be very little out of the ordinary in photographs showing people in natural attitudes going about their everyday work against a background of the harbour or of the open countryside. Yet in several ways, Sutcliffe felt himself to be breaking free from artifice and the photographic conventions which had developed over the years.

Some of these conventions had grown out of the limitations of photographic processes. The wet collodion process, introduced in 1851 and in use until about 1880, had led to skies being 'blocked out' in landscape and town views with a mask of paper or black varnish. Wet-plates were, in general, unable to reproduce sky tones in outdoor work, but the practical reason for 'blocking out' skies was to be found in the photographer's struggles in his dark tent. Sutcliffe said that 'it was almost impossible to coat a plate with collodion, sensitise it, develop it, and dry it without a certain amount of unevenness, to say nothing of comets and stars in the shape of dirt or air bells.'[1] This was one reason why photographers took to printing in skies (that is, the addition of clouds, taken on another negative, to a landscape) and, when occasion demanded, Sutcliffe used this process. The sky in *The Dock End, Whitby* (Plate 14) is printed in. Although this was introducing an artificial element into his photographs, Sutcliffe went to great lengths to see that the skies used were appropriate to the photographs they were printed into, and saw this as a way of increasing naturalism rather than adding artificiality. He felt that he was adding natural effects which his plates had, unnaturally, failed to register.

Other conventions which he came up against early in his career were based on personal preference rather than practical problems, and he eventually rejected them. The first portraits he ever took were taken with the sun blazing away on the sitters:

> Sometimes one side of the face would be in deep shadow; sometimes a halo of light would surround the head if the sun was behind it. I was only a boy at the time, and the photographers I showed these sunlit portraits to laughed at them and made game of them, and told me never to let the sun shine on my faces any more; but to get a studio with a North light or back yard with a North light, or anywhere where there was no sunshine. I followed their advice, but the portraits on which the sun did not shine seemed to me to be very insipid.[2]

But these were minor matters compared with the artificial means which other photographers were prepared to use to secure studies of 'rustic and picturesque figures':

> When a fisherman was to be taken mending his nets by the sea, the sea was painted on a piece of canvas, a few yards of net were carried into the photographer's studio, and a starfish or two were cut out of brown paper and posed on the floor. The fisherman as often as not was not a real fisherman, in all probability he was the photographer himself, who thought that the sou'wester, jersey or guernsey and seaboots (a real fisherman would not wear these things a minute longer than he needed, nor would he, unless his wife or daughters were 'badly', mend his nets himself) were becoming garments to wear. The success of the picture depended entirely on the excellence of the

artist. Even when he, like the famous musician in the Far West, had done his best, the result was often very wooden.* Only artists who, like Mr Robinson, had been through the mill were able to make pictures in which the art was sufficiently concealed to make them appear natural. The pictures of the less skilful were apparently so full of artifice that they led to laughter and tears more than anything else.[3]

Mr Robinson was H.P. Robinson, who had the portrait studio in Tunbridge Wells. Sutcliffe said that when Robinson went out into the countryside, he took with him one or two young ladies to act as models, and also a strong boy, who carried an enormous hand-box, full of suitable dresses for 'Miller's Daughters', 'Caller Herrin'', and other suitably composed pictures. The characters in his country photographs would have felt at home in the paintings of Yeend King, who often portrayed very graceful and refined 'miller's daughters' in idyllic rural settings.

Sutcliffe was not in sympathy with Robinson's fabricated reality and thought that it was better to risk a little awkwardness on the part of figures chosen on the spot—people the photographer had come upon by chance—than to import 'fisher girls' and 'country lasses'. However good the models were, he warned, the camera had sharper eyes than the photographer:

> To bring a fine lady from an inland town and dress her up as a fisher-lass, and plant her among the rocks beside the sea, and to photograph her with her hand shading her eyes, and to entitle the picture, 'My heart is on the wide, wide sea', is a very risky business, for the chances are that the fine lady may not look in the least like a genuine fisher-lass. Some little detail, her boots, or stockings or the kilting of her skirt, may give the picture away. For such work it is much better to search for good examples of the genuine article than to accept the help of one's cousins or one's aunts.[4]

Sutcliffe took photographs of Whitby fishermen for well over thirty years, and saw the sons of fishermen grow up to join their fathers on their fishing boats. Everyone knew Mr Sutcliffe, and, when he had time, he went down to the harbourside to chat with them and photograph them. They were on friendly terms, and he was accepted by the fishing community. The closeness of this link can be judged from some of the stories Sutcliffe tells. One year he couldn't find his tripod, which he used to leave in various places because it was so heavy to carry:

> I had not used it since last November, but where I had left it I could not for the life of me remember. There was nothing for it but to inquire, 'Did I leave my legs here last year?' at every likely place. I found it at last at a fisherman's house, to which a strange fate led me after I had given up all hope of finding it. I knocked, and walked into the kitchen, and asked the fisherman the question I had got so tired of asking. He was busy mending a crab-pot, and without speaking he pointed at a white petticoat which was stuck up on something near the fire to dry. His wife, I should say, was busy ironing in the scullery nearby. I am very thick in the head—at least I am told that I am—and when my friend the fisherman pointed to the white laundry

* For example, see Julia Margaret Cameron's fisherfolk narrative scene from the 1860s entitled *Pray God Bring Father Safely Home* of which Quentin Bell wrote: 'How surely one knows ... that father's only home is the photographer's studio and that it is furnished with props for the occasion.' (*Victorian Artists*, London, 1967).

in front of the fire in reply to my question, I could not understand what he meant. He smiled when he saw how stupid I was and said, 'I think, sir, if you don't mind lifting up them skirts, you'll find your legs underneath'. I hardly liked to take them away when I saw how useful they could be.[5]

The fisherman called Sutcliffe 'sir', but Sutcliffe was able to get along easily with the men by the quayside. In their spare time during the day, the fishermen willingly acted as models for him. Only one of them—David Storr—obstinately refused to be photographed. When he came in from fishing he walked off home rather than 'have his likeness took'. Several fishermen who saw him go asked Sutcliffe if he really would like a picture of him. Sutcliffe said that he would, as David Storr had striking, rugged features. So the fishermen marched into his house, carried him out onto the pier, and stood over him until the photograph was taken. As it turned out Mr Storr liked the print which resulted from this enforced sitting, and never again refused to be photographed.

This closeness and friendship with the fishermen allowed Sutcliffe to take photographs of them which other photographers would not have been able to get. Plate 6 shows a fisherman called Coulson just back from a long, tiring night out fishing. Sutcliffe describes how this picture was taken:

Coming along with my camera under my arm one day, the tripod legs sticking out behind, I noticed this big fisherman, considerably over six feet tall, crossing the road. In five seconds he would have been lost to sight. I ran up to him and asked to be allowed to make a picture of him. 'How long would I be, as he was very tired? He wanted to get to bed.' 'Not two minutes,' was my answer. To take him standing there in the middle of the road would never do, for in the first place he would not stand there, were no camera near, unless speaking to some one; and in the next the background was not good. 'Would he go back to the rail and stand there beside his wife,' who had been there all the while. That was better, but with one figure on one side and one on the other it looked as if they had been put there for the benefit of the camera. Then came a hasty look round among the small crowd that had gathered; a girl, not too big or too well dressed to look out of place, was pulled out from among it, and placed behind the woman, leaning toward her, and told to look anywhere but in the direction of the camera. The man was asked to look towards the woman. After a hasty look on the ground glass (no stop being used made this all the easier), and a smothered curse given to the camera maker who had made no provision for lowering the camera front (the print wants another half-inch of road badly, as the reader will see), the shutter was touched. Then a handful of coppers was poured in to the hands of the woman and girl, the man thanked heartily for staying there, and up went the camera, and the photographer back to his day's work, trying to amuse restless babies, and copying faded daguerreotypes.[6]

In fact he took two plates swiftly, one after the other.

He was also friendly with the children of the fishermen. They were rather ragged and cheeky, but they all seemed to like Mr Sutcliffe. They used to run off to find him whenever a big sailing ship came into the harbour, or when a timber ship which had unloaded its cargo was about to put to sea, and he would grab his camera, leaving the fisher lads to follow on behind with the tripod. These Whitby kids were not obvious subjects for photographs. They did not have the necessary redeeming qualities of coyness or picturesqueness which alone could make the children of the unwashed poor acceptable to the Victorian middle classes. Some visitors to Whitby were appalled by these children. In 1887 one correspondent wrote—anonymously—to the *Whitby Times* saying that he had visited the 'covered in market' and had found 'a wretched spectacle': 'It seemed to be the head quarters of a gang of rough and vulgar children, who, in their peculiar fashion, were enjoying themselves, in a way anything but pleasing to one even accustomed to the habits of this class of local society. Cannot this be altered?'[7]

Apart from enjoying themselves and annoying sensitive visitors, the children used to play truant from school. Whitby had its own School Board, and their 'enemy' was the attendance officer, Mr George Bonwick. Perhaps Mr Bonwick was a fast runner, because the local lads hit upon the tactic of stripping off their clothes and running into the water of the harbour, where he couldn't, or wouldn't, follow them. In the summer of 1886, Sutcliffe was walking along the harbourside looking for subjects, and he found some boys playing truant. This was the unlikely material which led to Sutcliffe taking what is probably his most famous photograph, *Water Rats* (Plate 10).

> One hot morning I saw three naked boys shoving an old box about in the harbour. I went to them; asked them how long they were likely to be there. They said all day, if I liked; for, though they ought to be at school, the kid-catcher could not come into the water after them. I offered them one penny each to wait till I fetched the camera. My offer of wages had spread, for, when I returned, I found thirteen boys naked. When they saw me, they all stood in a row in the same position, which was a cross between a soldier at attention and the Greek slave. I have regretted that I did not take them so. I was at a loss to know what to do with so many sitters, as the box would only hold two, till I saw an empty boat at the other side of the harbour.[8]

He told the boys to go and bring it over to where he had set up his camera on the harbour edge near the railway station, and then set about getting this unexpected army of naked little boys into some sort of order. Sutcliffe describes:

> How the big lad on the bow of the boat was most useful in pulling and pushing the rest of the crew into their places, after the camera, loaded with one of Sir John Swan's early dry plates, had been fixed on its tripod. How, when all was ready, one of the two boys in the soap box *would* sit up staring at the camera as if he were having his likeness taken. How the photographer cursed and swore at him for being so self-conscious. How the small boy in the red fez was sent to bring him ashore.[9]

The photograph was taken as he was getting out of the box. Each of the boys was given a penny, and he remembered: 'It was rather amusing this part of the business, as they were at a loss to know where to put their pennies.' The exposed plate was taken back to the Waterloo Yard darkroom and developed. It was nearly smashed when an inquisitive amateur lifted it off Sutcliffe's arrangement of clout-headed nails on the wall, where he rested his glass negatives to dry, and dropped it. Luckily it didn't reach the stone flags and the amateur caught it, 'buttered side up', on his knees as it fell.

Sutcliffe sent the picture to the 1886 exhibition of the Photographic Society in London, and it was awarded a medal, and was well received by the critics.* A review in the *British Journal of Photography* stated:

> A medal has been awarded this single picture, but it contains within itself artistic perception of a high order. The effect produced by young boys, 'rats', who are dabbling in the water from boats, with a background of buildings on the shore, is exceedingly well managed. It is hardly possible that the boys were controlled or modelled, therefore we assume that they were left to themselves; consequently the division of the group into two sections was accidental, but the artistic mind immediately saw the position, that it was good, and the negative was taken. The shore, being far away, is hazy in appearance; but here again we see the 'selection' referred to, for there must have been a haze present, which is confirmed by the stillness of the water. There is a wonderful sharpness about the focus of the boys, which suggests that the camera was kept waiting whilst the group assumed that phase which the artist felt to be right. Altogether the picture, though small, is well deserving the honour conferred upon it.[10]

The review and the photograph are a tribute to Sutcliffe's inspired opportunism in making the most of subjects and events which he came across. The older boys who helped by shoving the younger ones into place are sitting or standing where they were told, but there is no artistic posing of Tommy Ross in his fez, sent to fetch his troublesome brother Will out of the box on the left, and 'Cud' Heselton seems poised to spring out of the boat on the right. 'Rough and vulgar children', as the writer to the *Whitby Times* called them, would not stand much messing about and posing, and the commonplace nature of such a harbour scene can be judged from the lack of reaction by the people in the passing boat. The Prince of Wales, later King Edward VII, saw the photograph on exhibition in London and had an enlargement made to hang in Marlborough House.

The success of this picture seems to have inspired amateurs to bribe new *Water Rats*—a much better title than the sentimental *Water Babies* which *The Amateur Photographer* would have preferred—to pose in Whitby harbour for them. The result was that thirty or forty years after the picture was taken Sutcliffe used to be accosted by middle-aged men who would say, 'You won't remember me, Mr Sutcliffe, but I was a Water Rat'. The Sutcliffe family used to say that half Whitby must have been water rats. The boy standing on the left of the boat looking away from the camera is Mr James Edward (Ted) Locker. He was born in 1875 and died aged 93 in 1968. A few days before he died, he recalled the summer morning eighty years before when Mr Sutcliffe came along the harbourside:

> Well we were all school lads and 'dock end claggers'. We went be't name o' dock end claggers because we were allus ready for fighting and rowwing. … So *this* morning, *this* morning we were douwn an' it was fine, an' we all 'ad ower cleathes off an' we went int't watter, started dabblin' aboot an' enoow

* Sutcliffe said that he sent a print to Mr Lever, the soap manufacturer, 'in the hope that he would buy it and use it as a picture of the rising generation "whose only soap is sunlight". [But] the print came back from Port Sunlight with a polite note that it was not considered suitable for reproduction.'

thur was a man comes down an' it was sort a raised up like that an' we were down here y' know. That's Longburn Sand there an' we … we were larkin' aboot and he says 'Hey!' he says, 'Stop where you are boys, *stop where you are*' an' he says 'I want you to do it, now be good lads' an' he cum back, why, he had sticks up you knoa an' a cover owwer't top, a dark cover an' he put 'is he'ad underne'ath. 'Now', he says, 'I've got y''. Ar'way we was sorta bein' lads y' know an' he says 'Now', he says, 'Y'd better get y'r things on, time you were off now' an' he te'ak us all out as we stood an' he put 'is hand in 'is trousis pocket an' he gev us all a penny apiece an' tell'd us t' be good lads.[11]

The fact that *Water Rats* was a photograph of naked boys, a subject which was objectionable to some people however treated, did not escape notice. Sutcliffe says that the clergy of Whitby 'excommunicated' him 'for exhibiting such an indecent print in his shopwindow to the corruption of the young of the other sex'. There is no evidence to support this, and it seems highly unlikely considering Sutcliffe's friendship with the Rector of Whitby, Canon Austen. But there is no doubt that, to some people, the photograph would have been objectionable, and a local clergyman or two may have decided to rally to the banner of puritan opinion. Even in painting, which people assumed hung the veil of culture between the viewer and reality, the depiction of the naked human body was carefully circumscribed by a public predisposed to outrage.* The nude adopted disguises, as a writer in *The Studio* magazine describes:

> Covered with a garb of sanctity, or dignified by the literature of a past age, in almost every school of painting it has been held within the province of good taste to portray Adam and Eve, Susannah, St Sebastian, Andromeda, Leander, and other heroes and heroines, sacred and profane, even where a study of the Nude on its own merits was forbidden. Coming to modern times, we find the unwritten law on the subject still kept—at least in England—more rigidly enforced in America, and but slightly relaxed in France. … it is forbidden, as a rule, to depict contemporary humanity seen in the way that, as a matter of fact, it is rarely seen by contemporaries, and in this lies the chief argument of its opponents.

Photographs of the nude were more likely to raise objections than paintings because they were contemporary and not historical, particular and not generalised, and therefore more real and immediate in impact. The anonymous writer was not very brave in his support of photographs of the nude; they were, he said:

> not to be considered as pictures, but merely as charts for reference, or working drawings, as it were, for artists. … But all shortcomings granted, it would seem that, for a record of the Nude, photography is a distinctly useful ally that is not yet appreciated at its intrinsic value. In certain instances, notably a group by Mr Frank Sutcliffe, which, under the title of 'Water Rats', is too widely known to make it necessary to be reproduced here, one doubts if the most careful study of composition, or the most happy invention, had resulted in a more delightful picture.[12]

* It is interesting to compare *Water Rats* with the paintings of Henry Tuke. These often showed contemporary naked youths bathing from boats by the shore, and were—like *Water Rats*—considered objectionable by some people. They seem to have been the cause of Martin Colnaghi withdrawing his early support of the New English Art Club in March 1886, shortly before *Water Rats* was exhibited. He said that he was used to dealing with the work of Old Masters, and declined to become associated with the type of paintings produced by a certain (unnamed) artist, whose work had clearly shocked him.

The fact that local lads bathed naked in the harbour disturbed some visitors to Whitby. A letter to the editor of the *Whitby Times* appeared in 1887 under the heading 'The Bathing Nuisance'; the writer had noticed:

> a most decided retrograde movement towards the manners and customs of our remote ancestors. It is impossible now to walk at any hour of the day on the pier, cliff, or sands, without being obliged to see 'studies from the nude' in the sea or harbour, that may be charming enough to an artistic eye, but are decidedly disgusting to an ordinary observer. In no other watering-place to my knowledge (and I have visited several) is such a nuisance allowed to exist, and until the apathy and indifference of 'the authorities', which apparently exists towards it is removed, so long will Whitby feel its effects. I am no puritan, and am speaking from no prudish point of view, but simply in the interests of the town, and have been induced to do so from the many complaints that I have heard, and from an instance that has come to my knowledge of a gentleman of interest leaving the place with his family on this account. This may not be a solitary instance, but when the matter has gone so far, it is surely time for some interference, as, in the present depressed times, Whitby can surely not afford to offend those in whom so many interests in the town are centred.
>
> Yours faithfully,
> NUDA VERITAS[13]

The fact that naked boys bathing in the harbour was a common sight in Whitby has, in my opinion, a great deal to do with the success of *Water Rats*. Sutcliffe produced other photographs of nude boys, but compared with *Water Rats*, these seem posed and artificial. They seem to have been taken as follow-ups and were artificially contrived. One of them tells a story, as its title—*His First Bathe*—indicates; another shows three boys by a coble. Sutcliffe describes how it was taken:

> Some boys were playing about a boat in the harbour in the mud. Their dress exceeded by something the ideal garments these boys wear so gracefully. That something was not much, but it was quite enough to spoil the picture, and the background was a long straight mass of masonry hung with weed as far as the highwater mark. For some time from the opposite pier I watched these boys playing about the boat, until one of them climbed up on the side of the boat and sat there. I shut my eyes to impress his position on my mind, then I walked off. Some time after it was my good fortune to find a boat with a suitable background, and by the generosity of an amateur friend, who bribed three boys to wear Adam's clothes, I was able to repeat the performance which I had seen played before.[14]

The bribing of the boys to strip off and their posing, especially of the left-hand figure, seem contrived if one measures them by the yardstick of Sutcliffe's more characteristic, natural approach to his subjects. We know that the boy's name was Tom Pennock, and he stands gazing out to sea on a chilly North Yorkshire beach.* It seems that Sutcliffe's amateur friend had persuaded him to try to make his camera generalise about the nude. The figure is not Tom Pennock, but a carefully posed naked youth. The artificially contrived nude studies are exceptions to Sutcliffe's usual practice of taking photographs of figures and scenes as he found them. Time and again he stressed that photographers should avoid the artificial, and that to set up scenes to photograph, with posed models and fake props, was to perpetrate a falsehood and a sham—'the greater the attempt at reaching the sublime the more ridiculous are such got-up pieces likely to appear when finished'.

Sutcliffe's best photographs usually resulted from seizing an opportunity and exploiting it, waiting and watching for the right moment to let the shutter drop. *Excitement*† (Plate 2) is another example of this technique. The subject-matter is simple and would not have been given a second glance by most photographers. The photograph was taken by the harbour wall on Scotch Head, and Sutcliffe had originally gone to take a photograph of a completely different subject. Whilst he was taking this, a crowd of boys gathered. Probably to get them out of the way, he sent them off to run a race. When they returned, one or two of them went to lean over the wall to look at a boat below, and so, seizing the opportunity, Sutcliffe sent the rest of the boys to join them to make the excitement greater. Then the photograph was taken.

Both *Excitement/Stern Realities* and *Water Rats* were exhibited widely in this country and abroad, and it is interesting to see the extent to which these two photographs were copied—an indication of their popularity and of the power of the images. In April 1894, the *British Journal of Photography* carried a small item under the heading 'The Sincerest Flattery':

Detail of whole-plate print of three naked boys around a coble.

> Most of our readers are acquainted with Mr F.M. Sutcliffe's picture, *Water Rats*, which depicts a group of nude urchins in a river. Last week, at the Newcastle Exhibition, a photograph, bearing the same title and the inscription 'Copyright', which dealt with the same kind of theme as Mr Sutcliffe's, was received for competition. Mr Sutcliffe was one of the Judges of the Exhibition, the Committee of which, entering into the spirit of the humorous situation, arranged matters so that Mr Sutcliffe, who was ignorant of the imitative work, saw the latter under mock melodramatic circumstances, it being specially arranged amid draped surroundings, &c. Mr Sutcliffe's surprise and amusement can well be imagined. The 'copyrighted' *Water Rats*,‡ we may say, was not hung in the Exhibition.[15]

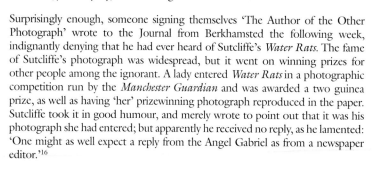

Surprisingly enough, someone signing themselves 'The Author of the Other Photograph' wrote to the Journal from Berkhamsted the following week, indignantly denying that he had ever heard of Sutcliffe's *Water Rats*. The fame of Sutcliffe's photograph was widespread, but it went on winning prizes for other people among the ignorant. A lady entered *Water Rats* in a photographic competition run by the *Manchester Guardian* and was awarded a two guinea prize, as well as having 'her' prizewinning photograph reproduced in the paper. Sutcliffe took it in good humour, and merely wrote to point out that it was his photograph she had entered; but apparently he received no reply, as he lamented: 'One might as well expect a reply from the Angel Gabriel as from a newspaper editor.'[16]

---

* Sutcliffe seems to have observed the scene at Whitby—he watched the boys 'from the opposite pier'—but the 'reconstructed' photograph was taken at the fishing village of Staithes.

† It is better known by its later title *Stern Realities* (or *Stern Reality*) which was probably given to it by Sutcliffe's friend R.E. Pannett, who had a liking for puns. It was exhibited in France with the utterly bewildering title *Triste Réalité*.

‡ Sutcliffe had taken the precaution of registering both plates he took of *Water Rats* as copyright at Stationers' Hall in London.

Stern Realities went on to even higher things. The journal *Photography* commented in December 1891 that although artists seldom had a good word for photography and looked down on photographs as 'contemptible things', they did not hesitate to make use of them when the opportunity arose, sometimes to the extent of copying them completely. The report continued:

> A friend lately returned from Copenhagen, who had the opportunity of going over the Czar's yacht, tells us that one of the six pictures which grace that luxurious craft is a copy in oils of Frank Sutcliffe's 'Stern Reality', commonly known as 'Excitement', and he tells us that not only is every figure painted from the photograph with faithful accuracy, but the picture bears the signature of a famous painter, who thus tries to pass off other people's ideas as his own.[17]

The little boys were transformed into young ladies and issued as a postcard, probably in the 1890s. The card seems to be taken from an oil painting, which may have been French. Somebody has written on the reverse of the only copy of this postcard I have seen that a good title for the picture would be 'Waiting for the Smack'. *Stern Realities* travelled still further down the road from the sublime to the ridiculous. The little boys were transformed into two stout fishermen and fat lady leaning over a harbour wall, presenting three enormous backsides to the viewer, by the postcard artist Donald McGill, on a card issued in about 1908. It was titled 'Waiting for the Smacks'.[17]

It is very doubtful whether any other photograph will ever have such a widespread influence—from the yacht of the Czar of Russia, to the seaside shop selling naughty postcards.

Postcard based on *Stern Realities*.

chapter 7

Sutcliffe's Style
The Changing Landscape

The weather on the North East coast was often harsh and unpredictable, but Sutcliffe believed that changeable weather was in the photographers' interest:

> If we did but know it, the weather we revile so in these islands is about as perfect for photographic purposes as it could be made. ... To this vile weather we owe our most charming effects. If there was no bad weather, there would be no clouds and no gales, no rain and no snow. If there is one time more than another when the country smiles the most, it is during rain.[1]

He advised photographers who wished to see stormy skies, and who did not mind getting wet, to visit the Yorkshire coast in March and April: 'when the sunshine and shower alternate at absurdly regular intervals; ten minutes sunshine followed by a rather shorter rainy period: then fine weather for ten minutes again, and so on until sunset, when the rain disappears till the morrow.'[2] From his house* with its wide views over the Esk valley, Sutcliffe could see the clouds and rays of sunlight providing an ever-changing display over the moors. His observations of the detail and atmosphere of changing weather conditions are very perceptive, and give an insight into the visual interests which are uppermost in his mind, and which he was able to express in some of his landscape photographs. In 1908 he wrote:

> There have been some fine opportunities this Easter for attempting atmospheric effects. With showers of hail following each other regularly every ten or fifteen minutes, with peeps of sunshine from behind stormy clouds, and with only a moderate wind, the weather might have been specially made for photographers. Commonplace subjects have been made beautiful—even a row of lodging houses looks well when seen, or rather imagined than seen, through a thick shower of snow. As for the fields and hills, they have been like fairy-land. Perhaps the curtain draws up and discloses a bare hillside. It is so thoroughly well-defined that one can see every tree, and every field, and every road for miles. Then the sun goes in, and in two seconds the landscape is blotted out completely. In ten minutes the curtain lifts, and the sun seems to be chasing the snowshower away over the hills. How very much bigger these look now that their tops are hidden with the snow-clouds! What charming colours the fields take when sprinkled with hail. The ploughed fields have turned a delicate pink, while the grass fields are the palest pea-green imaginable, the trees are like ghosts as they appear and disappear as the shower passes over them. Firstly one valley and then another opens out again as the wind drives the storm before it, and then, when it has passed, out comes the sun and very soon melts all the hail, except on the hilltops, where it glitters in the sunshine. Yet in such scenes as this the photographer generally leaves the camera behind him, and brings it out only in August, when the sun has it all his own way, when there are no showers and no mists to add poetry to common things, and no snow to shine brilliantly on the hilltops.[3]

He attempted to capture some of these fleeting natural effects with his camera.

His father, Thomas, had been trained in the traditions of the school of English watercolour painters, and Sutcliffe, carrying a camera in place of a sketching book, was following in their footsteps as he wandered all over the country in

* Sutcliffe had a house built for himself in Carr Hill Lane, Sleights—a village near Whitby—where he moved with his family in the 1890s.

all weathers observing nature, and thus learning to appreciate the grandeur and beauty of the countryside around him. Although the photographs which he produced of natural effects were not generally appreciated, his descriptions of the atmospheric conditions he tried to capture with his camera are poetic in their intensity:

> At times our cameras make what we think must be music, which any one would gladly pay for, but it is only when we become case-hardened with repeated disappointments that we get accustomed to having our best work thrown back to us. For instance one bright July day, when the sun had been shining since four o'clock in the morning, it became suddenly dark at mid-day. The birds of the air and beasts of the field became very uneasy, and all the faces of the people in the village turned white or grey, for every one thought the last day had come. There was not a sound to be heard, and it got darker and darker. Then an age seemed to pass, and the people simply sat and waited and waited for the sound of the trumpet. Then all at once, instead of fire and brimstone coming out of the black inky night above came rain. Such a rain. Then, after a time, away in the west, the dawn began to show, but still the rain came down. Seen against the brighter sky in the west, the rain, as it fell, looked like the long black hair falling from some invisible black beast in the sky. One would have thought that a photograph of such a weird scene would have found a buyer, or have been thought worth a place on the walls of an exhibition, but the plate which saw that dark, mysterious heaven, and blacker invisible earth, might as well have never seen the light at all, for any use it has been.[4]

Sutcliffe's early interest in transitory effects of this kind, which changed a scene minute by minute, brought him up against more photographic conventions, which he rejected because they refused to acknowledge that such effects were worth recording.

Sutcliffe was not the first photographer to react against the general belief that photographs should be as clear and sharp as possible, and show as much detail as the camera and its lens would allow. Lake Price wrote:

> From a want of knowledge of the principles of art in many photographers a morbid admiration and reverence of unnaturally *minute definition* tends to lead the operator away from what should really be the end and aim of his study. Instead of 'going in' for the broad vigorous effects of *light and shade* in the landscape he is led to look upon a mechanical 'organ grinding' kind of exposure consequent upon absurdly reduced aperture as the correct thing, whilst to the eye of the artist the much vaunted result appears like a landscape carefully black-leaded, and then executed in minute needlework, qualities which are no compensation for the want of the broad and vigorous effects of light and shade which have been given by the lens when skilfully applied to this class of subject.[5]

By using a whole-plate stand camera on a clear, still day, with the lens stopped right down a photographer could achieve great depth of focus and minute definition in the enormous negative which resulted. Such an overwhelming abundance of detail in a photograph is not always an advantage, as Sutcliffe realised. Excessive detail could be reduced in printing by the use of paper with a rough surface, or by placing sheets of celluloid or thin glass between the paper and negative whilst printing. Sutcliffe preferred to wait until natural atmospheric effects had softened and hazed away intrusive details:

> The first and best plan is to keep the camera at home till nature herself has wrapped the subject in a veil of mist. Little things are then hidden, and only the big ones are seen; a hillside which in clear weather might come out in a photograph like a map of the counties in England or the provinces in France, divided into so many spaces by hedgerows, would in a mist lose all its divisions and, like Cowper's ideal land, be 'mingled into one'. Seen through a hot haze, even prosaic houses and shops lose all their details and become one big mass.[6]

The closely-packed houses of Whitby often provided their own smokescreen from household coal fires. Sutcliffe makes use of this in Plates 13 and 25. But man-made smoke was nothing when compared with the fog which came rolling in off the sea, sometimes covering several miles inland from the coast. Sutcliffe had loved fog from his childhood, and never failed to be thrilled by its magical qualities. Fog transformed everything—a five-masted schooner in Whitby harbour for example: 'she fits the autumn sea-scape like a glove, and first thing in the morning, before any of the fog has lifted one could swear she was one of those phantom ships we used to read of when we were young.'[7] The familiar became unfamiliar in the fog:

> The photographer, anchored maybe on some street crossing, cannot fail to be struck with the pictures of humanity which the fog singles out from the crowds. To be sure they are but dark grey silhouettes against a lighter grey background, but their beauty and infinite variety are wonderful. Here a postman bending under his load. Before we have time to take in more than the graceful curve made by the letter-bag and his bent back, his curly fringe of hair, and his peaked cap, he has vanished, to be followed instantly by two workmen, one a few inches in advance of the other. One carries a shovel over his shoulder. Millet might have designed this group, but they, too, vanish in the mist. Here comes a boy with a parcel. He is walking towards us, and we have only time to notice how the parcel he is carrying adds grace to his movements and gives his outline an almost Grecian form. Figure after figure passes, each different. Were the light only good enough for photography, what an album of quaint and beautiful outlines the camera might secure! Strange that the fog should make such a difference in the appearance of the people passing along an ordinary street. Were the fog to clear away suddenly our pictures would vanish, even though the people went along as usual. The fog separates single figures for us, not only from the rest of the crowd, but from the distractions of the shops and roads and carriages and lamp-posts generally.[8]

The transforming effect of mist can be seen in the accompanying illustrations, for one photograph is an exact record of the stonework of the Abbey ruins and the other shows a powerful black mass rearing its jagged pinnacles towards the sky as it looms out of the mist.

Whitby Abbey.   Whitby Abbey in fog.

But to the general public, with their love of 'clear' photographs, fog was just fog. Sutcliffe won a medal with a photograph of a little white boat beside a big black fishing smack; the background he described as 'grey and tender', with the outline nearly lost against the sky. When the print came back from the exhibition, he put it on display in his window:

> If the judges who gave the medal could only have overheard the criticism of those who knew the place, they would never have ventured to judge at a photographic exhibition again. Part of the background consisted of the tower of a church. Now this tower was further away than the rest of the view, and came in for an extra share of the haze which was hanging about. Every local critic who looked at the view overlooked the fishing boat and the dainty little white boat and the reflections in the water, and tried to see the time by the parish church clock through the haze, but as he could not do so he damned the photograph and the photographer.[9]

Sutcliffe, looking back on his early career, said that the generation of photographers to which he belonged was criticised for anything unconventional about their work, as people had fixed ideas about what a photograph should be like:

> A photograph was a thing made by the help of the sun and the lens; the brighter the sun, and the more perfect the lens, the more successful the photograph. The photographer who went aviewing when the sun was not shining, and when the atmosphere was not perfectly clear, was the butt of all the knowing ones. Any person was at liberty to advise the photographer to wait till the weather was better. If the photographer ventured to put up his camera when it was dull, or the air was full of mist, a whole crowd of critics would soon swarm round him and pass remarks on the absurdity of expecting anything worth looking at without the help of the sun and a clear sky. If the photographer happened to be a young man, as he generally was,

he was advised to go home and not waste his plates by the knowing grey-beards. In those days, to take a photograph with the full aperture of the lens was an almost punishable offence; f.64, no more and no less, was the recognised standard of sharpness. To exhibit a photograph which did not meet all these conditions wanted no little courage. Some of us who saw how wild the critics were when their conditions were outraged went from bad to worse; from f.22 we went to f.8, and exposed plates not only when there was no sun, but when there was a sea fog on. The critics said that the only fit place for such work and such workers was the County Asylum.[10]

This was written in 1912, and it is not clear exactly when Sutcliffe began to move away from the microscopic detail of photography produced by using such tiny lens apertures as f.64. It must have been very early in his career. Sutcliffe was making use of methods of separating the various planes of his photographs, and was concentrating the viewer's attention on particular areas of his photographs by the use of atmospheric effects combined with differential focusing in the early 1880s. This was well before it became common practice, and several years before what became known as 'The Focus Question', which concerned the use of similar techniques, had the photographic world in turmoil.

Sutcliffe's method of working seems, as usual, to have resulted from a search for ways of taking the photographs he wanted, and from practical limitations imposed by his equipment. When he first took up photography, and it was still common to find cameras in use which were designed to take 12-by-10 inches, 15-by-12, and 18-by-15, the lenses which went with these large cameras had long focal lengths:

> If one tried to take near figures on a 12-by-10 plate with an aperture of f.8, any bright foliage behind the figures came out as circles of light. It was only when plain backgrounds could be found, or when the middle distance was obscured by haze, that it was possible to work quickly with large apertures.[11]

From 1876 on, Sutcliffe was concerned with photographing figures in natural lighting out of doors. Exposures were still long, and he said that as late as 1880, when the gelatine dry plate was just beginning to drive out the wet collodion process, an exposure of ten seconds out of doors was considered a quick one with a lens working at f.16. During this period it seems that Sutcliffe tried to work with as wide an aperture as possible, attempting to make figure photography easier. He had rigged up his Petzval portrait lens with its bonnet-box hood, to enable him to take photographs at f.4. At that time, lenses for outdoor work were not made with an aperture larger than f.8. In his description of how he took the photograph of the fisherman called Coulson (Plate 6), he says that he used no stop to the lens, which was presumably working at full aperture—f.8. The background to the photograph is out of focus—if one looks closely one can see that the skyline is blurred—but the effect seems a natural one because of the haze hanging over the water of the harbour. The reviewer of *Water Rats* (Plate 10) already quoted refers to the hazy appearance of the far shore, which he takes to be a natural effect, contrasting with the 'wonderful sharpness about the focus of the boys'.

In part, the nature of these photographs was predetermined by the physical situation in which they were taken. The west side of Whitby harbour consists of a harbourside and pier, which provided a natural standpoint for the camera tripod. The principal objects of interest in many photographs which Sutcliffe took by the harbour, are figures by the harbour rail. These are registered sharply in the foreground. As the harbour is fifty yards or more wide, there is nothing in the middle distance—unless a ship happens to be passing—except the water of the harbour, which poses no problem of focus. The background of the houses on the east side is a long way behind the foreground figures, and it seems quite natural that it should fade into the distance. The separation of planes—the foreground figures from the background—is achieved partly by haze in the atmosphere, and partly by Sutcliffe setting his sharply focused figures—the main points of interest in the photograph—against a background which is out of focus. He escapes being recommended for the County Asylum by the critics and 'knowing grey-beards' because his use of differential focus is not flaunted in their faces as a photographic trick, but, like many other techniques used by Sutcliffe, is used to enhance natural effects. The background varies with atmospheric conditions from a blank white—as in Plate 4, titled *Fog-bound fishermen*—to a hazy grey, which is to be seen in *Water Rats* and several others. This use of differential focus to emphasise the effect of haze hanging in the air is also to be seen in his country views, for example *Dinnertime* (Plate 54).

The readers of *The Practical Photographer* were let into 'one of Mr Sutcliffe's secrets' in an article on his work in 1904: 'He nearly always uses a long-focus lens and a large aperture, so getting the space feeling and quiet suppression of much that is not wanted. Thus on a whole-plate his favourite tool is a 14 inch R.R. [i.e. Rapid Rectilinear] lens working at f.8 or f.11.'*[12] Sutcliffe used these techniques to obtain photographs which reflected his view of the scenes depicted. Because he was able to put across his own feelings about a scene or a group of figures in his photographs, they began to develop a style of their own. It was not only their subject matter which made Sutcliffe's photographs unmistakeable at photographic exhibitions in the 1880s. Many would-be imitators found that Sutcliffe's photographs were deceptively simple, and could not be copied merely by reassembling figures and planting the tripod on the same spot from which Sutcliffe had taken a photograph. But although his photographs developed a distinctive look, he did not feel bound by any rules or restricted to use any particular techniques, and, throughout his career, his photographs were hazy or sharply focused, depending upon the particular effect he wished to capture.

Sutcliffe's own eyes were able to see many more effects of light than his camera and plates could register. He seems to have written one article which was published in *The Amateur Photographer* at the end of a sleepless night:

> The lamp is burning though the night is far spent. Where the window- blinds imperfectly 'shut out the darkness' come faint lines of blue, which show that the day is dawning. This battle of daylight and lamplight has many times bewitched me. Often have I watched the sun take the shine out of the lamp. To paint this would be easy; how to photograph it is what bothers me at this

* The article also states that: 'His favourite printing medium is platinotype, though he is a past master in carbon and silver printing in various forms.'

moment; how can I express in chemicals the glorious contrast between the
yellow lamplight and the blue daylight?[13]

The answer was that he couldn't, not only because of the low light level, but also
because the photographic plates which he used for the major part of his career
were colour-blind. Early photographic plates were sensitive only to blue light and
to invisible ultraviolet radiation. These blue-sensitive plates rendered blue colours
lighter on the print than they appeared to the eye, and green and red colours
darker, producing white skies in landscapes, and dark lips in portraiture. After
1873 work went on to extend the colour sensitivity of plates into the green range
of the spectrum by means of sensitizing dyes, and the resulting orthochromatic
plates were coming into general use in the 1890s. The colour sensitivity was
extended to yellow, orange, and finally to red and infra-red as new dyes were
discovered around the turn of the century. The first panchromatic plates—that
is, plates which reproduced all colours in their correct tone values—were not put
on the market until 1906. Sutcliffe worked in black and white, not colour, but
the false tonal rendering of colour by his blue-sensitive plates were a constant
problem to him, as they were to all photographers of the time.

   Sutcliffe saw brilliant colour, but had to accept that he could not photograph
in colour, and in order to take the best black and white photographs possible, he
had to train himself to see things as his camera saw them:

> It requires some years of practice to be able to tell in an instant what will
> make a good photograph. There are so many things which have to be taken
> into account. It is hard at first to see things stripped of all their colour, to see
> the blue sky as grey, red houses and green fields, rosy-cheeked boys and girls,
> gorgeous sunsets, purple hills, oranges, yellow buttercups—everything, no
> matter how fine in colour, all grey, light grey, and dark grey.[14]

If a photographer came across a scene which pleased his eye, he had to consider
carefully what alterations the plate would make in rendering the colour values:

> We used to study our subjects at dusk when it was nearly dark, for then they
> appeared somewhat as the plate would render them. The red geraniums
> and orange poppies, which looked so bright in the daylight, appeared quite
> black in the dim light of evening, while the blue gentians and cornflowers,
> which we had hardly noticed, seemed almost as light as the white phloxes
> and daisies. Our difficulty was to turn the colour of everything into that
> monotone which the camera delighted in.

One of Sutcliffe's friends was the photographer Valentine Blanchard, who found
that by looking at a scene through blue glass, a photographer could get an
idea of how the colours would register on the plate. The tones of the colours
would be lightened or darkened by the plate in a similar way that the blue glass
lightened or darkened them to the eye. Mr Blanchard bought a lot of blue glass,
which he cut up into small pieces, always carrying a few in his waistcoat pockets.
Whenever he met a fellow photographer he made a lifelong friend by presenting
him with one of them. As Sutcliffe said, 'Of course, these pieces of blue glass did
not make the photographers of that day any better; all they did was to enable

the photographer to know what pranks his sensitive plate would play with the subject or scene.'[15]

It is interesting that the landscape photographers with their blue glass were following the practice of landscape painters, who, over a century before, had been using 'Lorraine glass' to enable them to see more clearly the gradation of tone in a landscape. Similar devices were still in use in Victorian times, and Sutcliffe said:

> Painters often use a set of various coloured glasses, hinged together at one end like a pocket lens, when studying their landscape subjects. If the colours of a subject appear scattered all over, an examination of the scene through the different glasses will often suggest the best way of bringing them—the colours—together.[16]

The problems faced by landscape photographers and landscape painters were similar in many respects, though, of course, painters had complete control over colour.

Probably the most interesting of the techniques used by wet-plate and early dry plate photographers to obtain correct gradation of tone in their work was the practice of giving graduated exposures, a technique which lasted well into the 1880s. To give a graduated exposure, in order not to overexpose the sky whilst securing the darker tones of the landscape beneath it, a special cap for the lens was needed:

> Now, as the [normal] cap is circular, the gradation which would follow its use would be part of a circle; to get rid of this a piece of cardboard covered with black velvet was fastened to the edges of the cap, making the lens cap look like a miniature college cap or mortar-board. By taking off such a cap and moving it slowly upwards and downwards again, the foreground would get considerably more exposure than the sky. If the upper part of the view it was wished to photograph was considerably lighter than the foreground, then the upward movement of the cap was made, slow at first, and then as quickly as possible, the downward movement being made very quick, too.[17]

Sutcliffe went on to describe various other devices including flap shutters and special lens stops with masking arrangements, all of which were designed to cut down exposure on the sky area. If, even with these aids, it was still not possible to obtain sky and landscape on the same plate, the sky had to be printed in, if this was required. Following his usual guideline of keeping as closely as possible to nature, Sutcliffe recommended that the sky used should be that to be seen when the landscape itself was taken. This involved taking the landscape on one plate, which registered the dark tones, followed by the exposure of a second plate from the same position, but with a much briefer exposure, to capture the high-lights of the clouds and the sky. Balancing the two together to get the correct range of tones in the finished print needed experience and a keen eye:

> I believe the reason why natural clouds appear to be wrong is that photographers emphasise them by allowing them to print too deeply. As I look out of the window I see a hillside two or three miles away. This hillside

is considerably whiter than the paper I am writing on. Above this hillside are the first summer-like clouds I have seen this year. They are in bold big masses, piled high above each other—yet the darkest shadow of these clouds is lighter by many degrees than any part of the misty hillside. To render these clouds and the landscape at the same time would be a difficult matter. If we made the hillside as light as it appears, the clouds would have to be so faint that they would hardly show at all. If we could do this properly, we should have a most dainty picture in a high key. We should have to look at the picture once or twice before we noticed there were any clouds at all, but the surprise of finding them would add to the charm of the picture. To make the clouds show more plainly that the world may see how clever we, or at least our cameras are, we lower the tone of the hillside, and make it much darker than it appears. Then, and not till then, may we print our clouds more deeply. That is the reason why photographs are often depressing, the photographer is too afraid of using only the top notes of his scale, he is afraid his melody may appear thin. But by going down towards the base he loses much of the sweetness which he would get if he thought more about making music and less about making a noise.[18]

In 1856 a French photographer, Gustave Le Gray, had exhibited a print at the annual exhibition of the Photographic Society in London entitled *Brig upon the Water*, which showed a ship at sea and clouds in the sky above it. It created quite a stir because the clouds had not been printed in. Le Gray had managed to obtain this picture by pointing his camera towards the sun, which is shining brilliantly on the water, but which is itself momentarily obscured from view by a passing cloud. The effect was known as *contre-jour*—against the light—and the technique enabled photographers to obtain tones both in the seascape and in the sky. Because the sky was very much lighter than the sea, the effect was as if the ship was sailing along in bright moonlight, as the sea is unnaturally dark in tone due to underexposure. This effect could be achieved because of the slow speed of plates, which prevented the sun from blinding the eye of the camera, and the fact that wet-plates showed little or no halation—that is, the spreading of light from the bright areas of a photograph into the shadows. The early dry plates also were slow enough to be used in this way, especially in winter, when the sunlight was weak. Plate 7 was taken, probably in December 1882, with an exposure of a fifteenth of a second at f.8. Sutcliffe said that the sun was just over the lamp-post, and would have fogged any later, faster plates. He recommended photographs of this kind to photographers looking for subjects in mid-winter. In high summer, a landscape or seascape might fail to make a satisfactory picture because the sun is in the wrong position:

> Yet if we could see that view today, say, at three o'clock on a December afternoon, we should very likely find the sun exactly where we wished it to be, and, what is more, very likely sufficiently obscured with haze or light cloud to enable us to point our camera right on its face and find no blurring or reversal on development; and even if there is slight blurring and complete reversal of the disc of the sun,* the blurring might make our photograph more luminous, and as for the reversal, which makes the sun a black one instead of a white one, what is easier than to stamp a white sun out of a piece

of black paper with the perforating machine we use for our invoices and receipts, and gum it over the hole made by reversal. Even if the bit of round paper is a few sizes too large no one will be any the wiser, and very likely all who see it will say, 'There, now, that sun is of the right size, while in most of the photographs one sees it is too small'. The photographer will then pat himself on the back and say nothing. Pictures such as Claude Lorraine and Turner loved to paint, with the sun shining right into the eye of the spectator, can only be photographed properly when the sun is there in the right place.[19]

Sutcliffe took several photographs across the harbour waters into the sun under varying conditions. In Plate 37 the sun is almost obscured by mist or cloud; in Plate 20 the sun is shining through light cloud, and its image on the negative has reversed. Sutcliffe has stuck an opaque disc over the reversed image of the sun on the negative, in the way he described. Although other photographers condemned such 'moonlight' effects as facile, and Sutcliffe himself condemned the crude versions to be seen at the end of the century in postcard shops commenting that, 'If these things were not printed in greenish-blue, they would not deceive anyone', the image is strangely powerful. Why is the 'moonlight' so strong? Why are the houses so dark and sinister? What are the men in the boats doing? It would be more accurate to compare the light effects with an eclipse of the sun than with moonlight, as the atmosphere is unnatural and unsettling rather than dreamily romantic.

It is remarkable that a man working in a completely different medium should have produced an image so strikingly similar to this particular photograph as the accompanying illustration—an oil painting by another Leeds-born man, Atkinson Grimshaw. This is titled *On the Esk, Whitby* and is dated 1877. The painting contains many elements which also appear in Sutcliffe's photographs: the sailing vessel in silhouette, the boats at anchor in the haze, and the faint outline of the parish church and Abbey against the sky. As Grimshaw painted several studies of Whitby, one can play a game of visual snap with his paintings and with Sutcliffe's photographs; for example a Grimshaw painting titled *Whitby Harbour by Moonlight* and dated 1867 can be compared with a Sutcliffe photograph of the quayside in mid-winter probably taken over twenty years later.

Grimshaw was slightly younger than Frank's father Thomas, and both were working as artists in Leeds in the 1860s. After 1864, Grimshaw was living at Woodhouse Ridge, Leeds, only a mile or so away from the Sutcliffes, yet there is no record of the two painters having met. In 1870 the Sutcliffes moved to Whitby, and in 1876 Grimshaw moved to Scarborough, which was just twenty miles down the coast. He was painting scenes from the Whitby harbourside in the 1880s, and though one can imagine a bearded man with his camera passing yet another Whitby artist working at his canvas on the quay, there is no evidence that either was aware of the work of the other. One could trace precedents in romantic painting for the *contre-jour* effects seen in Sutcliffe's photographs. One could also suggest that Grimshaw had seen examples of 'moonlight' photography with its eery atmosphere—neither day nor night. Even when one sets aside speculation, the similarity in their images of Whitby harbour remains as a remarkable example of the close ties—in

Atkinson Grimshaw, *On the Esk, Whitby*, 1877.

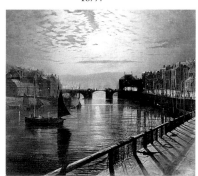

Atkinson Grimshaw, *Whitby Harbour by Moonlight*, 1867.

fms photograph. Winter scene along Whitby quayside, titled *A January Morning*.

* Reversal was a peculiar characteristic of the gelatine dry plate. Any subject which was grossly overexposed registered on the plate as a positive instead of a negative.

spirit, if not in fact—to be found between painting and photography in the late Victorian period.

Grimshaw's paintings are gentle and full of calm serenity. Some of Sutcliffe's photographs were taken in the teeth of a howling gale and, under these conditions, the paths of the painter and the photographer diverged sharply:

> Sea-side photographers are often asked why they do not get more pictures of storms. Now, a photograph of a storm is one thing and a painting of a storm is another. In the first place, the sky is seldom as black as painters make it, and the waves seldom as big—for when the wind is blowing its hardest it seems to flatten the sea down and keep it from knocking about. Then those picturesque groupings of fisherpeople are, I may safely say, never seen in real life. What you do see is a black mass of humanity sheltering as much as possible out of the wind. The force of the wind is seldom taken into account. You see people in paintings standing in places where nothing less than an elephant *could* stand. In fact, sometimes the only way of getting along is to go on your hands and knees. I have seen a man too proud to adopt this undignified method of progression twirled round and round, and thrown down on his face insensible. In a gale of wind one man can do nothing with a camera; even in a sheltered corner one man is wanted to hold on to the legs while the other looks after the plate and exposing. But worse than the force of the wind is its keenness. On our coast we only get rough seas when the wind is north-easterly. Standing beside the camera when a piercing wind is blowing is often more than a joke. I have felt the wind go through my coat, and cut my arm like a knife. Sometimes after waiting maybe for a gleam of light for half an hour, the photographer finds his hands so benumbed that he has lost the power of using them, and do what he will he cannot even take hold of his camera legs to take it away, much less take his camera down and pack it up. One feels very stupid to have to ask a passer-by to be good enough to take up the camera, and carry it along till the blood, like melted lead, begins to flow again.[20]

Sometimes his eyebrows and moustaches froze to the focusing screen of his camera, and sometimes the wind blew so hard that it was impossible to stand in the face of it. It was blowing a gale when Sutcliffe took the photograph of the ship driven aground on Whitby beach (*The Flag of Distress*, Plate 57):

> The wind was so strong that it was impossible to walk: all one could do was to crawl along on all fours; in this case a heavy camera stand shook like an aspen, a focusing cloth was an absurdity. By the way in a high wind a focusing cloth only increases one's troubles, for the wind seems to be determined to send the corners of it into our eyes; besides which it seems to hold the wind and increase the vibration. If it had not been for the help of a big heavy soldier, an artillery man, who was on the beach at the time, who curled himself up under the tripod and held on with both hands to the two legs which caught the most wind, it would have been impossible to have done anything.[21]

Despite his cumbersome equipment and 'colour-blind' plates, Sutcliffe delighted in the countryside around him and tried to capture with his camera some of the beautiful effects which changed minute by minute and season by season. In 1920 he wrote:

> As I walked home today in the mist, unable to see more than twenty yards ahead, I ran into dozens of Japanese pictures, now a pine branch hanging down behind a grey background, now a gnarled hawthorn purple against the pink mist, now a lot of brownish yellow sedges, by the edge of an invisible pond. What countless pictures we lose by not taking any cameras out into the fog.[22]

Over twenty years before he had taken a picture of a similar effect of mist in response to a warning from the organisers of a photographic exhibition in Japan that 'as the standard of taste in Japan was so superior to that of Europe it was quite probable that they might not be able to hang any European exhibits at all'.[23] He decided that he would take a picture of trees half lost in mist. To judge the exposure and depth of focus required for such a photograph was a problem which presented enormous difficulties. Sutcliffe had only his skill and guesswork to go on. Determined not to be outdone by 'superior' Japanese photographers, he got a man to carry his camera to a suitable spot on a misty day. With him he had six dark slides loaded with 12 whole-plates, and he exposed them one after another on the same scene, pausing only to change the stop of the lens, and, in addition to changing the aperture, gave each plate a different exposure. The result was the beautiful and ethereal study of trees in a misty valley (Plate 12). It is very simple, and yet remains mysterious, with a suspicion that the sun is about to break through and drive the mist away. It was sent to Tokyo and was given an award—a piece of lacquer work instead of the usual 'gold' medal given in England—in 1893.

The success of this picture was, no doubt, due to its beauty, but it also stands as a tribute to Sutcliffe's skill as a landscape photographer. When one looks at Sutcliffe's landscapes and seascapes, one responds primarily to the pictorial qualities of the photographs. I hope that by giving some details of the methods he used and the difficulties he faced, I have given an insight into the vast experience and mastery of technique which was necessary to produce such outstanding work.

chapter 8

Photography

'Art's Youngest and Fairest Child'

From the moment that photography was introduced in 1839, painters had regarded this scientific marvel with a wary eye. Paul Delaroche, a leading French painter of the time, was shown one of the first photographs and, on seeing it, he declared, 'From today painting is dead!' Not everyone took such an extreme view, but all were able to see that images could now be produced without the aid of the painter's hard-won skills. Most artists saw photographers as rivals or potential rivals. Photography was such an innovation that no-one knew into what category it should fall. It was by no means clear whether it was an art form or a scientific technique, or both. Supporters of photography hailed 'Art's youngest and fairest child; no rival of the old family, no struggler for worn-out birthrights, but heir to a new heaven and a new earth.'[1] More down to earth, the Commissioners of the International Exhibition held in 1862 denied photography the right to take a place among the Fine Arts, and lumped it together with carpenters' tools and agricultural implements. Painters were accused of copying photographs; photographers were ridiculed for styling themselves as 'artist photographers' and for making absurdly high claims for their work. As the photographer son of a painter, Sutcliffe felt torn between the supposedly rival claims of art and photography and said that: 'If photographers in the past had not claimed too much for photography, I believe that their work would be set at a higher level today than it is.'[2] If his support of photography sometimes seems a little muted, it is probably because he saw himself in the role of mediator between the two opposing camps. Typically, he never claimed the status of works of art for his own photographs, and ridiculed the use of such terms as 'painter photographer'.

The death of his father, soon followed by the disastrous start to his own career as a professional photographer, seems to have left him with a sense of inferiority which sometimes distorted his view of the merits of photography as a creative medium. Perhaps he thought that he should have become a painter and won for the family the admiration and success which had been denied his father because of his early death. Despite Sutcliffe's own international success as a photographer, one can sense Thomas's shade looking over his shoulder as his son wrote, for example:

> If necessity is the mother of invention, laziness is the father. Whether there
> was any real need for photography is doubtful, but it is certain that some lazy
> person, who was too idle to sharpen a lead pencil or wash the paint out of his
> brushes, said to himself, 'Why cannot we let the light make pictures for us
> while we sit by with our hands in our pockets.' So photography was born of
> poor, and not too admirable, parents. The offspring of this couple, need and
> sloth, was, as might have been expected, a mixture of the two, ravenous at
> times, indolent at others, utterly careless of what happened, limited in scope,
> yet, like the London guttersnipe, wonderfully cute. If photography today has
> not come up to the expectations of its earliest admirers, it is because it has
> grown too quickly, and, like other things which have overgrown themselves,
> is loose-jointed, and wanting in grit.[3]

In part, this sense of inferiority belonged to photography in general. It was still a very new medium. It had potential as an art form and, unshackled by a past heritage of great achievement, it could look forward to a future wide open to experiment and development. At the same time it lacked self-confidence and, in its search for security, turned away from the new and untried towards the old and respectable. In this case of photography, the search for established, accepted values always led to painting. The fact that Sutcliffe—at least on occasion—thought that photography was very much the timid newcomer can be seen when he writes:

> Unlike the art of painting, photography cannot look up to any old masters whose work the student may be sure is right. We photographers have no Rembrandts, no Franz Hals, no Constables, no Whistlers. So the student had better not look at photographs after all till his taste is perfectly broken in. It will be safer for him to look at pictures, or at the many beautiful reproductions of our best painters. In time he will find that all these men have much in common, and that they must have had the two words 'Simplicity' and 'Breadth' ever before them. Although a photograph is but a little insignificant thing compared with a big fresco on the wall of a church or a palace, there is no reason why the author of a photograph should not be guided by the same will as that which inspired the painter— to do his best with the tools and the material at hand.[4]

When it was a matter of setting a good example for budding photographers, writers on photography always turned to paintings. Sutcliffe was certainly aware that painters were making free use of his own photographs to aid them in their work. He once managed to take an 'impossible' view of a local church by persuading a farmer to build his haystack in the corner of a nearby field. It was from the top of this that Sutcliffe secured the otherwise impossible view of the tower and north-west side of the church. He said that since then the church had often been painted from that point of view, 'but as the stack up which the photographer climbed has been eaten long ago, and no other stack was ever built there, it is very puzzling to know where the artists plant their easels when they paint their pictures.'[5]

In addition to the fact that photography could not record colour, one of the main differences between it and painting was that a photographer had to take a scene more or less as he found it. A painter, on the other hand, could move trees, rivers and mountains about as he pleased, or as the composition and balance of his work dictated. Sutcliffe was aware that whilst the camera's vision was limited, an artist was not restricted to depicting 'the literal truth', but could draw upon all the best points of any scene. Some photographers tried to redress this balance which lay in favour of the painters by trying to ape their ability to 'compose' pictures. One method they adopted towards gaining this end was combination printing; another involved composition by the sweat of the brow, as they physically built up the view they were seeking.

He thought that the scene-setting undertaken by some photographers was ludicrous, although such prominent workers as his friend Horsley Hinton, the editor of *The Amateur Photographer*, used to 'do a bit of gardening', as he put it, to arrange his foregrounds. When a landscape photographer with a passion for foregrounds went out into the countryside:

he took with him, as well as his camera, plates, and legs, a spade, and a bill-hook. The two latter were for the purpose of trimming his foreground with. It was great sport watching these artists, as the sweat rolled down their faces, digging up ferns and planting them again in front of their tripods, chopping down little trees and trying to make them stand upright behind the ferns, and filling their arms full of bramble sprays to finish off their wonderful foregrounds. No foreground in those days was considered to be complete unless the photographer had laboured at it for a couple of hours or so.[6]

This was another artificial convention in photography against which one must set Sutcliffe's more honest and straightforward work.

Compared with painting, photography allowed anyone who could master the process to make detailed representations of views in a very short time, and Sutcliffe believed that: 'The weak point of photography is that except in the hands of one who has been trained from infancy to *see*, it 'draws' too much, and the eye is vexed at having to reject so much.'[7] He believed that the most important skill which one should develop to produce worthwhile photographs was that of selection:

To know what to take and what to leave is one of the most difficult things the photographer has to do. There are so many bits which are almost good which tempt him to expose a plate on them, and it is so much easier to fix up the camera and make an exposure than to go to the trouble of finding something more complete.[8]

Sutcliffe said that to those who used their eyes, Nature revealed wonderful compositions of her own, and told the story of a landscape painter who looked through a collection of photographs and, when he had finished, declared that he had not realised that Nature could compose so well (see Plates 26, 46 and 50).

In landscape photography, he said that the work of selection was often merely a question of waiting and watching. Having lined up a view on the ground glass screen of the camera, the decision had to be taken whether or not to include any figures in the landscape:

When out with the camera the photographer must *feel* whether he wishes figures in his landscape or not. He must say to himself, 'This view wants a figure *exactly there*, and it must be a light figure or a grey figure or a black figure.' For the life of him he may not be able to say *why* he wants a figure *there*. It is sufficient for him to know that its addition will make his photo-graph more satisfactory. If he has patience and waits long enough the figure will come. Then his friends will say, 'What a lucky snapshot; how well that figure comes there; an artist could not have put it in a better place.'[9]

This technique demanded patience, but Sutcliffe found that it usually worked, and that the 'natural' models who came along were usually well worth waiting for. He once took a friend out on a photographing trip, and they found a view they thought would make a good photograph—a ford overhung with trees and a footbridge to one side:

> I remarked how a white horse would improve the picture, if it could only be persuaded to stop and drink. My friend wished to scour the countryside for a white horse, and it was all I could do to curb his impatience. We had not been there five minutes at the most before an old white pony did come along, and it stopped to drink without any invitation on our part. My friend would not believe that the appearance of the pony had not been pre-arranged.[10]

Sutcliffe freely acknowledged the debt he owed to the work of painters, and said in 1904: 'I believe that J.F. Millet has shown me more than any others'. His knowledge of painting was extensive, and he sometimes saw the landscape before him in terms of the work of painters:

> The other afternoon I saw from the train some harvesters setting up the last few rows of stooks in a cornfield. The sun was shining on to the field—that is, it was directly behind my back. I was astonished at the amount of light reflected by the corn. Had Whistler painted it, he might have called his picture A *Symphony in Cream*.[11]

Like Millet, Sutcliffe depicted the farm labourers at work in the fields (see Plates 22 and 29).

His photographs, by showing the beauty of the countryside without becoming romantic in outlook or dishonest in pretending that working in the fields wasn't sweaty and backbreaking, helped to drive the bonneted aunts and cousins posing as shepherdesses and milkmaids out of photographic exhibitions. A contemporary critic wrote: 'Millet's supreme quality in his power of creating general types of men and things. His peasant is certainly the French peasant to begin with, but beyond that he is the peasant of all times and all places.'[12] Millet generally used a dark range of tones in his paintings, and often deliberately sets his figures against a featureless landscape, which concentrates the viewer's attention on them. In several photographs Sutcliffe seems deliberately to be copying this technique.

Another obvious parallel which could be drawn between Millet and Sutcliffe is that they both buried themselves in the heart of the countryside—Millet in the village of Barbizon close to the forest of Fontainebleau: 'a place so primitive that it might have been hundreds of miles from Paris' and Sutcliffe in a remote corner of North Eastern England. Both these places of refuge were, for a short while, insulated against the shock which was to come from the industrial revolution, which was to transform the countryside as well as the towns, and both Millet and Sutcliffe worked hard to capture the feel of a country life which both suspected—quite rightly—could not survive for very much longer. In both cases, their work stands as a testimony to a way of life which has been swept away by the advance of the modern world.

Many artists saw photography, which made accurate representations of everyday scenes and perspiring humanity, as a natural ally of Realism, which, despite all warnings, continued to exert its influence on the work of English painters. George Clausen, an English painter much influenced by the French *plein-air* school of painting and the work of Jules Bastien-Lepage, was an almost exact contemporary of Frank Sutcliffe (born in 1852 and died in 1944). In an essay on Bastien-Lepage published in 1892, he describes how he has seen painting change over the past few years:

> It will be generally admitted that if painting has made any advance in our day, if it shows in any direction a new departure, or fresh revelation of the beauty that exists throughout nature, it is in the development of the problems which have arisen from the study of landscape and of the effects of light. There now prevails a close and sincere study of nature, founded on the acceptance of things as they are, and an increasing consciousness on the part of artists ... that a picture should be the record of something seen, of some impression felt, rather than be formally constructed. And men have awakened at length to see that all nature is beautiful, that all light is beautiful, and that there is colour everywhere; that the endeavour to realise truly the natural relation of people to their surroundings is better than to follow unquestioning on the old conventional lines.[13]

In many respects the preoccupations of painters who adopted what Clausen calls 'the modern standpoint' were remarkably similar to the more adventurous photographers of the period, such as Frank Sutcliffe. Both painters and photographers based their work on 'the study of landscape and the effects of light', believed 'that a picture should be the record of something seen, of some impression felt, rather than be formally constructed', and tried to capture in their work 'the natural relation of people to their surroundings'.

The influence of French painting brought into being the 'Newlyn brother-hood' of painters in Cornwall, who settled in Newlyn to enjoy the benefits of a climate which made painting out of doors possible all the year round. St Ives also began its rise as an artists' colony in the 1880s, and a writer in the *Art Journal* in 1889 described the subjects to be found in the two villages: 'Both places, being fishing villages, have an always paintable population. A fisherman in a jersey is one of the few modern Englishmen not burlesqued by his garments. And the man who wears a blue jersey generally holds his head in the manner of one familiar with the sky and with horizons.'[14] The similarities with Sutcliffe's Whitby fishermen are obvious. Sutcliffe describes them: 'Their distinctive dress of sou'-wester guernsey, and sea boots, would be worth taking alone, but when you have besides a handsome, open, bronzed face, absolutely without guile, or deceit of any kind, the photographer, and not the model, will be at fault if the photograph turns out a failure.'[15] Walter Langley was the first painter to settle in Newlyn, in 1882, but, before he finally decided to move to Cornwall from his home in Birmingham, he had visited Whitby and other Yorkshire fishing villages to see if they would suit his purpose better. His painting of the *Departure of the Fleet for the North*, dated 1886, shows figures of fishergirls and all the nets and gear used in fishing which are familiar features of Sutcliffe's photographs. This painting illustrates the direct link already referred to between Cornwall and Whitby. The men of Newlyn are taking their fishing boats North to the Yorkshire coast to take part in the herring fishing, leaving behind the boy mending the nets, the old fisherman with his telescope, and their wives and sweethearts.

Walter Langley, *Departure of the Fleet for the North*, 1886.

The French Realist painters looked mainly to the peasants for their folk heroes; English painters often found their heroes among the fishermen around the British coastline. French peasants were steadfast toilers in the fields; English fishermen faced dangerous conditions in their continual battle with the sea and the changing weather. They are the noble, sturdy heroes of everyday life:

> More than with most other sailors, the seafaring life brings to fisher folk many reasons for a certain grave tenderness and quiet heroism. For one thing, the ties of home are stronger to them; they have more on land than any others of their sort; they see more of wives and bairns; often enough they have their own growing lads tending the smack alongside of them; they risk not their own lives only, but also the lives of those that are dearest to them. Then, again, the ship and trade are more of a family affair than elsewhere; each man has his friends and relatives in other smacks; he has been bred to the sea and the fisheries from his childhood upward; his ancestors have been fishermen on both sides for countless generations before him; his good woman herself is a fisherman's daughter, a fisherman's sister, and a fisherman's wife. There must be a great deal of unconscious and instinctive recognition on the part of the world at large of this deep-seated difference between the fisherman and the ordinary wandering sailor, for you will see fifty pictures, and read fifty poems, of the true fisher life for one that you find devoted to common seafaring.[16]

Both Sutcliffe and the Newlyn painters depicted this strong, simple heroism to be found in the fishing communities.

Sutcliffe's photograph of Henry Freeman (Plate 30), the sole survivor of the disaster when the Whitby lifeboat capsized in 1861, captures the spirit and strength of the Whitby fishermen, and his photograph of little 'Dandy' Storr sitting on the knee of his great-uncle Tom Storr (Plate 31) points to the continuation of the fisherman's skill and bravery passed down through the fishing families of Whitby from generation to generation. One of the most famous paintings by a Newlyn artist—*A Hopeless Dawn* by Frank Bramley—shows the mother of a missing fisherman comforting his young wife. A candle placed on the window-sill as a beacon has flickered out. The painting was exhibited at the Royal Academy in 1888 with a quotation from Ruskin's *Harbours of England*:

> Human effort and sorrow going on perpetually from age to age; waves rolling for ever and winds moaning, and faithful hearts wasting and sickening for ever, and brave lives dashed away about the rattling beach like weeds for ever; and still, at the helm of every lonely boat, through starless night and hopeless dawn, His hand, who spreads the fisher's net over the dust of the Sidonian palaces, and gave unto the fisher's hand the keys of the kingdom of heaven.

Sutcliffe returned to Whitby to photograph the fishing community in 1876; Walter Langley moved to Newlyn in 1882. In the spring of 1881, the American painter Winslow Homer rented a cottage in the fishing village of Cullercoats, near the mouth of the Tyne. He found there a fishing community very similar to Whitby and Newlyn; a writer in the *Art Journal*, which devoted several articles in the 1880s to life in fishing villages, describes the people of Cullercoats:

Winslow Homer, *Flamborough Head, England*, 1882.

> The men—and women too, for that matter—have not only to bear with the elements, they have to battle with them for daily bread. They must perforce be quick, strong, and self-reliant in their dealings with wind and wave. So perhaps do they gain that look of—how shall I describe it?—mental power— hardly that perhaps—complete development, which, added to their fine, strong, robust looks, raises them far above any other section of the working classes that I know.

Winslow Homer painted there in the summers of 1881 and 1882, producing watercolours which reflect in their sombre colours the grey skies over the North Sea and the hard life of the fishermen and their families. The article continues:

> The life they lead is a picturesque one, full of vigorous action and variety. But the work is toilsome and laborious, and often very unprofitable. Many people think their occupation is quite an easy way of earning a livelihood. Poets and artists are fond of dealing with it in a fanciful manner, calculated to mislead. The pretty harbour, the shimmering sea, the boats sailing out at eventide to cast their nets and wait for the silvery shoals. It sounds simple and idyllic, but the reality is no pleasant idyll. There is a lot of patient, disagreeable work to be done on shore before a sail is set or a boat is ready to start.[17]

There is no evidence that Winslow Homer, Walter Langley or any of the other painters of fishing communities knew or were influenced by Sutcliffe's work, although photographic qualities can often be traced in their paintings. A painting by Stanhope Forbes, whose work came to epitomise for many people that of the Newlyn School, titled *Home-Along: Evening*, shows people returning home from work and gathering by the harbour rail to stop and chat as dusk falls. The figures against the rail are placed in a way which is typical of Sutcliffe's photographs. Sometime shortly after 1900 Sutcliffe visited Newlyn and took several photographs from the quayside and slipway and many of the details to be seen in the painting are also seen in these Sutcliffe photographs. *Home-Along is* dated 1905, and the Sutcliffe photographs were taken sometime

Stanhope Forbes, *Home-Along: Evening,*
1905.

fms snap-shots of the Newlyn harbourside.

after 1900.* Like the Sutcliffe/Grimshaw comparison, there is no direct link, but the similarity of viewpoint and subject-matter reflects the similar interests of Sutcliffe and Stanhope Forbes, who both delighted in portraying the life of the fishing communities they chose to live among.

Walking up a hill one day towards the church at the top, Sutcliffe noticed a large cloud blowing across the sky towards the church, and timed with his watch how long a photographer would have had the opportunity of using the cloud as a background to the tower of the church. He found that it took the cloud five seconds to get into position, that it was in the right place for about two seconds, and that in another five seconds it had moved away from the imagined picture.

* The photographs were taken on a No. 3 Cartridge Kodak, which was introduced in England in October 1990.

He once timed how long it took to unpack and set up his stand camera, and without including focusing and inserting the dark slide, it took one and three quarters of a minute to set up. When using a stand camera, the photographer had to use a good deal of deliberation and forward planning. Even then things could go wrong. One winter morning he went down to the harbour:

> The tide was unusually high, the air as calm as it often is on a frosty December morning, and there was one solitary Scotch boat riding grandly on the lake-like water in Whitby upper harbour, its mast towering up to the sky. Behind, in grey pearly mist, was the old town crowned by the Abbey and the Church. The sea was perfect, but for one little cockle shell of a boat, which was moored at right-angles across the immediate foreground. I gave a man tuppence to move this away, and while he was doing so I fixed up the camera and put on the lens I usually use. Instead of exposing straight away, when the small boat which looked so big in the foreground had been moved away, I thought I would try and make the Scotchman look bigger by putting on a long-focus lens which I had in my pocket. I had just made the necessary alteration in the length of the focus of the camera, and was setting the shutter to a quarter of a second, when suddenly, from behind an ugly gin palace to the left, appeared a paddle-wheeled tugboat, churning up the lovely reflections and belching out dirty smoke. Then, turning round, this beast of a boat was made fast to the quay between the Scotchman and my camera. If I had only had one lens my picture would have been boxed long before.[18]

Over the years spent using stand cameras and trying to overcome the handicaps which they imposed when the photographer tried to capture the vital moment, Sutcliffe developed an acute sense of timing—an ability to hit upon the split second which produces the best photograph (see Plate 24 and many others). He was able to make full use of this skill when, at the turn of the century, he took to using hand cameras which gave 'snapshot' results.

In the 1890s, members of the Bath Photographic Society went on an excursion to Bradford-on-Avon, and it was reported that: 'Bradford and environs are so picturesque that it is hardly advisable to attempt too much on any one visit; for this reason the party made all possible haste to the weirs at Avoncliffe in order to secure some views ere the light should be unsuitable.'[19] Presumably Bradford was 'picturesque' in all weathers and from all angles.

Sutcliffe saw the stupidity of this approach, and pointed to the fact that by rushing up and down the country pointing their cameras at scenes which had been called 'picturesque' or places which had been declared 'beauty spots', photographers were not only producing a great many worthless images, but were also missing the chance of photographing many beautiful subjects which did not bear the label 'picturesque' and, because of this, went unrecorded.* Sutcliffe found innumerable subjects in the streets of Whitby and was staggered one day when, crossing Whitby bridge, he met a photographer coming in the opposite direction from the old east side of the town, who said to Sutcliffe as he passed: 'There's nothing worth doing over there: I've just been.' This confident statement so amazed Sutcliffe that he could only reply: 'Oh, thank you very much,' and he turned back, abandoning the work he had set out to do.

* P.H. Emerson was of the same opinion as Sutcliffe, stating in his book *Naturalistic Photography* (1889) that: 'the present method adopted by inartistic writers of publishing 'Photographic Haunts' is strongly to be deprecated, such guides can but lead to conventional and imitative, therefore contemptible work. The fact of the matter is nature is full of pictures, and they are to be found in what appears to the uninitiated the most unlikely places.'[20]

Many photographers—especially as the ranks of the unskilled amateur photographers grew in numbers—seemed to undertake photography by guidebook rather than by eye. Sutcliffe said that Whitby Abbey and Scarborough Castle both bore the label 'picturesque', and yet he doubted whether anyone had taken a really outstanding photograph of either.* A contributor to *The Amateur Photographer* wrote in 1891:

> Whitby Abbey I did have a look at, and found fourteen amateur
> photographers spoiling plates as hard as they could. One gentleman informed
> me that he had been at Whitby a fortnight, and had had a turn at the Abbey
> almost every day: 'In fact', he said, 'there is nothing else in Whitby to take,
> except the church.'[21]

Sutcliffe asked:

> Is it because we have been so in the habit of going only for the labelled
> objects that our eyes are not sufficiently alert and our senses properly tuned
> to respond to the greater charms of the rarer beauties? The man who labelled
> all these old ruins 'picturesque' in the first case could not have known that a
> picture must have a pattern. And it is this pattern most of them lack. It is this
> pattern, or pleasing combination of line and mass, that the artist considers
> of greater importance than any historical facts which may be found in his
> subject, and he does not hesitate to sacrifice the latter to the former.[22]

Sailing ships and fishermen might carry labels announcing them as suitably picturesque subjects for the photographer, but no-one had stuck them on an alleyway (Plate 42), a dredger (Plate 37), a barn (Plate 28), or a valley which was little more than an overgrown gully (Plate 12).

One can trace a development in Sutcliffe's photography away from the early object-centred work—such as the photographs which he took of abbeys and castles for Mr Frith, which had to be clear shots of ruins and places, without figures—towards work which was visually motivated—photographs which came from the photographer's eye acting as a viewfinder, rather than from a guidebook. Sutcliffe's development was part of a more widespread movement among the leading workers towards photographs which had pictorial qualities of their own, and which went beyond the limitations of the old traditions which had guided photographers. In his opening speech to the 1894 Photographic Convention of the United Kingdom, the president, Sir Howard Grubb, outlined the changes which were being brought about:

> In the early days of photography a photographer never thought it worth
> his while to point his camera to any object that had not some particular
> interest connected with it. It might be a building having historical interest
> or architectural beauty, or it might be a well-known and favoured landscape
> celebrated far and wide for its beauty; the aim, in fact, of the photographer
> at that time was to produce a representation, or, we might say, a portrait
> of some particular object which had a special interest in itself; but what
> photographer of that time would have thought of wasting his plates (as
> it would have been considered) in pointing his camera at those little

* This seems unduly modest: see Plate 18.

bits of moor or fen, or some nameless brook, out of which the modern photographer has produced his most exquisite pictures? I say pictures advisedly, because that is just the difference between the photographs of the present day and the photographs of the past. The superiority of the later efforts of photographers depended much more on the fact that, whereas in former time the photographer's aim was to produce a representation or a portrait of a particular scene, that of the modern photographer is to produce a picture.[23]

The 'pictures' produced by photographers such as Sutcliffe were beginning to be seen as photographic images in their own right, and not as monochrome mock-paintings. Sutcliffe's career spanned the years from the time when the photographer who attempted more than a straightforward portrait or a topographical record shot was an 'artist photographer', to the time when the prefix 'artist' could be discarded. Though he may not have realised it at the time, he was moving in a direction which led to photography coming of age in the 20th century, which was to see the world through the eye of the camera, and not through the eye of the painter.

chapter 9

New Movements in Photography and Painting

In 1861 Dion Boucicault produced a play called *The Octoroon*, which has passed into oblivion except for one phrase which has survived to become a photographic cliché. One of the characters is given the line, 'The apparatus can't lie'. Sutcliffe recalled the origin of this saying* and added that: 'Photographers of that day, and after, were not slow to make the most of this free absolution from the errors of their ways, though they knew all the time that camera pictures were far from being true.'[1] He never deceived himself into thinking that his camera could produce completely truthful representations of the real world, and realised that the 'reality' produced by the camera could be modified by the photographer:

> The photographer lives in two worlds, the world as it is, and the world as it is photographed. It is the difference between the two which gives him so much trouble. To make matters worse, people are continually telling the photographer about this difference, as if he did not know it too well. The whole art of photography is in knowing when this difference is small enough not to be noticed, or, at any rate, not great enough to give offence.[2]

The real world was transformed in its reflected image seen in a photograph, because subtle modifications were made to 'reality' by both the eye of the camera and the eye of the photographer using the camera:

> The man who always gave his camera legs a gentle kick at the moment of exposure was no fool—he knew what he was about, and he knew, too, the shortcomings of his camera. Many photographs fail to please us because we never can see things as the camera does. At the precise moment when the camera is recording its impression it is as fixed as a rock. We never see anything as a rock would see it. Even if we are sitting on the ground or leaning against a gate or wall, there is a certain amount of play in our point of view. We see round the corners of things; none of our outlines are sharply defined. Yet our outlines are not double, nor so undefined as we find them in some photographs which are made by men who, seeing that the camera's eyes were different from theirs, set about to remedy the defect.[3]

To be a successful photographer, one had to learn to see with a photographer's eye, attuned to the behaviour of the camera:

> The trained eye of the observer of nature, by long habit, is accustomed to seize on every pleasing combination of line or composition of masses; this it does instinctively. If this observer is a photographer, he will probably stop, and try to see the scene in a different way from that which he was doing before. Instead of deriving pleasure from looking at those things which first struck him, maybe some graceful lines formed by the branches of some trees, maybe the contrast between some mass of cloud and some hill-top, he will run his eye over the rest of the scene, looking for faults, looking for anything which would spoil the photograph made by the all-seeing eye of the camera. Let a photographer go out into the country with a sketch-book in his hand and his camera on his back; let him draw or paint his impression of any subject which appeals to him, draw only those things which made him stop. He will doubtless make those things which appeared most beautiful more distinct than they really are; but this does not matter, his eye will not

---

* This is the only source I have seen given for this saying, which was presumably adapted to become the universally-known untruth: 'The camera cannot lie.'

tire so soon as his hand; then, when what appeared to him to be the 'motive' of the place has been put down, let him take his camera off his back and photograph the scene. On the ground glass he will, in all probability, see many things he had not noticed before; perhaps he will find that the principal object in the photograph is a line of bright light running right across the view, caused by the water in the gutter by the roadside; the beautiful curves of the branches may be quite lost.[4]

The camera's eye saw more than the human eye—and this did not apply only to detail in a photograph. When instantaneous exposures became possible, the camera was enabled to see things which looked, to Sutcliffe's eye, ludicrously unreal. He said that instantaneous photographs of horses jumping fences made them look like rocking-horses, and referred to people 'photographing acrobats and jumpers in such strange ways as if hung from the clouds by invisible wires'. Sutcliffe's time-and-instantaneous outdoor shutter was usually set to 'Time', which was the setting he almost invariably used:

long experience having proved that the subjects which will stand a shorter exposure than a brief 'Time' exposure are few and far between; of course, if any one wishes to make caricatures of that noble animal the horse, he must use an instantaneous shutter if the horse is to appear as if in a fit or stricken with a stroke.[5]

He even used time exposures of brief duration to photograph breaking waves, as he believed this gave a more truthful effect of the movement of the sea.
    Sutcliffe was aware of how the human eye could fool the brain:

Many of the wonderful pictures we see and regret that we cannot take because we have no camera with us are not really there to take; they are greatly the result of imagination. We catch a glimpse of an unusual effect of sunshine or cloud and pass on; by the time we reach the hilltop that glimpse has been developed in our mind into a wonderful fairytale. The other day as I turned a corner of a street the afternoon sun seemed to run a stream of molten gold across the houses and elm trees seemed quite black; the distance melted into a purple haze. I ran for my camera, and even as I looked into the finder, and then onto the ground glass the stream of gold seemed to dry up, the big black houses and trees turned grey, and the distance seemed no distance at all. Yet the sun had hardly moved, and no cloud was in the sky.[6]

The difficulty was to transfer the impression received by the mind's eye to the photographic plate.
    In one of his articles, Sutcliffe describes the sort of natural effect which was very difficult to translate into either medium:

It is two by the clock, one by the sun; I am looking sou'-west by south. Twenty yards away, between me and the sun, are two willow trees, some twenty feet high. The greater part of these willows has for a background the blue hill of 'Blue bank'. There, the leaves, where the sun catches them, appear to be speckled with white; they shine like diamonds. Nothing unexpected in this. But against the sky, they shine brilliantly also. Even when seen in front of a white cloud floating across a blue sky they are more than twice as white as the sun-lit, snow-white cloud. As the Americans would say, these willow leaves are 'some highlights'. Suddenly the cloud comes between the sun and the willow leaves, and all their sparkle has gone, they are merely silhouettes against the white clouds. Now they are scintillating again. It would be impossible for a painter to render the sparkle of the leaves against snow-white clouds, unless he mixed diamond dust with his chinese white. White paper or canvas would be far too drab.[7]

It was exactly the same problem—how to reproduce objects seen in bright sunlight—which was later brought forward by the two champions of the new movements in photography and painting which both claimed the same object as their goal—Naturalism. Francis Bate, as an honorary official of the New English Art Club, acted as spokesman for the rebellious painters and laid down the challenge to the established order of art in a series of articles published in 1886 and titled *The Naturalistic School of Painting*. Peter Henry Emerson was the brilliant but volatile champion of the new movement in photography, of which he assumed the leadership, challenging traditional attitudes in photographic circles, first in articles and lectures in 1885-6, and then in his book *Naturalistic Photography* published in 1889. Sutcliffe became directly involved in the controversy which followed its publication because Emerson, Gale, and other leading photographers saw in his work examples of 'naturalistic' photographs produced before the naturalistic movement was fully under way.* Sutcliffe was to become a founder member of 'The Linked Ring' of forward-looking photographers, which in turn led to the Photo-Secession in America, announcing the arrival of the modern school of photography.

It was the conservative, exclusive attitude of the Royal Academy which led to the formation in 1886 of the New English Art Club which was, as its first chairman, W.J. Laidlay, said,

> the outcome of a movement or feeling expressed at divers little meetings between the years 1880 and 1886, with a view to protesting against the narrowness of the Royal Academy and to obtaining fuller recognition for the work of English artists who had studied art in France. The idea at the outstart was simply to supply a want and start an exhibiting society.[8]

The Club appealed to those younger artists—including, incidentally, Clausen and many members of the Newlyn School—who were in their work trying to escape from the bonds of obsolete traditions in painting. Francis Bate spoke for the members of the Club when he said:

> Sentence of death has been passed on conventional folly. Art is now to be judged by a different standard than the old one—pictures will receive a very different criticism, from a very different audience. ... New fields will be found for it to labour in, new chances for its outlet. For knowledge of art the people will go to that source whence they gather all their knowledge—Nature.[9]

* It has been stated by several authorities that Sutcliffe was a follower of Emerson. This is a gross distortion of the truth, and probably stems from the fact that, whilst Emerson never missed an opportunity of blowing his own trumpet, Sutcliffe was a retiring man, and remained hidden away in Whitby for most of his life.

The Photographic Society was suffering even more than the Academy from the stiffness and lack of movement of advanced old age. This was personified by the Society's venerable president, James Glaisher, who was born in 1809. The champion of the new photography, P.H. Emerson, drew on the same artistic traditions which had guided the founders of the New English Art Club. He looked to the French school of painters—men such as Corot, Millet, Bastien-Lepage and Monet—and said that 'these were the first painters who understood Nature; studied her, lived with her, and loved her'.[10] He proposed that all judges at photographic competitions should be artists, and that they should be drawn from the painters 'of what is called the Impressionist School', such as Stanhope Forbes, Clausen and Tuke. This stress on the artistic side of photography was a counterbalance to the importance the Photographic Society placed on photographic technique. Sutcliffe joined in the criticism of what he called 'the worship of technique':

> How long will photographers continue to pride themselves on their technical skill? ... At no exhibition of paintings are works admitted because the canvas has been neatly stretched, or the flies kept from sticking to the paint while the picture was in progress, yet grown-up men are not ashamed to exhibit photographs which have no other merit than technical excellence. It seems as if many overlooked the fact that a photograph is nothing at all in itself, only a means to an end.[11]

Both Bate and Emerson come closer to the essential features of Sutcliffe's photographs when they discuss what the eye sees, and what the painter or photographer should attempt to capture. Bate stated:

> Wherever and in whatever direction we may look our vision centres itself in one point called the centre of vision. Some objects near and around the centre of vision we may see very distinctly; others, not so near, are seen less distinctly: others, again, still further from the centre of vision, are seen very indistinctly, until outside the circumference of the base of the cone of visual rays all things are blurred quickly, and we see nothing. In one glance unvarying in direction we have one centre of vision in our impression of Nature, and it is held by some painters of what is known as the impressionist school that there should be but one centre of vision in a picture, which consequently requires that the subject of the picture should consist of and reflect only so much of Nature as may be seen in one unvaried direction.[12]

Emerson translated these observations into photographic terms:

> The principal object in the picture must be fairly sharp, *just as sharp as the eye sees it, and no sharper*, but everything else, and all other planes of the picture, must be subdued. But, at the same time, it must be distinctly understood that the so called 'fuzziness' must not be carried to the length of *destroying the structure* of any object, otherwise it becomes noticeable, and by attracting the eye detracts from the harmony, and is then just as harmful as excessive sharpness would be ... . Nothing in nature has a hard outline, but everything is seen against something else, and its outlines fade gently into that something else, often so subtly that you cannot quite distinguish where one

ends and the other begins. In this mingled decision and indecision, this lost and found, lies all the charm and mystery of nature. This is what the artist seeks, and what the photographer as a rule strenuously avoids.[13]

The principle of focusing he describes is exactly that which Sutcliffe used throughout the 1880s—the separation of planes, foreground from background, and the concentration of attention on the principal object by the use of differential focusing, and the blending of one feature into another by the skilful use of atmospheric conditions combined with technical expertise.

In an editorial published in 1895, the *British Journal of Photography* scoffed at any claim Emerson might make that his ideas on focus were original, stating that: 'Dr Emerson's plan of focusing the principal object, and keeping the remainder of the picture in subordination, is precisely what every one worthy the name of a photographer has ever done, be he portraitist or landscapist.'[14] But although differential focusing had been used in the past, Emerson was the first to put it forward as a principle which could be used to produce more effective photographs. In an article published in October 1890, he revealed that he was aware that some leading photographers were already following the lines he had laid down in his book, when he stated that: 'Mr Sutcliffe, Mr Coles, Mr Valentine, Mr Steiglitz and many other able photographers work on the differential focus principle.'[15] Sutcliffe said that: 'One good thing Dr Emerson did was that he proved up to the hilt that hard, spotty, or brilliant photographs were quite untrue to Nature.'[16] Emerson's method of avoiding hard photographs with excessive contrast was an exact description of that evolved independently by Sutcliffe: 'As the tendency of "atmosphere" is to grey all the colours in nature more or less, and of a mist to render all things grey, it follows that "atmosphere" in all cases helps to give breadth by lessening contrast, as it also helps to determine the distance of objects.'[17]

The same issue of the *Amateur Photographer* contained a letter to the editors from Frank Sutcliffe. It is worth quoting in full because it not only gives Sutcliffe's own view of the 'naturalistic' controversy, but also comes as a cool breeze of common sense in a debate which was to become more and more heated:

SIRS, It seems to me that the long and short of natural photography is that, as everyone *sees* differently, so some like to make their photographs sharp everywhere, others just the opposite. Living in this age of freedom, I do not consider myself bound by any rules, but free to take a subject that pleases me, either as it appears in the twinkling of an eye, or as it looks after a lengthened inspection. In the former case my eye would not have time to see anything clearly, in the latter everything before me would in succession be focussed [*sic*] on the retina of my eye; but as I am not in the habit of standing and gazing at the beauties of nature for hours at a time, preferring to look at her as I walk along, I do not think I ever see so sharply as my lens does. Some people may be able to focus their eyes in succession on every leaf, and twig, and stone, and ripple that is in front of them as they travel round this world; but I fear if I tried to do so my poor brain would soon begin to spin, and my eyes ache, as they do after a lengthened visit to a picture gallery. By looking at the world in this fashion no doubt I miss seeing most of it, and when out with my camera I fear I see less still, for I find myself continually half closing my eyes, and so see less clearly than ever. I cannot think that I am doing very wrong when I allow my lens to photograph just what I can see without an extra effort. After all on examining the results I generally find that the lens has seen more than I did, sometimes it sees things that had slipped my observation altogether. If I had been born with a piercing, penetrating eye, things might have been different, and I possibly should not have been content with slices of nature, but have taken the whole loaf. Perhaps the continual rubbing against painters has spoiled me, for I do not like to think that those artists who work out of doors, and study nature and picture making as no photographer has done yet, are going backwards, now that they do not elaborate detail as they did in their youth. I think you will agree with me that the worship that has been paid to detail by photographers is one reason why photographers have been held in such low estimation by the educated public. In the hands of a worker like Mr Gale detail is no doubt kept in its proper place, but generally the opposite is the case, the detail forcing itself on the spectator. That some people who consider themselves judges of photographs can see nothing and care for nothing in a photograph but the detail shown, may be seen by the way they examine them. They take out a pocket microscope, and, placing the eye to one end and the photograph at the other, go over it, then put it aside, and exclaim either, 'How beautifully sharp!' or, 'What a funny photograph! Why, it isn't sharp at all!' Such people do not think it right to take photographs except when the air is clear, and look upon the photographer as a fool if he sets up his camera when nature is veiled with fog, or blurred with rain, or almost lost in the shades of evening. —I remain, yours truly,

FRANK M. SUTCLIFFE.
October 29th, 1889.

P.S. Of course, when I am taking map-like views, and soldiers in their war paint, and ladies in their best dresses, and architectural and scientific subjects, I do not give people the opportunity of saying that my eyesight is getting dimmed by intemperance or by old age.[18]

By 1893, when Emerson spoke on 'Naturalistic Photography' to the Photographic Society, he had moved even closer to Sutcliffe's views as expressed in his letter reproduced above and as shown in his photographs. Emerson now saw that it was 'self-evident' that

there is no *absolute* truth to Nature from the visual standpoint, for, as each man's sight is different, the only absolute truth to Nature for each man is his own view of her (though certain broad features remain true to all). On the other hand, from the mathematical standpoint, or perspective drawing standpoint, there is an absolute standard, such as the sharp photograph taken with rectilinear, and otherwise duly corrected, lenses.[19]

He had come to these conclusions in the course of writing a pamphlet on 'Perspective Drawing and Vision' and said that 'Dr Griffiths and Mr Sutcliffe were the only two photographers who were acute enough to see and acknowledge in public the force of the pamphlet'.

Emerson's *Naturalistic Photography* was a milestone on the road to modern photography. However, it did reveal a rather biased view on the part of Emerson as an art historian—one writer said that 'it has been reserved for Mr Emerson to convert the Temple of Fame into a slaughterhouse'[20]—and his own arrogance as a writer.

The old school of photography, which Sutcliffe had moved further and further away from as he developed new methods of expressing himself through his photographs, met the new school in head-on collision. H.P. Robinson was still dressing up his 'peasants' and 'fishergirls'. The year 1889 saw both the publication of *Naturalistic Photography* and a second edition of Robinson's *Picture Making by Photography*,* originally published in 1884. Robinson's methods of working were once more expounded, and he gave an example of the taking of one of his photographs which was titled *A Merry Tale*:

> In the drawing-room of a country house in North Wales five young ladies in evening costume were amusing themselves after dinner. One of them was relating some funny circumstance to the others, who arranged themselves in a picturesque group round the story-teller. Here was the germ of the picture. … It was arranged that the group should form part of our work for the next day. … Off we started to a quiet lane about a mile away. The photograph conveys no idea of the picturesque effect of the five girls in their humble but brilliantly-coloured garments. … Arrived at the selected spot, the camera was unpacked, and the models placed approximately in their proper places, interfering branches cut away, and everything got ready, so that the last moments might be devoted to the quite final touches, expressions and other little things. … A few last words—at the special request of the models I use fictitious names—'Now, girls, let this be our best picture. Mabel, scream; Edith, a steady interest in it only for you; Flo, your happiest laugh; Mary, be sure you don't move your hand, or all the good expressions will go for nothing; Bee, I will say nothing to you, but leave you to fate. Steady! Done!' and two seconds' exposure settled the matter.[21]

Davison attacked such artifice as combination printing and dressing up models on behalf of the naturalists:

> It is not in man, even in f.64 man, to over look the unnaturalness of joinings in photographic pictures, and the too visible drawing-room drapery air about attractive ladies playing at haymakers and fishwives. Naturalism does not stand or fall upon a question of how much or how little softness of focus is admissible, but it certainly is diametrically opposed in its view to the much worship of register marks, and to all *un*naturalism in figures and their attire. Its creed is, *Truth, and the best of everything*.[22]

It is only when one realises the early stage at which Sutcliffe broke with artificial picture-making that one can appreciate how advanced much of his work was compared with that of the members of the old school, who were not put onto the defensive until the late 1880s.

Although Sutcliffe's and Emerson's views on photography seem to coincide on several important points, Sutcliffe was not always impressed by Emerson's work. However, on another occasion he made a special visit to the library of the British Museum to look at Emerson's photographs in his book *Life and Landscape*

* This second edition contained a chapter refuting Emerson's theories.

of the Norfolk Broads (published in 1886). The two men seem to have got to know each other fairly well during the 1890s. They served together as judges at photographic exhibitions and wrote to each other regularly. Unfortunately their letters have not, to my knowledge, survived.

At the annual exhibition of the Photographic Society held in 1890 two photographs which were each awarded medals revealed the gulf which was opening up between the old and the new photography. One was Lyddell Sawyer's *Two's Company*, a photograph in the style of Sawyer's acknowledged master, H.P. Robinson. A reviewer in *The Photographic News* described the picture: 'we get a laughing damsel engaged in a very hot flirtation with a laughing swain. ... Further away is a second swain with an intolerable scowl upon his good-looking face.' The new school was represented by George Davison's *An Old Farmstead* which was so far removed from the 'sharp' school of photography that it had been taken with a pin-hole in place of a lens, which produced an effect some thought went beyond the bounds of naturalistic photography into the realm of impressionist images.* The reviewer said of Davison's exhibit:

> The effect of this picture is exceedingly pleasing to the eye, and if it be that the quality of a photograph is that it should look as unlike a photograph as possible, then Mr Davison has succeeded admirably. ... It would seem that such photographs as 'The Old Farmstead' can scarcely be criticised on the principles which have hitherto governed photographic art criticism; and it may be necessary to wait until further examples familiarise one with the intentions of the exponents of the new style.[23]

Frank Sutcliffe commented on the conflict in a paper read at the Photographic Convention in 1892:

> There has been, as you all know, a lot of strife between what has been called the old school and the new, or the sharp and the unsharpened; it seems to me that, if both these parties had looked at their work and at that of others in the right way, all this bickering would not have been. It would almost appear as if many consider their photographs as an end rather than a means to an end, and as if all that is expected of the spectator is that he should admire the skill of the worker as shown in his work; sometimes even it appears to be the *author* of the work who expects to be admired.

Sutcliffe does not identify himself at this point with either school. His suggestion that photographs and the theories they are said to exemplify were being used as a form of self-advertisement among photographers was a point unnoticed by others at the time, but which has come to bedevil the work of photographers and artists of our own day. Sutcliffe said that 'if a photographer thinks he can tell his tales better by making his works microscopically sharp, let him do so by all means'. But he added that an extremely sharp picture could be, to some eyes, 'positively painful', and that it could perhaps disturb or break the observer's train of thought, 'whereas a less-defined one would allow the mind to wander at its own sweet will'.

Sutcliffe, as his work shows, was aware of the evocative power which photographs could carry. He describes an example—'an almost ideal photograph' he

* In the previous year, 1889, the *Amateur Photographer* had commented that: 'We trust the time will never come when examples of photography will in any way resemble the "Impressions" now being exhibited by Claude Monet and others in the Goupil Gallery.'

says—by George Davison, who came to be seen as the leader of what one critic called 'this new photo-woolly-graphic school'. Sutcliffe saw the advantages of a certain lack of definition, as he says in his description of Davison's photograph of a windmill:

> I don't mean that it was so uncertain and undefined that it could have represented anything the spectator might have been pleased to wish, but it was just enough to start the mind along a pleasant channel ... one heard the wind blowing and whistling through the mill sails, then it almost died away, only to come again in louder and louder gusts. Now the miller and his man come out and look anxiously, first at the yellow sky, and then at the wands, from which they take in nearly all sail. Yet the arms rush round at a fearful rate as the sky gets darker and darker. What an enormous size the mill looks!—did you ever go underneath a mill's sails in the dark? What terrible things the arms are—they are more like a nightmare than anything real, as they come down threatening to crush you at every turn, yet never getting any nearer. ... All this, and much more, did Mr Davison's simple photograph say. Had it been taken by one of the cast-iron school, the same pleasant train of thought might have followed, if one could have kept at a distance of ten yards; but where is the man who is content to look at a photograph from this distance? No, it would have drawn us nearer and nearer, and every step would have disturbed the train of thought by forcing other subjects forward. Most likely the excellence of the lens would have been impressed upon us, and, once started on such a subject as cameras and lenses, good-bye to all pleasure.[24]

The Photographic Society took no action to meet the objections of those among its ranks—members of both the old and new schools of pictorial photography—who protested against the practice of hanging work of a scientific and technical nature alongside that of the pictorial workers. This led to a secession from the Society of the pictorial photographers led by H.P. Robinson. On 9 May 1892 a meeting of photographers took place at the *Restaurant d'Italie* which led to the formation of the Linked Ring—an informal grouping of some of the most prominent pictorial photographers in Britain and overseas. Their common opposition to the policies of the Photographic Society brought the old and the new pictorial workers together, and the Linked Ring had as members both George Davison and H.P. Robinson. Frank Sutcliffe became a founder member in 1892.

The Linked Ring held annual exhibitions, which they called Salons,* in the Dudley Gallery in London, which also housed the exhibitions of their counterpart in painting, the New English Art Club. The idea of a photographic exhibition which consisted of pictorial work alone, without any examples of scientific or technical work, was a new one, and the photographic press was very critical of this attempt to put forward photography's claim to a position as an independent art form. Sutcliffe said in 1908† that the Salon organised by the Linked Ring set the highest standard of any exhibition in Britain:

* This was the name given to the great exhibitions of painting in France. Sutcliffe said that he thought the name had been put forward in a sense of fun and without pretentiousness.
† 1908 saw the last Salon organised by the Linked Ring before it disbanded.

It was here that virtue found its own reward, and no other. No medals or plaques or other bait was even dangled in front of the exhibitors' eyes. Quality, with a personal note in it, is what The Salon asks for. Perhaps at first there was too much personality, and not enough quality but this cannot be said today. The number of prints hung is never very large. The number of frames unhung is always large. ... There are no classes at the Salon—anything which is a photograph may be sent, but unless it has great pictorial quality, it will be a waste of time and money sending it. The sharpest, clearest, f.64 print on smooth paper has an equal chance of admission with the vaguest, faintest gum-print, if it has anything to say for itself, and can say it in the best way.[25]

In 1890, the *Amateur Photographer* had congratulated the New English Art Club on one of their early exhibitions:

We, as photographers, can hold out the hand of fellowship to the members of the Club and encourage them to persevere in the road along which they have made so excellent a start, for they (with a few notable exceptions) have realised at least one of the truths artists are ready to acknowledge, that they owe in no small measure to the advance of photography along the artistic path, namely, that 'nature out-of-doors cannot be mimicked by paintings in a studio, and that to handle a subject dramatically it is not necessary to be theatrical'.[26]

Now, in 1893, it was the turn of the painters to offer encouragement, and the *Studio* gave the first Salon a favourable review:

The exhibition just closed has done more almost than any previous one to prove that photography allows the artist free play for his own individuality. The photograph of today is something more than a mechanical production. The individuality of the photographer is being expressed in his work almost as much as that of the painter; and while critics are discussing if there be Art in photography, photographers are settling the question by themselves.[27]

Despite being attacked as 'decadents', 'fuzzyites', and 'neuropaths', the exhibitors at the Salon began to exert an influence on photography which reached beyond Britain. In 1894 the Photo-Club de Paris held its first Salon, where for the first time in France photographs were shown for their aesthetic qualities alone, and in 1899 the Royal Academy in Berlin opened its doors to photography. In America, attempts were made to organise photographic Salons in the late 1890s, and in 1902 Alfred Stieglitz, who was himself a member of the Linked Ring, organised the American photographers in the Photo-Secession.

Sutcliffe welcomed the movement towards photography becoming recognised as a valid and independent medium of self-expression, but he was unhappy with the recently introduced manipulative processes such as the gum bichromate and later the oil process, which allowed the photographer to modify his work to such an extent that it was difficult to tell whether a finished print was a photograph or a sketch produced by hand. 'Where is the line to be drawn,' Sutcliffe asked, 'and is a photograph to be simply a photograph, or may it be a cross between a photograph and a chalk drawing? May it even be very much chalk drawing and very little photograph?'[28] He saw excessive manipulation of the photographic image as a reintroduction of artifice—the enemy of the straightforward approach to photography for which he had fought throughout his career. Artifice was now re-emerging in a new guise. He saw photographers once more posing as artists: 'It is very sad to see so many excellent photographers turning into bad oil-painters. Men who used to delight us with splendid photographs year after year now ask us to admire their attempts at oil painting.'[29] To Sutcliffe this was a step in the wrong direction and could only lead towards deception—deception of the public by the exhibition of doctored prints, and self-deception by photographers who were twisting photography to meet their 'artistic' purposes.

chapter 10

Whitby

'The Photographer's Mecca'

In 1894 the *Whitby Gazette* published an article on Sutcliffe, who was by this time a well-known and respected figure in Whitby: 'Mr Sutcliffe has achieved honour and profit, not only in the place of his biding, but also distinction in the highest corporate bodies of his art; his work and skill have been sealed, emblazoned and gold-medalled, not only in England, but in foreign countries, on more occasions indeed than at this moment we would care to enumerate.'[1] Between 1881, when he won his first photographic award at an exhibition in Newcastle for the best photograph on the newly-introduced Swan dry plates, and 1905, he won 62 gold, silver and bronze medals and other awards at exhibitions in Britain and all over the world. His photographs won acclaim at shows from Dundee to Falmouth, and from New York to Tokyo. A list of the places where he won awards reads like the gazetteer of an atlas—Dublin, Cardiff, London, Chicago, Boston, Berlin, Paris, Vienna, Calcutta and Tokyo, to name but a few.

One of the first photographic exhibitions to which he sent prints was held in Dundee in 1882. A friend—a lady water-colour painter—gave him some frames covered with crimson plush, which Sutcliffe used to frame some silver prints of shipping scenes. The hanging committee at Dundee, their eyes dazzled by the frames and not their contents, hung them as near the ceiling as possible out of harm's way. Luckily for Sutcliffe one of the managers of the show—James Valentine—noticed these crimson frames which had been 'skied', and climbed up a step-ladder to see what they contained. He obviously felt that the frames were harming the prints and had them reframed at his own expense, and they were hung 'on the line' in new wooden frames. They won Sutcliffe a silver medal, and, in addition, all of them were sold. This was the happy beginning of a friendship with Valentine who invited Sutcliffe up to Dundee to see his photographic printing works, where his firm produced local views, and, later, postcards.

Sutcliffe was excluded from the amateur classes of photographic exhibitions, which in the 1880s were usually divided into amateur and professional sections, which were then further sub-divided into various classes. Thus at Keighley in 1890 he took the bronze medal in the class for subject pictures in the professional section, taking second place behind H.P. Robinson, who was awarded the silver medal. Sutcliffe also took the silver medal as champion photographer overall at the exhibition. But although he was very successful in winning medals, he was not in favour of photographic exhibitions dangling them as bait for photographers, who often sent exhibition prints round the country from exhibition to exhibition in search of awards. Sutcliffe thought that exhibitions should be thrown open to all photographs—as the Salon was later to be—and said that: 'As long as exhibitions are hampered with regulations and distinctions, often difficult to understand, and classes are tolerated, they will not ever be looked on as a show of pictures in the highest sense of the word.'[2]

In October 1888 George Davison, the honorary secretary of the Camera Club, wrote a letter which was printed in *The Photographic News*:

> Will you allow me to draw attention to the first of the series of 'one-man' exhibitions of photographic pictures which are being organised at the Camera Club. The first exhibition will be devoted to the work of Mr Frank

> M. Sutcliffe of Whitby. By the kind co-operation of Mr Sutcliffe, we shall be able to present a fully representative show of his work, and believe that the exhibition will prove of great interest to photographers and artists.[3]

The idea of a 'one-man' show giving the public the chance to see a representative selection of the work of one photographer was quite new. Photographic exhibitions usually contained a jumble of work of very varied standards by many hands. For Sutcliffe to be asked to mount an exhibition showing about 250 of his photographs was a great tribute to his stature as a photographer, and the fact that he was the first man* to be given this honour is an indication of the respect in which he was held in photographic circles.

A reviewer in the *Amateur Photographer* saw the nature of the show as a tribute also to photography as an art:

> The title 'One Man Exhibitions' has provoked inquiry, and has attracted the attention of photographers and of the Press. Photographic art having advanced to the point where complete exhibitions may reasonably be devoted to presenting the works of single exponents, becomes worthy of notice and even of serious criticism. The name points directly to this, excites curiosity, and assists in raising public opinion in regard to the possibilities of photographic art.

The photographs on display were silver prints in mounts pinned onto backboards covered with a gold coloured sateen, which served 'to throw up the silver prints exceedingly well'. On entering the room the visitor saw on his left the best lighted and most important wall. The central frame on this wall carried nine of Sutcliffe's best and most famous photographs, including *Water Rats*. The reviewer said of Sutcliffe's work:

> It is the work of a true amateur, a lover of his practice, an enthusiast for art, and one with natural taste and high culture. Almost every picture evidences Mr Sutcliffe's power to sympathetically command his models, and his fine perception of the beautiful in nature, and skill to render the effect he aims at, both in the negative and by judicious printing … Altogether the exhibition is of a very high order, full of variety of subject, and showing skilful work. … It will be difficult to follow Mr Sutcliffe.[4]

Despite acclaim by the photographic world, Sutcliffe found little financial benefit to be derived from his widespread fame, and, often working over twelve hours a day during the Whitby holiday season, he felt shackled to his portrait business. He found expression for his bitterness in several articles written in the 1890s and early 1900s:

> A painter who has made a reputation finds his name worth so many thousands a year to him. It is doubtful if the reputation of a single photographer in the world has got beyond his own town; that he may be known to his brother photographers is outside the present question. Ask any travelled educated man if he knows the work of Rejlander, H.P. Robinson, Craig Annan, Barnett, Hollyer. No, he has never heard of one of them. Therefore we may say that reputations made by photographers are valueless. That is, they do not bring in any more customers.[5]

* Future shows were planned for the photographs of Robinson, Emerson, Gale and others, but Sutcliffe was given pre-eminence over these respected names. Emerson had a one-man show at the rooms of the Royal Photographic Society in Russell Square in June 1900, followed by an exhibition of Sutcliffe's photographs in January 1901.

It would be wrong to give the impression that Sutcliffe was constantly harping on about money, but past financial difficulties cast long shadows over the years of his success. He saw men with little ability make fortunes out of photographic businesses. 'Success is a matter only of capital,' he complained. 'The man with the most capital is able to buy the best lenses and machinery, and is able to do the best work in the best way.'[6] He became more and more disillusioned with the portrait photography which took up almost all his time—especially after the success of his Skinner Street studio, opened in 1894. The final years of his work as a portrait photographer seem to have been carried out in an atmosphere of grim necessity, although he maintained a polite attitude to his sitters:

> It would seem that he always commences any acquaintanceship with the perhaps sane idea that they are Philistines, and that they will want him to make their photograph in the commonplace, orthodox style, and that, although he has to do it, he has no sympathy with them or they with him; and after he has done it as conscientiously as he can, and as well as he is able in their way, he won't be sorry when he sees the last of them.[7]

The photographs which won worldwide fame at exhibitions he sold copies of at his shop, and also arranged for carbon prints to be made by G.W. Wilson & Co. of Aberdeen, who were in the 1880s the world's largest publishers of photographic views and lantern slides. In an interview published in the 1890s, a member of the firm was asked 'if the public had shown any desire to be supplied with pictures of the art type seen in these latter days at our exhibitions'. He replied: 'No, none whatever. ... We once tried to introduce a series of pictures of a much higher order, but the venture was an absolute failure.' It is very likely that he is referring to the venture in printing copies of Sutcliffe's photographs in 1891. Sutcliffe quotes this interview in an article in *The Practical Photographer* and adds: 'Absolute failure, yes, that is what photographers, who try to make a living by making pictures, see staring them in the face at the beginning of the year 1897. Would that instead they could see the coming of success!'[8]

He likened the professional photographer who had been born with artistic instincts to a swift runner who finds himself in a sack 'which prevents him turning his abilities to account, that is into pounds, shillings and pence; his artistic powers are of no use to him as a professional.' The taste of the general public he considered deplorable, but they provided him with his living and, in addition to demanding that their portraits should be taken as they wanted, influenced Sutcliffe's work in producing local views, which were popular with tourists before the introduction of picture postcards:

> Why do people buy local views? Are they allured into spending their money because they are offered such exquisite examples of photographic art? No; all the tourist wants is something to remind him of the places he visits, something to strike a note in his memory. A few years ago I took a view, but somehow or other it did not sell at all, though it was as clear as the most fastidious could wish for. No; the view which sold was taken by the other man, though he ought to have been ashamed of it, for the grass was black and his whites were white without any mistake. But his prints sold; do you know why? At one corner of his view was a whitewashed public-house.

Frank Sutcliffe with his family, c.1895. From left to right: Kathy, Horace, Irene, Eliza, Frank, Zoë, Lulu.

I learned afterwards that visitors called there to refresh. My view did not include that ugly public-house. What I gained in artistic excellence I missed in sentiment and £ s. d.[9]

From 1875, when he contributed a short piece to the *Year Book of Photography and Photographic News Almanac*, Sutcliffe wrote a great many articles on photography, which must have provided a healthy supplement to his income as a professional photographer and an outlet for his pent-up feelings. He wrote for *The Practical Photographer*, was an 'editorial contributor' to *Photography*, writing many of the leading articles in the 1890s, and also had articles printed in *The Photogram*, *Camera Notes* (the American journal edited by Stieglitz) and many others. The *Amateur Photographer*, edited by his friend Horsley Hinton, a colleague in the Linked Ring, printed dozens of his articles between 1895 and 1913, many of them illustrated with Sutcliffe's photographs. Horsley Hinton wrote a weekly column called 'Photography Notes' for the *Yorkshire Weekly Post*. When he died in 1908 at the early age of 45, Sutcliffe took over the writing of his column. His first contribution was printed in the issue dated 29 February 1908, and he contributed articles almost every week for the next 22 years. He wrote 'Photography Notes' almost as an open diary, and addressed his Yorkshire audience as if they were old friends. Compared with these 'Notes', his articles for other journals—especially for *Photography*, which called itself 'The Journal of the Amateur, The Profession & The Trade'—are much more impersonal and less revealing. The mass of information, incidental details and personal reminiscences which have been preserved in his 'Photography Notes' have provided much of the material for this study.* The immediate and personal nature of the 'Notes' can be judged by the way in which several of them begin, for example: 'As I sit in the train, about to start ...'† or: 'As I sit here, waiting for my breakfast ...' Photography was not the only thing in Sutcliffe's life either. In 1921 he brusquely ends an article on photographic printing: 'But we must leave our toning till next week. There is a cricket match in ten minutes of more importance than all the photographic prints in the world.'

Another activity which took up an increasing amount of his time after he had become a familiar name in photographic circles was judging at photographic exhibitions. Although he was not a member of the Royal Photographic Society, he acted as a judge at their exhibitions on at least three occasions in the 1890s. He was also the 'honorary judge and critic' of the Whitby Camera Club. Between the lofty heights of the 'Royal' and the shows of the local club were dozens of provincial societies who organised photographic exhibitions and asked well-known photographers such as Sutcliffe to select the prints to be shown. This usually meant travelling by train to a strange town and trying to judge exhibits among the chaos of last-minute arrangements for the show. 'Those who have had any experience in judging know too well how rarely their expectations are met,' Sutcliffe said. The judges might hope to enter a well-lighted room with all the photographs tastefully hung and a cup of coffee waiting for them, and at well-organised exhibitions in the large towns this was occasionally the case. But usually the circumstances were very different:

> How often are they, instead, on entering the exhibition rooms, greeted with the smell of an escape of gas, and a plumber groping about with a bit of tallow candle! Here and there may be a few photographs hung, but most of the exhibits are just being taken out of their packing cases, which cover the floor. Joiners are busy hammering at trade exhibit stalls. It is impossible to hear what is said. You proceed to take off your hat and coat when the secretary, using his hands as a trumpet, shouts, 'Keep your hats and coats on, gentlemen; we tried to light the fire, but it smoked, so we thought it better to let it go out.' The lids are nailed on two or three of the largest packing cases, and on these the judges are invited to sit and pick out the best pictures as the frames are brought before them. ... One of the judges is very difficult to please, he cannot see any beauty in any of the exhibits; it turns out that one of the nails in his packing case had not been hammered down.

Having survived the allocation of awards for photographic prints, the judges descend into the depths of the building to judge the lantern slides:

> In the basement of the building, the floor, half an inch deep in water, planks had thoughtfully been provided to keep the judges' boots dry; the lanternist had lost his screw-key or something, and could not turn on the light till he had gone home and found it. Then for a minute or two a white circle of light is given to the judges to blind them, and their work began. 'Good heavens, was that a rat?' 'No, that is a blackbird on the snow.' 'You don't understand me, it ran over my knees.' 'Yes,' breaks in the lanternist, 'they come out of the drains.'[10]

The details of the story have no doubt grown in the telling, but their vividness gives the ring of truth to the description, and Sutcliffe is probably writing from personal experience of nightmare-like meetings of selection committees.

* Many of Sutcliffe's articles were published in later life, after his main work as a photographer had been completed, and he felt that he could pass on his experience to the rising generation of photographers. Many of the ideas put forward in his articles are quite original, but I have nevertheless been careful not to credit Sutcliffe with foresight which, upon the examination of the dates of the article and the subject he is talking about, proves to be hindsight.
† He travelled the three miles from his home in Sleights to his work in Whitby by train.

Sutcliffe entered his own prints in so many exhibitions that he must have become familiar with seeing his work criticised in print. Sometimes the reviewer attempted to influence Sutcliffe to change the type of photograph he usually took. In 1889 the *British Journal of Photography* reviewed three prints which had won a medal at the Photographic Society's exhibition:

> These consist of three specimens of the usual productions which this exhibitor produces every year. They consist of pictures with an artistic perception of arranged or waited-for moments, when the figures combine into what will eventually prove to be a pictorial study. Whilst admitting that there is very great artistic construction shown in these photographs, we feel compelled to state that some choicer specimens have been shown by this exhibitor. ... However, as evincing an exceedingly effective capacity for utilizing the picturesque in simple seaside and country-life figures, this photographic art worker keeps up the even tenor of his way, which we venture to suggest is capable of higher possibilities in photographic representations of more emotional scenes.[11]

Sutcliffe had the good sense not to let himself be persuaded to change his genre scenes into narrative photographs in the style of Victorian narrative paintings, though he does occasionally introduce a narrative element into his photographs. *The Young Orthographer and his Grandfather* is an example of this style, which was not well received by his critics. Sometimes reviewers decided that Sutcliffe was well-established enough to take hard-hitting criticism. A reviewer in the *Amateur Photographer* described Sutcliffe's work in the 'Subject Picture' class at the Keighley Photographic Exhibition in 1890:

The Young Orthographer and his Grandfather.

> Mr Sutcliffe takes second place with a fine study of an old woman, truly
> a splendid portrait of a most admirable model. Mr Sutcliffe exhibits other
> pictures; we have his everlasting Whitby fishermen and women, taken in
> front and behind, standing, sitting, kneeling, crouching, and so on *ad
> infinitum*. We have seen these men and women at every exhibition for years,
> and are tired of them. Lately Mr Sutcliffe has thought fit to 'haze off' the
> distance, until in some that he exhibits Whitby is completely enveloped in
> fog, although there is a bright light upon the men and women on the jetty.
> Mr Sutcliffe is an old exhibitor, and ought not to give us the opportunity of
> calling attention to careless work, but it is a fact that on one print exhibited
> there are no less than *five blemishes;* of course, in these days such a thing is
> inexcusable.[12]

The same reviewer dismisses Sutcliffe's landscapes 'which, in our opinion, are
neither of artistic or technical value'. Petulant outbursts such as this were rare;
Sutcliffe's photographs were usually well received by the critics.

Sutcliffe was very critical of his own photographs, and saw them as personal
statements rather than as potential medal-winners. His photography was an
extension of his own personal development and he looked on its progress in
the same way that a painter might regard personal development in his work:
'Whenever I see any old photographs by Hollyer, Blanchard, Mudd, Rejlander,
Heath, Hill, Fenton, etc., it is impossible to keep from thinking that we get "no
forrader". Each of us knows quite well what prevents us *individually* from making
progress, but we think it wiser to keep our own counsel.' Unfortunately he does
not expand this point. He said that to produce good work a photographer must
be a sensitive person:

> There must be some degree of fine mechanism within the worker before
> it will respond to the touch of nature—in other words, photographers
> must be born and not made. Now this fine stringing, which makes the
> photographer susceptible to what the man in the street never hears, makes
> him also susceptible to other things. A thoughtless, unkind word from one
> whose opinion he values will make him kick his camera into the sea. ... Little
> do we know how many promising photographers have been cruelly nipped
> in the bud by having their artistic and gifted work ignorantly condemned
> by photographic critics. It is not given to everyone to have a dogged
> determination to try and try again in spite of jeers and failures.[13]

He never harshly criticised anyone's work—even the bungling amateurs who
brought him their 'mistakes'—and it seems likely from reading between the lines
in some of his articles that he took criticism hard.

The English coastline, including Whitby, had for many years attracted
painters—Turner had visited Whitby on his tour of the North Riding in 1801—
and photographers were also attracted by the town. Lewis Carroll (C.L. Dodgson)
visited Whitby in the summer of 1856 when he was just beginning to master the
technique of wet-plate photography,* and no doubt many other photographers
had visited the town before Sutcliffe. But it was Sutcliffe's photographs which
turned Whitby into 'The Photographer's Mecca'. Photographs of Whitby
were everywhere. The Keighley exhibition referred to above contained *Whitby*

* A photograph taken by Lewis Carroll across
Whitby harbour from St Hilda's Terrace has survived
in an album now in the Gernsheim Collection,
University of Texas.

Harbour by Mr Ernest Beck, and *Up the Harbour, Whitby* by Mr Alf Nicholson. Francis Frith's photographers produced photographs of Sutcliffe-like Whitby urchins. An advertisement for 'The Kodak' placed in *Royal Academy Pictures* for 1894* showed a coble beached in Whitby harbour. In the holiday photographs competition organised by the *Amateur Photographer* in 1891, most of the photographers who entered seem to have made a beeline for Whitby and the Yorkshire coast, and photographs with titles such as *Natives, Setting Sail, In Whitby Harbour, A Misty Morning, Whitby Abbey, Gossip—Staithes* and *Mending Crab Pots* abounded.

Amateur photographers travelled to Whitby to spend their holidays taking photographs—some seem to have hoped that their cameras would be inspired by their surroundings, and were disappointed when their developed films did not produce Sutcliffe-like photographs. In 1906 Sutcliffe said:

> There cannot be many devout photographers who have not made the pilgrimage, if one may judge from the queues of people with hand cameras which are to be seen any fine day in summer, winding their way towards the Abbey. But among these pilgrims there have been some who said that Mecca did not come up to their expectations, while there are others who come year after year, who would as soon think of going anywhere else for their holidays as a good Mahometan would think of going to Rome. It all depends on whether the pilgrim is alive to the possibilities of the place whether he gets any good out of it or not.[14]

He was at a loss to know what to do when he saw visitors attempting to take photographs which he knew would never come out. The photographer in him fought with his natural reserve:

> What should a photographer do when he sees a stranger wasting film? Go up to him and say: 'Excuse me, sir, but your film exposures will be very much out of focus unless you move further away'; or, 'May I venture to tell you that at this time of day, in such a dull light, there will be no image at all on your film when it is finished'; or, 'You may not have noticed that the sun is shining into your lens'—this last excuse would naturally not apply to this country   or, should the photographer do as the man in the Bible did, pass by on the other side?[15]

Usually he cringed inwardly and said nothing. His reserve was not restricted to photographic matters. A man came striding towards him over the slippery weed which covered the rocks on Whitby Scar. Sutcliffe thought of warning the man, who was carrying a huge reflex camera 'about as big as a hat box', to mind his step, but decided against it:

> Our ways had not crossed more than six paces when I heard behind me what I took for the explosion of a charge of blasting powder or the firing of a big gun. I turned round quickly, and saw the man from Leeds sitting on his camera. I had no idea that a camera could make so much noise when sat on.[16]

* The Royal Academy Supplement to the *Magazine of Art.*

The magic of photography seemed to mesmerise some amateurs. Sutcliffe recalled seeing one man buy a packet of dry plates and, although the label stated that they were sensitive to light and should only be opened in a dark-room, proceed once he had left the shop to open the wrapper and carefully examine both sides of each plate, before replacing them, presumably for use on some future occasion. Sutcliffe told the readers of his 'Photography Notes': 'Amateurs must realise that it is the exposure which makes a good picture and not the skill of the person who developed, or any imaginary magic power of the chemicals used in development.'[17] He said that it was thankless work developing other people's films and plates, because if they had made a mistake in taking their photographs, they would try to blame the man who did the developing for their errors:

> Once I developed a plate for an amateur which he said was an instantaneous picture of a flock of sheep going up Bay bank, if you know where that is. When the plate came to be fixed, there was Bay bank right enough, very fully exposed, but not the ghost of a sheep could be seen; there was a kind of dusty haze all over the road, that was all there was to be seen of them. The photographer evidently had had his camera on a stand, and had given a time exposure long enough for the sheep to have walked away in. I was called all manner of names for having spoilt such a beautiful picture in the developing, but how the owner of it thought I had been able to obliterate the sheep he did not say.[18]

The pier was a favourite spot from which to take photographs. Some of the amateurs Sutcliffe saw there were of a quite superior type:

> I have seen, on Whitby Pier, an amateur photographer, too proud to carry his own machine, followed by his manservant carrying his camera, which he handed to his master when the latter thought he had spotted a subject. The exposure having been made, the camera was handed back to the manservant, who did the menial work of turning the handle to roll on fresh film, and the shutting up the camera and putting it into its leather case.[19]

The two piers at Whitby were quite different in character; Sutcliffe described the West Pier as 'given up to fashion and frivolity', whilst the pier starting from the old east side was usually deserted, except for fishermen and photographers:

> One evening last summer, when the band was playing 'Ehren on the Rhine', and the sitters on the seats were tapping their feet on the ground to prevent the band playing out of time, a solitary photographer might have been seen on the other pier unpacking his apparatus. At last he had got it all unpacked, and his polished mahogany camera and lens 'shone like a burning flame together' in the rays of the setting sun, towards which it was pointed. Slowly the sun sank, till it nearly touched the sea. What was the solitary photographer going to take at this time of night? The crowd on the other pier began to be interested in him. Soon the end of one pier was crowded with people watching the solitary photographer on the other pier. 'He expects a ship coming in,' said one. 'No, he is waiting till the lamps are lit,' said another. 'He wants to take a moonlight photograph,' said a third. 'No,

he wants to take the sun as it dips into the sea,' said a fourth. 'What beautiful legs he has got!' said a fifth. 'Yes, but his coat does not fit', said a sixth. 'And his ears stick out,' said a seventh. 'Look! Look!' said everyone at once, 'he is taking off the cap.' And so he was, but just as he was putting it on again, the cap fell down on to the pier; it fell on its edge and began to roll. The photographer looked at the rolling cap, then at the lens, undecided whether to rush for the cap and put it on the lens, or to take his coat off and throw over the whole camera. He decided to run after the cap, which by this time was perilously near the edge of the pier. As he did so, one of his legs got entangled with one of the tripod legs, which had called forth such admiration from one of the crowd. Down came the tripod, camera, and all, with a crash; the cap gave a little jump and went into the sea. The photographer stood aghast. The crowd cheered to a man. The photographer slowly picked up the pieces and went home.[20]

The fishermen who had acted as models for Sutcliffe for years found an increasing demand for their services as 'old salts' to feature in photographs taken by amateurs. When Sutcliffe had the time to stop and talk, they had as many stories to tell about the antics of amateur photographers as he had:

> There was one of 'em this season. She was a woman—a lady, I oughter have said. She came up to me and said she wanted to take my likeness beside the coble. ... So I said, 'Well then, marm, how am I to stand; shall I get inside the boat and pretend to be rowing?' That's how one daft chap, who gave me half a crown, made me sit. The coble was drawn up on the sand just as she is now. No, the lady said she wanted me to stand beside the boat ... she said I might stand near the starn. 'Can't you take hold of the boat with one hand ?' she asked. 'To steady her, marm ?' I asked, innocent like. ... When she had got all ready fixed she said to me, 'Now then, I want you to look *straight* at me, and put on your sweetest smile.' She had hardly got the words out of her mouth before she was half drowned with a pailful of dirty water. I had see our Emma [his wife] come to the rails [which are some twelve feet above the sand where the boats lie] with a bucket of water, but I never thought she would have thrown it over without looking to see if there were any photographers about.[21]

When the danger to the amateur photographer did not come from above, it lurked expectantly beneath him. The dock end (see Plate 14) was another favourite spot for taking photographs, partly because it was the first view the visitor to the town had of the harbour and abbey on emerging from the railway station. Unseen in these photographs was an open sewer which discharged its untreated contents directly onto the harbour mud. This was the scene of yet another tragi-comedy witnessed by Sutcliffe:

> One Easter Monday, at low water, I saw a young man with a camera in one hand and an exposure meter in the other, so intent on reading this meter that he neither saw nor cared where his feet took him ... he walked right over the Dock End into the mud where the sewage falls. Fortunately, the mud there is deep and very soft, so he broke no bones. A crowd soon gathered, but no one was inclined to go and help him. The crowd was even

so rude as to laugh. Not content with laughing, it shouted and cheered. It was impossible to keep from laughing at the attempts this lover of photography made in gaining terra firma. The mud was so soft he could not stand upright, but kept embracing mother mud every few minutes. Eventually someone threw him a rope, which he got hold of, and he was dragged to one of the flights of steps, used by the fishermen in unloading their boats. As he reached the steps he clutched at them with both hands, and then, as if remembering something, looked out, not to sea again, but towards the scene of his late exploit. Was he looking for his camera? I expect so. When he got to the top of the steps the crowd made way for him. They wished to have the wind between him and their nobility. I heard that when he got to his lodgings, his landlady would not let him in, and he had to go into a stable yard and pay a man half-a-crown to pump cold water on to him.[22]

The camera which fell with its unfortunate owner over Dock End into the stinking mud and excrement was very probably a Kodak, and it was the introduction of hand cameras such as the range produced by Kodak—then the Eastman Company—which had led to photography being made available to those who had not dared to attempt to take photographs with a stand camera. In 1897 the Eastman Company hired the New Gallery in London and mounted an exhibition of photographs which had been taken with Kodak cameras. One gallery was devoted to photographs and enlargements of photographs taken with Kodak cameras by leading photographers; among them was Frank Sutcliffe. George Davison had in June 1897 joined the management of Eastman's and the idea of helping to sell the company's products by showing what could be done with their cameras in the hands of expert photographers came from him. The arrangement which Sutcliffe had with Eastman's was that they supplied him with the latest models of the cameras which they put on the market, and he was given the opportunity to try each camera out. The company seems to have supplied Sutcliffe with film, and in return for all this, merely asked that they could use copies of the photographs taken with their cameras for their own purposes. This arrangement lasted until Davison resigned as Managing Director of the company in 1907.

Sutcliffe reviewed the 'Kodak' exhibition at the New Gallery in 1897 and said that instead of buying copies of 'focal views' the tourist could now 'with the intelligent use of the Kodak get his own views of the places he visits, as he sees them, and these photographs will remind him, as no stock view can, of the places visited'.[23] The new range of pocket-sized cameras which produced 'snap-shots' rather than the carefully-selected images which were arranged and scrutinised on the ground glass screens of stand cameras added a new dimension to Sutcliffe's photography, and his work saw a second flowering in his photographs taken with Kodak cameras. He rapidly became enthusiastic about the possibilities which these hand cameras opened up, and a friend who met him in 1900 said that Sutcliffe had four Kodaks slung round him. One might have expected a certain amount of gratitude towards the Eastman Company in handing out free photographic equipment, but Sutcliffe seems to have been genuinely impressed by the advantages which the Kodaks had over stand cameras, especially when out walking:

> Photographers who have only tried to make pictures with heavy stand cameras have no idea of the comfort of working with a Kodak. To begin with, the apparatus takes care of itself; it is not heavy enough to make the photographer think of it every other minute; it does not want a man to carry it home, it need not be left at an inn or a railway station, on account of its weight. When the photographer has reached his destination he does not feel compelled to expose plates if his subjects do not please him, as he is too often tempted to when he has carried a heavy camera a long way. The Kodak need never be left at home, it is not much heavier than a walking stick, and every photographer knows that the best subjects appear when he has no camera with him.[24]

He found that it was quite possible to work with a Kodak under unfavourable lighting conditions, and made time exposures when necessary.

Sutcliffe saw both the advantages and the disadvantages of hand camera work. A Kodak could not produce the same quality of image as a whole plate taken with a stand camera; hand camera lenses were not usually of the highest quality, and the films of the time had a coarse grain. The different methods of working with the two types of camera each brought different aspects of photography to the fore. The stand camera produced images which were usually the result of careful deliberation. 'A photograph, to be of real value,' Sutcliffe said, 'must express some little thought on the part of the photographer, and there is no doubt that the stand camera helps him to think.'[25] But then stand cameras were much more cumbersome than hand cameras, which could mean that pictures were lost in the time taken to set the camera up: 'In some cases, if the photographer hesitates a single second, the picture is lost. This is the case when the beauty is dependent on figures, or quickly-moving clouds. To be able to raise the camera to the eye and fire it off instantly is a great help towards pictorial photography.'[26] Sutcliffe realised that one could often get closer in to a subject with a hand camera. The accompanying illustration was taken on the same occasion as Plate 25—the unveiling of the Caedmon Cross. Sutcliffe must have taken a plate with a stand camera from the top of the parish church tower, and then come down into the churchyard to take a snapshot of the crowds jostling around the gravestones, trying perhaps to catch a glimpse of the Poet Laureate who performed the unveiling ceremony. The stand camera produces an objective view of the occasion; the Kodak photograph gives a view which is much closer and more intimate.

Snap-shot taken at the unveiling of the Caedmon Cross in 1898.

A stand camera with slow plates had imposed restrictions on the photographer, but with faster films, a shutter that worked quickly and a camera that was small enough to be unobtrusive, Sutcliffe said that one could now steal impressions rather than beg them. The accompanying illustrations show such 'stolen' impressions. He toyed with the idea of shooting through a 90° prism or into a mirror in order to take photographs of people unaware of his presence. Snapshots taken with a Kodak, Sutcliffe said, were quickly and easily taken: 'There are certain things which have a delightful precision or snap about them, which may be seen any day or every day— combinations of natural forms which arrange themselves in a certain way for an instant or two, and then alter entirely.' The Kodak made it easy for the photographer to capture such moments, and enabled

Snap-shots of Scottish fishergirls gutting and packing herring on Scarborough quayside.

him to 'snap' the everyday scenes which caught his eye, 'with that slickness which is becoming part of our lives in this hurried age.' He added:

> It might be better to go more slowly, to stop and gossip with this old man, or look over that gate at that weasel wriggling along. It might be better to sit down on a camp-stool and draw what strikes us; but some of us … are greatly distracted all the time by thinking of other things we know are waiting to be done. This is the best of photography with a Kodak. We feel that the work is so quickly done that no time is wasted.[27]

The element of time entered Sutcliffe's photography when he took sequences of photographs in quick succession, such as the launching of the lifeboat. The world shown by the wet-plate camera was a world that had paused momentarily for the photographer; the world revealed by the Kodak was full of life and movement— moments in time frozen at the split second the shutter opened. The hand camera was easily manoeuvrable and allowed photographs to be taken from angles and positions which would previously have been considered impractical. Of course Frank Sutcliffe had not been deterred by the problems of taking difficult subjects with his big stand camera. However, on one of the few occasions he tried to take photographs from a tripod mounted in a rowing boat, he was rammed by another boat full of visitors and, although he did not fall into the harbour himself when the collision came, his camera went overboard. But luck was with him and another unexpected advantage of the stand camera was revealed—the air in the camera bellows brought it bobbing back up to the surface.

Sequence of snap-shots of the launching of
the Whitby No. 2 lifeboat from the beach.

Snap-shot of a Lowestoft fishing boat at sea.

Snap-shot probably taken from a boat of two boys swimming in Whitby harbour.

Snap-shot of Whitby children taking part in a procession.

Several of Sutcliffe's articles in the *Amateur Photographer* were illustrated by snapshots 'taken at odd moments, snatched when sitters were few, or before or after working hours, by a portrait photographer, all within a few hundred yards of his workshop or house. They may, perhaps, show what people who have the time and money to spend, might do with a Kodak.' His hand camera became the photographic equivalent of an artist's sketch book, and Sutcliffe used it as a kind of visual diary to record the world around him. He said:

The Kodak has freshened my interest in outdoor photography in a marked degree, though my friends chaff me and ask if I sleep with 'that thing' under my pillow, and take it to church with me on Sundays. 'That thing' helps me to remember what I might otherwise forget—the countless charms which nature puts on for the pleasure of all those who have eyes to see. ... My only regret is that I did not have it years ago, for it would then have written a diary for me of many things I can never see again. ... Perhaps the coming century will see many diaries so written.[28]

Sutcliffe saw the possibilities of photo-journalism before it was developed by newspapers and illustrated magazines. An article entitled 'Striking a Bargain' published in the *Amateur Photographer* in 1902 was in fact a photographic report with descriptive text on the annual horse fair at Yarm.* Sutcliffe said that 'everyone looks at pictures first and only reads any letterpress when the pictures have no more to say'. But the text gives a vivid description of the activity at the fair which adds to the immediacy of the photographs:

As my Kodak and I went up and down among the groups of men and horses, it saw and I heard many bargains in process of making. ... At the end of the fair, where the grass-grown High Street ended, and the road into the country began, horses were being put through their paces for the benefit of their would-be buyers and for the benefit of a motley crowd as well. If a horse had never picked up its feet, and ran as if for its life, before, it did then with a crowd of men and boys shouting at it, and waving sticks and hats behind it; but no horse seemed to bolt. As soon as they got away from the shouting and sticks the pace slackened. ... As the day wears on, the horses get thinner—thinner individually and collectively. Men with one hand in

Snap-shot taken of horse-dealing at Yarm Fair.

*Yarm Fair is still held in October each year. One hundred years on there is a fun fair instead of a commercial fair for cheese, horse and livestock sales. But travellers' horses are still run up and down the High Street on the Saturday morning to display those for sale, and this is called the 'Riding of the Fair'.

their left trouser's pocket, and the other carrying a saddle and bridle, are to be seen walking home or up to the railway station. At the railway station the stationmaster and his men have their hands full of horse-boxes, which go off by every train. The merry-go-rounds and their piebald horses are lighting up. You hear the incessant ting-ting at the shooting galleries, and the fun of the fair is beginning as my Kodak and I start for home, leaving the old town, where, for the next three hundred and sixty-four days, the grass will grow in the streets again till next fair day.[29]

Sutcliffe once said of himself that: 'He was unfortunately born forty years too soon, for the photographs he made when he stole a few half-days away from his studio showed what he might have done as a press photographer working for modern illustrated journals and books.'[30] To judge by the way in which his photographs and text bring the horse fair of seventy years ago to life, he would have made as successful a photo-journalist as he was a pictorial photographer. In this, as in many other aspects of photography, Sutcliffe was ahead of his time.

Snap-shot of beach photographer at Whitby.

chapter 11

Epilogue
The Passing of Sutcliffe's Whitby

The beginning of the First World War marked the end of Sutcliffe's work as a photographer. Photography was forbidden by law on the North East coast. Sutcliffe covered up the names 'Zeiss' and 'Goerz' on his camera lenses with sticking plaster so that he was not suspected of 'pro-Germanism'. He carried on his work as a portrait photographer in his studio: 'Hardly a day passes in any photographer's shop but someone goes in and asks, "Can you make anything of that?" and then when the photographer shakes his head comes the pitiful addition, "It is the only photograph I have of my boy who was shot in France."'[1] Sutcliffe did his best to make enlargements from the badly-focused smudges which were often the only remaining photographs of local men who had died in the trenches, and charged cost price for this work. He was revolted by the idea of making a profit from the war.

Sutcliffe had hoped that his son would follow in his steps as a photographer, and together they had planned a series of photographs of the herring packers at Scarborough. *Photograms of the Year* 1902 carried a view of fishing boats at anchor titled *A Crowded Harbour*—'by Horace G. Sutcliffe (Son of Frank M. Sutcliffe)'. But he died young, and the war brought more bereavement to the family. Sutcliffe's wife Eliza died in 1915 and his youngest daughter Zoë, who was working as a nursing volunteer with the Red Cross, died in the military hospital in Ripon. Sutcliffe had been warned about overworking by his doctor, and was weakened by an attack of the influenza which swept Britain just after the war.

In 1922 Sutcliffe sold his photographic business, and the right to reproduce his exhibition photographs, to T.W. Gillatt, who had been one of the young photographers he had taken as 'articled pupils' before the outbreak of war. Inactivity would probably have killed Sutcliffe and, after a retirement of precisely one week, he became—at the age of 70—the curator of the museum of the Whitby Literary and Philosophical Society, which now has Sutcliffe's glass negatives in its collection. This was no leisurely occupation for a retired gentleman, but involved moving the whole museum from its old premises on the Pier to the new museum in Pannett Park, built with money and on land bequeathed by Sutcliffe's old friend R.E. Pannett. His problems in retirement were no longer photographic; not the least of them was how to move *Ichthyosaurus crassimanus*—a huge fossil reptile—up the hill to the new museum. His daughter Irene wrote in 1942:

> Once, after he had sold the business and had taken up museum work, as we were walking up Skinner Street I asked him, 'Do you ever wish you were going back to the studio?' His reply was explosively emphatic—'Never!' Then, with the usual twinkle in his eyes, he said, 'It was an awful life, shut up in a dark room with only babies to talk to.'[2]

As the years had passed, Sutcliffe had seen Whitby change, and he mourned the passing of the traditional way of life of the inshore fishermen and of the farmworkers, which had been established over generations and was swept aside within a few years by 'progress' brought by the modern world. For Sutcliffe, the coming of steam marked the end of the Whitby he had known from his childhood, and he lamented: 'Much beauty is fast leaving these islands, and we wish over and over again that photography had been invented at least a hundred years before that great leveller, steam.' The number of sailing ships using Whitby harbour declined every year, and with the passing of the age of sail and the advent of the steamship, Sutcliffe felt that much of the beauty and poetry had left the sea. Once he had been able to climb to the clifftop and see a continuous procession of sailing vessels passing up and down the coast, moving briskly or sluggishly along, depending on the strength of the wind. In 1904 he said that the only sign that the sea was a highway was a trail of smoke left on the horizon by the occasional passing steamer. The inshore fishing fleet was transformed by the arrival of the steam trawlers. The characteristic dress worn by the fishermen to protect them from the worst of the weather and the sea as they fished from open boats went out of use. Sutcliffe said: 'The men who man the steam drifters look more like sailors or enginemen than thoroughbred fishermen.'[3]

One can feel that Sutcliffe bitterly resented the manifestations of progress which were transforming the town he had grown to love over the years. He felt that the change was gradual and insidious:

> Some of us who have lived for half a century or more in some small circle
> of a few miles in diameter have been conscious of a gradual spoiling of
> our surroundings. No great change may have taken place, but thousands
> of little things, which have been altered have in the course of years almost
> entirely changed the appearance of the place. It is surprising how slight an
> 'improvement' will destroy the beauty of a scene.[4]

Snap-shot of fishermen aboard one of the new steam-powered fishing boats in Whitby harbour.

When an old house was demolished, Sutcliffe said, 'Jerry the builder' invariably put up something cheap and ugly in its place. The famous view of Dock End was ruined for him when a gable was demolished and replaced by 'a little drinking bar which might have been built with a box of toy building bricks'. It became increasingly difficult for any photographer to take pictures of Whitby which did not include modern additions to 'The Photographer's Mecca'. Sutcliffe said that it was only when there was a good deal of fog or haze about that one could keep these recent intrusions into old Whitby in the background of photographs:

> The modern practice of covering conspicuous frontages with large
> advertisements also makes the pilgrim's way much harder. The roads and
> footpaths, too, in the narrow streets which were paved with cobblestones,
> which made such good foregrounds, have now been nearly all levelled up
> and flagged or cemented. The old street lamps which leaned about in the
> most intoxicated positions, have been replaced with electric standards of the
> regulation pattern. The old pantile roofs are being replaced by blue slates
> from Wales, and the old brick and tile yards are closed for want of orders. In
> time, when every old brick wall is cemented and chalked over with lines to
> make it look like stone, when all the old chimney-stacks have been replaced
> with 'ornamental' chimney-pots, when all the old wooden rails and balconies
> which remind us of Holland, have given place to iron ones, then Mecca will
> be like everywhere else, and photographers will have to find another gate to
> heaven.[5]

The countryside around Whitby was changing as well. In the 1920s Sutcliffe saw hay being carried on the back of a motor-lorry instead of a horse-drawn wagon for the first time, and later wrote in astonishment: 'Having moved with dignity for thousands of years, it seemed quite indecent for hay to be travelling at such a speed. It was as if a seventy-year-old dowager had picked up her skirts and had frisked along the promenade after a toy balloon.'[6] The leisurely progress of loading a large hay wagon which enabled Sutcliffe to take photographs when the lighting and positioning most pleased him was replaced by the speedy efficiency of the petrol-driven lorry—work that had taken days was now over in hours.

In his 'retirement' from business, Sutcliffe found the colour which he loved and which his camera had always failed to capture in the flowers which grew in his garden at Sleights. The photographic world seemed to have forgotten him, and it was only through the prompting of another Yorkshire photographer— Harold Hood, FRPS—that in 1935 Sutcliffe was made an Honorary Fellow of the Royal Photographic Society. This was the highest honour that the Society could bestow upon a photographer, and was a tribute to the contribution which Sutcliffe had made to the advancement of pictorial photography almost half a century before.

He still travelled by train into Whitby early every morning in all weathers, and it was not until March 1941, at the age of 87, that he stopped his work at Whitby Museum, and even then it was only because the Second World War had cut off the flow of visitors to what was, once again, a defence area. Sutcliffe now said that he would, at last, be able to find time to devote himself to a serious study of botany, and he tended his garden all through the very cold April of that year. At the beginning of May he took what was to be his last photograph—of his forsythia in flower. He died on 31 May 1941 and was buried in Aislaby churchyard.

Sutcliffe had first visited Whitby in the 1850s, and the eighty years during which he knew the town saw the greatest period of change and upheaval that Whitby had known. The busy fishing port with a history which went back centuries was being transformed in the space of a few years into the modern town and resort which can be seen today. To Sutcliffe's eyes, it seemed that the modern world, which was making itself more and more evident in the town and which was speeding up the pace of life which had gone on steadily for generations, was robbing Whitby of its beauty: 'It would seem as if Beauty is like the lichen on old walls, a thing which grows slowly, and refuses to have anything to do with bustle and speed.'[7]

As he felt the pace of change accelerate, Sutcliffe placed increasing stress in his articles on the importance of photographs as records:

> There are many things to be seen today which are not likely to be visible in ten years time, except in museums; some will not even get into the museums. … There is smoke, a common thing today, but we do not know how soon it may be done away with. One touch of the magic wand of Science, and chimneys and chimney pots will be useless clay, and chimney sweeps must learn new trades. Bathing machines, once common on our shores, are now being sold as henhouses, canvas tents having made the machines of our boyhood, and the bathing woman clad in coarse blue flannel, useless things of the past. Sailing ships, or wind-jammers, are getting scarcer and

scarcer; even boats rowed with oars are giving place to petrol-driven ones. The travelling tinker, sitting on the ground as he mends the farmhouse kettle, the pedlar with his pack, the scissors-grinder, the pot-hawker, the village blacksmith, professional rat and mole-catchers and many other rural professors, are dying out, leaving their shoes to none. If our cameras do not catch these passing shadows they will soon be forgotten.[8]

As he saw the Whitby which he had grown to know so well transformed by forces which he saw as coming from outside the town, he began to campaign against 'improvers' who, in their haste to bring the area 'up to date', were 'turning the country and town alike upside down'. Sutcliffe had served on the Whitby Local Board and was no impractical idealist; he saw the benefits which progress could bring as well as its darker side, but still believed that unthinking change was ripping the heart out of Whitby, destroying beauty and unfailingly replacing it with ugliness:

> Some of us have made use of our cameras with the intention of holding unbecoming objects up to ridicule, but I fear we have done little good, for the slums are still there, and the houses the medical officer of health had photographed to show that they were unfit to live in, are still occupied. We have sometimes photographed ugliness for a lark, and have made lantern slides of bill-posting hoardings, and roadways full of puddles and pot holes; of flamboyant lamp posts, where the surroundings called for simplicity; of painted advertisements in beauty spots of somebody's pills, or someone's pianos, and have talked by the hour to big congregations, pointing out how much easier life would be if all such abominations were done away with, but all to no purpose.[9]

He knew that, thanks to progress, Dock End was no longer full of sewage, and that the fishermen who managed to get jobs on the steam trawlers found their working conditions vastly improved. He also knew that cottages which looked 'picturesque' from the outside might be wretched places in which to live. Sutcliffe dropped in to see an old fisherman who was crippled with rheumatism and said that: 'The walls of his cottage were simply running down with water. His sea boots, which he had not been able to put on for some months, were green and white with fungoid growth.'[10] But despite the improvements in living standards which the modern world brought, Sutcliffe bitterly regretted the wanton destruction of the environment which he saw taking place, and believed that Whitby was rapidly squandering its heritage of beauty.

Whitby had, in its heyday, been a bustling port, but in 1905 Sutcliffe described the place as 'a city of the dead—no ships, no shipbuilding,* no music of the caulkers' hammer, no jet, no picturesque jet turners covered with rouge, nothing but idleness. ... Here they do nothing for ever and ever.' He had gone out to take a few photographs by the harbourside:

> On turning out of the empty street of Flowergate one comes suddenly on to the harbour; by the harbour railings, day after day, year after year, stands the manhood of Whitby. ... As I came in sight of the harbour, with its foreground of men in every conceivable attitude leaning on the railings, I hid

* In the years around 1880 the Whitehall Shipyard employed about 800 workers, and the shipbuilding industry contributed greatly to the prosperity of the town. The last ship to be built in the yard was the SS *Broomfield*, launched in April 1902. When the shipyard closed the skilled workers left Whitby for other shipbuilding towns, and many of the unskilled men became unemployed.

my Kodak as well as I could and then suddenly turned it round to the mass
of mankind (but they) had melted away like the snow in summer. Only three
men with their backs turned to me were visible. The rest had gone up or
down the pier on the first sight of a photographer. I turned the camera the
other way, up the harbour, where, when I was a boy, I could have counted
two hundred ships or more. Today there was not one, only two tiny fishing
boats, waiting for next season to come to take the visitors out to sea to fish
for whiting.

He warned against the town relying entirely on the holiday trade, and saw the
lifeblood of Whitby draining away:

No matter how beautiful the old town may look through a sunlit November
mist, a delicate pearl-covered veil, almost transparent, it is impossible to take
any pleasure in this beauty, because the moving spirit of all that is good—
work—is absent. One feels that all ones [sic] energy is oozing away at ones
[sic] finger ends because there is no evidence of any work being done. ... As
one looks into the eyes of the schoolchildren, hoping to see signs of energy
in the next generation, one seldom finds anything but a hopeless dawn.[11]

Shipbuilding was no longer carried on in Whitby, the fishing industry no longer
required the manpower it once did, and the jet industry was almost dead. Sutcliffe
saw the young people of Whitby leaving the town to seek work elsewhere, and
calculated that 'the amateur who comes here for the week-end in 1975 will have
the unique opportunity of snapshotting the last native of the place'.[12]

   He felt the loss of the spirit of Whitby even more than the loss of its beauty. When he had first known the town it was prosperous and enterprising. It
was tucked away in a remote corner of Yorkshire, but it stood squarely on its
own feet as a town where men earned an honest living by the sweat of their
brow. Sutcliffe saw the growing reliance of the town on its tourist industry,
often controlled by people who came to Whitby to make their living from the
visitors, as a development which had reduced the manhood of the town to
a life of idleness. In what was probably the last article he wrote, in February
1940, Sutcliffe sorrowed over the change that had made Whitby, once an
independent, self-reliant community, a town which catered for the whims
and fancies of holidaymakers: 'If only Whitby would start some honest work
again, such as boat building, quarrying, furniture making, and other trades
on which she founded her former prosperity, or even begin some of the
newer industries, ... instead of relying entirely on the taking-in of visitors.'[13]
Like many local people today, he preferred the town out of season when it
did not try to cater for the entertainment of outsiders: 'all through the summer German bands, barrel organs, and hurdy-gurdys never stop their noises.
Without their help, the quietness of the place might be too great a contrast
to the hum of big cities.'[14]

   Sutcliffe's photographs give such a loving and faithful view of Whitby and its
inhabitants of almost a century ago that they retain the immediacy of the present
moment. The girl standing jauntily with her hand on her hip in Plate 48 has
lost her good looks, grown old and died, and the shop no longer exists. Yet she
and the children are so real that one feels that it is almost possible to step into

the picture—just as Alice stepped through the looking-glass—and enter a world which now exists only in Sutcliffe's photographs.

Sutcliffe said that: 'Photographs, unlike pictures, do not improve with keeping. It is improbable that there will ever be any "Old Masters" of photography, for the best photographs of each age will be so much behind those of the succeeding one that they will have no lesson to give to any who follow.'[15] But in fact Sutcliffe has become as near an 'old master' as photography is likely to produce. Techniques have changed and tastes in photography altered, but nothing can detract from the power of the images which he produced. If his shade were to return, he would certainly deny that he was an 'old master', and would probably find the use of such a term applied to him ludicrous. He always denied that his work could be called art, and said:

> Pleasure, and not art, has been at the bottom of all the best photographs which have been made. When you feel that a certain subject gives you pleasure, you don't go to the trouble of analysing it, and seeing whether the rules of art are properly exemplified, but you know that if you can with the aid of the camera reproduce on your plate those elements which please you, others will be pleased with the shadow you catch.[16]

He could have been speaking about any of the photographs in this book, for the 'shadows' he caught at the end of the 19th century in and around Whitby are still giving pleasure today.

Plates

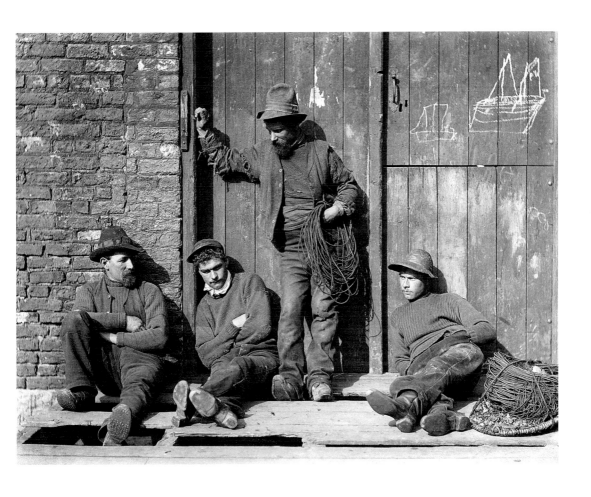

Notes to the Plates

The reference numbers given for each plate refer first to the number given to his negatives by Frank Sutcliffe (the index books in which these numbers were entered have not survived) and, secondly, to the number by which each negative is now identified by the Sutcliffe Gallery, Whitby.

Plate 1: Two young boys playing with model sailing ships. The stillness of the sea provides the reflections and at the same time intensifies the dreamlike atmosphere of one of the timeless moments of childhood. The photograph was taken at Runswick Bay.
(Ref. 138 fms; 2-60)

Plate 2: One of Sutcliffe's best-known photographs. Titled variously *Excitement*, *Stern Reality* (or *Realities*), and *Scotch Head*. (See Chapter 6 for a description of how this was taken, and the influence it had.)
(Ref. fms 507; 24-9)

Plate 3: Taken in 1893 and titled *Free Education*. This shows a fisherman called Robert Ledley with a group of children on the Tate Hill Pier, Whitby.
(Ref. fms ?; 17-43)

Plate 4: Titled *Fog-bound Fishermen*. Six Whitby fishermen by the harbour rail. On the left is Mr Coulson, facing the camera on the other side of the rail is Joe Tomlinson, who lived on the Cragg, and third from the right is probably Henry Freeman. The fog which has rolled into the harbour blankets the background of the East Side. A reviewer in the *Amateur Photographer* criticised Sutcliffe in 1890 for 'hazing off' the distance 'until in some that he exhibits Whitby is completely enveloped in fog, although there is a bright light upon the men and women on the jetty'. The implication is that this was a piece of trickery, when, although it is possible that some work was done to eliminate background detail on the negative, natural conditions would probably have produced this striking image.
(Ref. fms 400; 24-15)

Plate 5: Nine Whitby fishermen against the harbour rail. Among them can be seen familiar faces, as several appear in other Sutcliffe photographs—for example Henry Freeman and John Batchelor. Despite its casual appearance, the figures are very carefully—and very beautifully—arranged, so that the group is carefully balanced to provide a tightly constructed composition which relates the figures not only to each other, but also to the Parish Church on the far side of the harbour, and to the passing ship.
(Ref. fms 401; 17-32)

Plate 6: Titled *Saturday Afternoon*. A print of this

photograph on 'Blanchard's platinum paper' was awarded the Society's medal at the Photographic Society's Exhibition in 1889. For a full description of how it was taken, see Chapter 6. The fisherman, Mr Coulson, was drowned while salmon fishing. His wife was left with five children and was paid a shilling a week for each child. Canon Austen gave her a mangle and she supplemented the family's income by taking in washing.
(Ref. fms 397; 24-49)

Plate 7: Taken on a dull December day looking towards the *Marine Hotel*, Whitby. This was called Coffee House Corner and was where the fish auctions were held. For a description of how it was taken, see Chapter 7. Bill Eglon Shaw of The Sutcliffe Gallery admires this photograph but adds his own practical insights: 'For the technically minded, the photograph was taken on an 8½" x 6½" glass dry plate and is a difficult one to print, with dense highlights in the sky area and extremely subtle tones running through the rest of the image. Added to this, the original negative is very blemished requiring hours of hand finishing to obtain a presentable result.'
(Ref. 62 fms; 11-34)

Plate 8: Titled *A bit of news*. Taken around 1884 in Cliff Street, Robin Hood's Bay. In this photograph Harrison Alison, reputed to have been the only literate member of the group, is reading to Tommy Baxter, Mary Emmerson—who lived at the Almshouses—and Lumar William Storm. The baskets they are holding are pots for catching lobster and crabs.
(Ref. fms 81 or 91; 24-38)

Plate 9: Taken *c*.1895 at the slip top near the *Cod and Lobster Inn*, Staithes. The old lady is Mrs Margaret Shordon, known locally as Emma Ward. The smallest of the boys is her grandson, Robert Ward. Staithes was at this time a thriving fishing village. In 1891 George Du Maurier wrote to a friend recommending visits to make when on holiday in the Whitby area: 'tell them especially to manage Staithes *circa* 4, 5, 6 p.m., a little before high tide, to see some 40 (or 50) cobles disembark to herring-fish, with all the town, women and children, pushing the boats off—the loveliest sight I ever saw!' Sutcliffe wrote of this photograph: 'The group of the two little boys and the old lady under the crab-pots is quite wrong by all canons of art, but that is the best of photography; no one expects a photograph to be perfect, and the photographer may do things in the way of composition which would be quite wrong for an artist to do. The two boys with the pony have no business to be where they are. The photographer had been taught so much, but for the life of him he could not find it in his heart to ask them to go away. I believe he asked them to

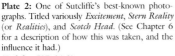

stay, and emptied his pockets of all the money he had among the five.' (*Amateur Photographer*, 11 August 1904).
(Ref. fms ?; 19-28)

Plate 10: *Water Rats*, taken in 1886. (For full details of how this was taken, see Chapter 6.) Charles Noel Armfield wrote of this, Sutcliffe's most famous photograph: 'The scene is no set picture, but is one of a kind of daily occurrence during the summer in Whitby Harbour; yet at what a happy moment has Mr Sutcliffe seized upon it, and what a happy point has he taken it from— the whole thing is full of "go" and vitality—see the strained shoulder muscles of the boy who is evidently going to splash with his right foot while balancing himself on his hands underwater, then see the pained face of the poor little chap in the boat who has just hurt himself, or note the grip of the hands of the boy in the left hand group who is trying to reach a higher standing place on his slippery perch, or mark the vibrating reflections in the water; indeed, look where you will the whole thing is full of life, and is a splendid specimen of what photography can achieve in the hands of an artist.' ('Mr F.M. Sutcliffe', in *Sun Artists*, 1891.) Seven of the 'Water Rats' can be identified: by the box on the left, wearing a fez, Tommy Ross, with his brother Will climbing out. James Locker stands by the boat, and Isaac Coates lies in front of it; Kit Corpse, with his back to the camera, and 'Cud' Heselton, facing the camera, are in the boat; standing with his back to the camera on the right of the boat is Arthur Ross.
(Ref. fms 115; 10-38)

Plate 11: A view across Whitby upper harbour towards the Abbey. The stumps in the water are probably the remains of old slipways leading from boatyards. (The Whitby wife who dried her washing over the harbour waters was presumably equipped either with a boat or with seaboots and tide-tables.)
(Ref. fms ?; 25-44)

Plate 12: The study of trees in a misty valley which won Sutcliffe a prize in Tokyo in 1893. Sutcliffe wrote that: 'The selection of landscape compositions is, and always will be, slow work, for only with the help of the sun and other outdoor forces, such as the wind, the snow, the mist, the seasons, is the photographer able to get what he wants. He will often come to a bit of landscape which will say to him, "There is a picture wrapped up in me for those who have patience to unfold it." By continually watching that bit of landscape under varying conditions, that picture may be found.' (*Yorkshire Weekly Post*, 27 May 1911).
(Ref. fms 263; 4-17)

Plate 13: When Sutcliffe heard that Whitby was to get a new bridge over the Esk, his first reaction was to make a record of the old structure

before it was replaced by 'an up-to-date cast iron affair'. He wrote a full description of how this photograph came to be taken. 'The other day, though I found the tide and sun both in the right place for photographing the old bridge, my first impulse was to let the camera rest in its case and go back home again, for not only was there a lot of haze about, but the wind was so strong that no reflection of the bridge in the water could be seen … The weight of the camera and plates, however, made me decide to wait a bit and see if the haze would clear off and the wind go down. After half an hour the haze was less dense, and after an hour the wind suddenly went down. By this time I had rigged the camera up and had got a long focus lens on the front. I had time to expose two plates, and intended to get a third one with a shorter focus lens; but as I was changing it the wind came back again worse than before.' (*Amateur Photographer*, 14 January 1908). The photograph was taken from Spion Cop near Whitby's Khyber Pass, and the chimneys below are those of the fishermen's cottages on the Cragg. The effect of mist and smoke is enhanced by the elimination of hard details and bright reflections in the upper right hand area of the photograph, by working on the negative.
(Ref. fms ?; 5-16)

Plate 14: Titled *The Dock End, Whitby*, a view taken in 1880 across Whitby upper harbour from the dock end (now covered over as a car park). The *Alert*, on the right, was built as a sloop at Whitby in 1802 by G. and N. Langborne, and later converted to a schooner. When this photograph was taken she was owned by Anthony Jackson and Edward Barker. Lying at the left are the *Lively*, *Sara* and *Hopewell*. Charles Noel Armfield described the details of this photograph: 'in the immediate front to the right hand is a top-mast schooner moored to the dock end, in most picturesque disorder, just as she has run into harbour, with her double topsails loose and half down, yards all awry, jib and fore staysail half run down and mainsail partly "scandalised", altogether a charming chief object, balanced in composition on the left of the picture by a long curved line of schooners, brigs and nondescript colliers broken in upon here and there by a few fishing cobles, backed up by the old houses on the staithe side; indeed, so admirable is it as a composition, that it might almost be taken for a photograph from a picture, rather than the result of artistic selection of an accidental combination.' ('Mr F.M. Sutcliffe', *Sun Artists*, 1891.) This was one of Sutcliffe's most successful photographs, from a commercial as well as from an artistic point of view, and Irene Sutcliffe wrote: 'We often used to wonder why "The Dock End, Whitby", was so popular. The slanting sail of the little boat in the middle distance did not look quite right, my father used to say, but if this sail had not been there then the slanting sail of the big timber ship on the right would have looked wrong, and we would agree that this was the first glimpse that visitors to Whitby had of the old town, and also the last they saw of it on their departure, so this was probably why it sold so well.' (*The Photographic Journal*, December 1942.) Most visitors arrived by train, and this was the view from Whitby railway station. (Ref. fms 174; B-17)

Plate 15: Penzance boats leaving Whitby harbour. This is probably the 'Study' which was exhibited at the Photographic Society Exhibition of 1887 and which won a medal. A reviewer wrote that the picture succeeded 'by combining well-chosen contrasted clouds with a number of upright lines arising from buildings and boats, and waiting (ah, there is the mental design)! for a vessel with dark sails to come into close proximity with the highest lights. Then follows an artistic picture, which is looked upon with intense pleasure both by the painter and the public.' (*The British Journal of Photography*, 11 November 1887.) The highlights of the clouds which contrast so effectively with the dark sails of the boats, seem at first glance to have been added to the print. Sutcliffe said that: 'The clouds in this were taken at the same time as the rest, though one of the most successful landscape photographers in Great Britain once found fault with the way they were printed in, and said it was a pity we could not have found a sky which looked as if it had been taken at the same time of day as the rest.' (*The Practical Photographer*, July 1899). This may well be a case of Sutcliffe exposing two plates on the same subject which were then printed together (see Chapter 7).
(Ref. fms ?; B-8)

Plate 16: Titled *Stoking Up*; three men in a mud-hopper. One man is lighting his pipe from another, and it is likely that Sutcliffe had just passed round his tobacco pouch, which was kept handy to tempt likely subjects. The man on the left has been identified as Freddy Kingston. The mud-hopper was a primitive type of harbour dredger. Being flat-bottomed, it could be floated over mud at high tide and allowed to settle there as the tide receded. Mud was then shovelled aboard until the boat was floated off by the next rising tide. The mud could then be dumped either at sea or wherever else it would cause no obstruction.
(Ref. fms ?; 20-36)

Plate 17: Sheep-washing in progress in a stream, probably in Glaisdale.
(Ref. fms ?; 25-6)

Plate 18: Whitby Abbey from the South-East. An example of Sutcliffe waiting for the right moment to take his photograph, as cows, unlike people, cannot be posed to suit the photographer. Their importance in the picture can be assessed if one mentally removes the drover and his small herd

from the photograph. The tails of the two cows on the right have flicked during the exposure and so are not seen. Sutcliffe wrote that: 'In days to come the date of a photograph will doubtless be estimated by the speed at which it was taken. In the early days, when the exposure ran into minutes, such appendages as a horse's ears or a cow's tail would be absent.' The exposure for this photograph would have been seconds at the most—not minutes—but cows were still liable to lose their tails.
(Ref fms 599; 4-3)

Plate 19: *Through the Station Doorway, Whitby.* Taken on 19 September 1895, this shows Whitby Dock End in the upper harbour, framed by the entrance to the North Eastern Railway Company's town station. This area has changed considerably since Sutcliffe's time with quite a large section of the harbour having been reclaimed and developed. A contemporary commented critically: 'It is hardly fair … to produce this as one of Mr Sutcliffe's photographs. Those who know his work will recognise that it is anything but one of his best. Still the end of Bagdale Beck, which has been filled in within the last year or so, will always be of interest to the town of Whitby, for hard by, Cook's immortal ships the 'Resolution' & 'Endeavour' were built.' (H.S. Percy in *The Art Journal*, 1895.)

Sutcliffe said of such views: 'How often in passing under a railway or other arch have we not heard "What a pleasing view." Nothing of the sort, it is simply that the railway arch does what everyone ought to be able to do, frame the landscape as they go along, not with a frame of the same proportion always, now long and narrow, now square, or occasionally oval or dome topped. Once having acquired the power to see the world bounded by an imaginary frame at each step, the next thing required is a retentive memory, which will enable the student to see whether the finished print is what it was expected to have been, and whether the print appeals to him in the same way as the actual scene did.' (*Photography*, September 1895.)
Ref. (fms ?; 28-12)

Plate 20: A view taken into the sun across the waters of Whitby upper harbour. The unusual visual qualities of this photograph are discussed fully in Chapter 7.
(Ref. fms ?; 4-21)

Plate 21: Titled *Sunshine and Shower*. This shows a topsail schooner with the sun shining through the fabric of the sail. Charles Noel Armfield wrote a first-hand account of how it was taken: 'I have a particular interest in this photograph, for I happened to be passing at the time Mr Sutcliffe

was taking it, and one of the most charming effects of it is one which, so far as my knowledge goes, no painter has ever attempted to paint, ... I refer to the fact that owing to the shower the direct rays of the sun behind the topsail of the schooner were refracted by the particles of moisture right through the sail, and so we have a point of semi-transparence of an opaque object against the light.' ('Mr F.M. Sutcliffe', *Sun Artists*, 1891). This is an example of Sutcliffe catching a passing effect of light to produce a photograph of great beauty, and one which few other photographers of that time would have dared to attempt, let alone have succeeded in overcoming the technical difficulties involved.
(Ref. fms 8; B-42)

Plate 22: Titled *Among the Turnips.* Irene Sutcliffe wrote of this photograph after her father's death: 'One or two people seem to remember my father telling them that "Among the Turnips" was the first of his "snapshots". Really, the plate had, I think, quite a long exposure, but as the horses were standing so still and the farm lad kneeling on the ground was so absorbed in his work, it was not thought necessary for the photographer to announce his presence.' (*The Photographic Journal*, December 1942.)
(Ref. fms 187; 16-39)

Plate 23: A photograph with a quiet, even sombre mood. The sea is almost unnaturally calm. In the absence of any figures the cobles look abandoned, and the seaweed-covered rocks and the drifting smoke become slightly menacing. Taken looking across Runswick Bay. (Ref. fms 2007; C-16)

Plate 24: A coble drawn up on the harbour edge near Tate Hill Pier, Whitby, with the Parish Church in the background. A deceptively 'simple' shot which on closer examination proves to be a carefully balanced image taken at exactly the right moment to enable the viewer to 'read' the photograph easily. Sutcliffe has waited until the man sewing the sail of his coble has his hand carrying the needle upraised. This acts as a focal point in the photograph as well as being the centre of interest for the figures looking on.
(Ref. 2092 fms; 20-29)

Plate 25: Taken from the tower of Whitby Parish Church, this photograph shows the ceremony of the unveiling of the Caedmon Cross which was performed by the Poet Laureate, Mr Alfred Austin, on 21 September 1898. The various dignitaries can be seen around the foot of the cross, and the crowd of onlookers seems ready to spill over the edge of the churchyard. The houses below and the harbour are almost lost in smoke. The *Whitby Gazette* reported that. 'The weather was delightfully fine, there being an unclouded sky and a September sun, whose heat was nicely tempered by the gentlest of breezes, and this indeed made the scene on the brow of the hill one so remarkable and striking. The old Abbey ruins, the grey tower of the ancient Church, the red tiles of the houses below, and the vast expanse of ocean; all tended to carry the mind back many centuries; and strange, but true, it was that the people of Whitby were standing almost within the shadow of the very spot where English Christian poetry had first been put into verse.' (23 September 1898.)
(Ref. fms ? (12 x 8 neg.); 22-25)

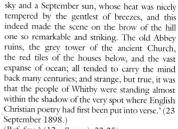

Plate 26: A waterfall in Mulgrave Woods, in the grounds of Mulgrave Castle, the home of the Marquis of Normanby. These woods were extensively altered and planted under the direction of Humphry Repton, the landscape designer, in 1792. This photograph is a good example of Sutcliffe's skill in balancing contrasting masses of light and shade.
(Ref. fms 725B; 9-26)

Plate 27: Whitby Market Place on a busy market day—which in Whitby was Saturday—in 1884. On the right, Whitby housewives are buying fruit and vegetables from the stall of Richard Hodgson, known as 'Pickering Dick' because he came from Pickering every week. In the background on the right are the churns displayed by John Hunter, a cooper who had a workshop on the Fish Pier, Whitby, and also made washtubs or 'poss' tubs. In the centre background, a girl sits pensively among the pots belonging to Mr Dale who brought them from Loftus. In the foreground are two ice-cream stalls, the one on the left with the fancy awning belonged to William Jackson. While their mothers bought in food for the weekend, the children clustered round the stalls to eat 'hokey-pokey' (ice-cream) served in glasses which were then washed in the buckets which can be seen on the stalls. The old gentleman in the foreground, who stands stolidly immobile amongst all the bustle, is Mr Purvis who had a cobbler's shop at the top of Pump Ghaut, Church Street. The building on the left in the background is the Old Town Hall, or 'tollbooth' for the market. It was designed by Jonathan Pickernell and erected by the Lord of the Manor, Nathaniel Cholmley, in 1788. The rents for the stalls were collected by John the Bellman (John Stephenson, the town crier) on behalf of the Lord of the Manor, and stall-holders paid from 1s. 6d. to 2s. per day.
(Ref. fms 559; 12-11)

Plate 28: Titled *Barn Door Fowls.* Taken at Lealholm Hall Farm, Lealholm, a small village approximately eight miles from Whitby which was a popular location for many of Sutcliffe's rural photographs. This is a very strong photograph made up of such simple elements that most photographers would not have given the scene

a second glance. Knowing the acuteness of Sutcliffe's eye as a photographer and his attention to detail, it is safe to assume that the ladder and wheelbarrow are just where he wanted them, and the fact that the hat covers the face of the child, and that the shadow of the woman on the barn door is not obscured by a passing hen is due to more than 'happy accident' alone.
(Ref. fms 341; D-11)

Plate 29: Milkmaid with milking stool and pail, wearing a traditional bonnet. Taken in about 1902. She is Laura McNeil of Longstone Farm, Low Hawsker, who used to work at Hawsker Hall for sixpence a week and was described as 'the bonniest lass for miles around'. Most of the McNeil family, including Laura with her brothers and sisters, emigrated to Reston, Manitoba, Canada around 1910. Laura married and had two sons and later settled in White Rock, Canada where she died around the age of ninety-eight.
(Ref. fms 376; 14 -9)

Plate 30: One of Frank Sutcliffe's best known portraits. Henry Freeman was the sole survivor of the Whitby lifeboat disaster of 9 February 1861, when 12 lifeboatmen drowned within sight of their distraught relatives, who were among the hundreds who watched helplessly from the beach and from Whitby's West Pier. A storm had raged all night, increasing in intensity towards morning. At 8 a.m. the lifeboat was launched. By 2 in the afternoon five crews had been saved from vessels in distress, and the crew of the lifeboat were exhausted by their battles with the raging seas. Two schooners were then seen being driven onto the shore, north of the piers. One of them succeeded in crossing the harbour bar to safety, but the other, the *Merchant*, drifted helplessly onto the beach. The exhausted lifeboat crew put to sea once again, and in attempting to get close to the ship the lifeboat, which was self-righting, capsized only fifty yards from the beach. Perhaps the greatest tragedy of all was that the men had lowered their lifebelts, because they had rowed so much that day their arms had become sore with chafing. Because of this, many of them were 'dipped' to death, and only Henry Freeman was safely brought to shore. His escape from death was attributed to the then recently introduced Board of Trade cork life jacket which he is seen wearing in this photograph. He was a lifeboatman for over forty years and died in December 1904 aged sixty-nine.
(Ref. fms 259; 20-23)

Plate 31: John Robert 'Dandy' Storr sitting beside his great-uncle Tom Storr, an old Whitby fisherman. Taken in 1884. In *Heroes of the Whitby Lifeboat* (Peterborough, *c*.1905), W.B. Pickering describes a typical Whitby fisherman like Tom Storr: 'He is of medium height, rather stout, rough looking, with shaggy eyebrows, weather-

beaten face, keen eyes despite his many years, and old fashioned clothes. He is much in request. His many pockets contain stray pennies, small packets of sweets, and many other things may be found therein, therefore the children love him. He is careful yet generous, large hearted, keen witted, not much of a scholar, but a positive hero of the sea. He is a man who says very little, unless appealed to, and keeps his breath to cool his porridge, or that he may have it when putting out to sea.'
(Ref. fms 2171; E-17)

Plate 32: A wet-plate portrait of an old man, which dates from the period 1876-80.
(Ref. fms 468; 3-66)

Plate 33: A studio portrait of a Whitby fisherman's wife, Mrs Nan Pennock, who lived in Henrietta Street. Sutcliffe presumably asked her to the studio in order to take the portrait, which reveals a beauty not to be found in bottles of cosmetics, even though her hands are rough and her fingernails black. It is typical of Sutcliffe that he produced this portrait not of a society lady or of a famous actress, but of an ordinary Whitby woman, whose natural nobility so outshines that of those more used to having their portraits taken.   (Ref. fms 2076; 19-3)

Plate 34: Two fishergirls by a large rock. The girl on the left is Jane Fordon, who lived in Henrietta Street, Whitby. The shallow baskets for collecting bait on the seashore were known as 'skiffs' or 'swills', and many were made at Runswick. Sutcliffe wrote: 'The amount of hard work these fishermen's wives and daughters undertake is marvellous. Let the photographer follow them when out flither picking on the rocks [flither was the local name for a limpet], he will soon be wet through up to the waist, and then when they have got their baskets and sacks full, let him climb with his apparatus, but a featherweight compared to the weight of their loads of flither, with them, up a cliff side some 500 ft. high, he will then think that the woman's work by daylight is even harder than the fisherman's toil and danger at sea by night.' (*Amateur Photographer*, 24 July 1896). Although the two women in the photograph are working girls, the seaweed hanging from the 'swill' is on this occasion a mere token, and Sutcliffe has posed them on a rock to take their portrait rather than asking them to pause for a moment from their work.
(Ref. fms 260; 19-5)

Plate 35: Four Whitby fishermen. Left to right: Bill Hawksfield, Jack Fordon, John Batchelor, and either Jack Dryden or Ben Weatherill. In a fishing community like Whitby, even the children's drawings reflect the all-pervading influence of the fishing industry, and the sail of the ship chalked on the door carries the detail of the Penzance registration letters—PZ (see Chapter 3). (Ref. fms 236; 4-34)

Plate 36: This photograph was published in the *Amateur Photographer* for 8 November 1904 under the heading *An Illustrated Note* by F.M. Sutcliffe: 'The photographer has one advantage over the painter; he can stick his camera up in the darkest hole, and if there is anything light in front of it, his plate will copy all it sees. Not so with the painter; he must have daylight on his canvas or paper, or he is not able to see what he is doing. There are many subjects which photographers have fought shy of in the past, when plates were given to halation more than they are now. Such a one I beg to send with this.' The photograph is taken into the light from the dark interior of a warehouse and shows men unloading sacks of coal from a collier brig. (Ref. fms 349; 19-34)

Plate 37: A bucket dredger moored in Whitby upper harbour. Although Sutcliffe was far from enthusiastic about many of the 'improvements' brought by 'Progress', his eye was not prejudiced against seeing the momentary beauty of this massive and functional piece of machinery. Many years later he wrote: 'Today the dredger and its long chain of buckets is but a memory, though it remains in the affections and albums of many an amateur. I heard one lady amateur only yesterday remark, "I do so miss the old dredger; I was never tired of watching the buckets go round. I once tried to count those buckets," she added; "I got to two hundred and forty, and then the Parish Church clock struck twelve, and they stopped, so I never got to the end".' (*Yorkshire Weekly Post*, 26 June 1926.) (Ref. fms 368; 10-6)

Plate 38: Horace and Irene Sutcliffe—two of Frank's children—fishing for newts. The pond is at Hart Hall Farm, Glaisdale, a village in the Esk Valley approximately ten miles from Whitby. (Ref. fms 494; A-47)

Plate 39: A landscape view with three children on the banks of the beck at Sandsend. The fine detail and the idyllic rural scene remind one of the children in pastoral settings to be seen in the paintings of Myles Birket Foster (1825-99). The negative carried so much minute detail that Sutcliffe deliberately left his thumbprints on

the emulsion of the plate, over the trees in the background, in order to blur and soften a sharpness which he realised could become intrusive. It is very likely that this is an early landscape work in the 'f64' tradition. (Ref. fms 709; 9-9)

Plate 40: George Scarth with his wife Ann at 'Long Steps', Glaisdale. He is holding a scythe as he lights his pipe, but he earned his living by making 'besoms' (brooms made out of birch or ling) and 'scuttles' (oval baskets used in farm work). Sutcliffe is here following his own advice: 'When including figures in his views the photographer should take care that they are not placed in such a position as to hide "the way out" of his picture.' (Ref. fms ?; 20-48)

Plate 41: *Drinkings*; a group of haymakers at the edge of a field, probably at Lealholm Hall Farm, having 'drinkings'—the Dales term for mid-afternoon refreshment. Among the figures are 'Tailor' Bill Readman, Willie Wren and Alice Chambers. They are all very carefully not looking towards the camera. The dog was the only one of the group unable to keep still for the time exposure required. His tail is faithfully recorded, but the rest is the blurred image just to the left of the basket. A close look at what at first glance might seem to be a chance grouping of figures reveals the care and skill with which they and the minor details which make up the whole have been organised. The eye is led from the arm of the man drinking from his mug on the left to the girl dressed in light clothes carrying the basket on the right with deceptive ease. (Ref. fms ?; 20-6)

Plate 42: Two women talking by a doorway in New Way Ghaut, which was one of the many alleyways running between the houses in old Whitby. Tin Ghaut was a similar alleyway leading down to the harbour, and Sutcliffe wrote that it was 'generally crowded with artists and photographers. After noon the Sun shines into the spectacles of the former and the lenses of the latter, and as the houses on either side are very dark and the sky and the water outside are very light, few plates will stand the contrast. ... There are also many other yards and courts, but as some of these are only about three or four feet wide, it is difficult to get enough light into them to work by.' (*Yorkshire Weekly Post*, 25 July 1908.) In this instance, Sutcliffe has overcome these technical difficulties to produce a photograph which owes much of its beauty to the subdued light in the alleyway. (Ref. 533 fms; E-4)

Plate 43: Girl baiting lines. Taken *c*.1880 at Shop Alley, Runswick Bay. The young woman is Dorothy Taylor, who was to marry Thomas Patton, 2nd Cox of Runswick Lifeboat. The wives and daughters in the fishing community had to prepare the long lines for the fishermen. This involved 'mucking' (clearing old bait etc. off the hooks), 'skeining' (cleaning mussels), and baiting the hooks, as well as collecting the bait itself. The ring hanging by the window on the right was known as a 'roll' or 'wreath', and was used as a cushion to enable the fishergirls to carry heavy loads on their heads. Sutcliffe said that: 'It is no uncommon thing for bait gatherers to walk thirty miles in a day, fifteen of the thirty with heavy loads on their heads, wet through to the skin.' The women of Runswick often went as far as Robin Hood's Bay for bait. If they were lucky, they stayed overnight in Whitby on the walk there and, after collecting bait, made the long trek home the same day, while the bait was carried back to Runswick by cart.
(Ref. 32 fms; 4-8)

Plate 44: A team of three horses pulling a load of hay into the farmyard, probably at Lealholm Hall.
(Ref fms 336; 25-36)

Plate 45: Titled *The Ingathering*, taken at Four Lane Ends Farm, Whitby. In the background are Mr and Mrs John Agar, and their son Richard stands with his back to the camera. The girl in the bonnet is Annie Raw. The farm lad on the left was a 'daytal man' (that is, a man who worked and was paid by the day), who helped at farms on 'throng' (busy) days. Sutcliffe arranged the figures to his satisfaction, but was then bothered by the restlessness of the leading horse. The farm lad tried to soothe it, but it still kept moving about. Sutcliffe suggested that he should try giving it a bit of hay, and as the lad stooped down to get the hay, the horse turned and began feeding. Seizing his opportunity, Sutcliffe asked them to hold still and the picture was taken. The arrangement of this photograph is unorthodox, and its impact is derived as much from differing textures—the fuzzy outline of the pile of hay, the sharp lines of the trimmed stack, the wind-blurred foliage of the tree, and the orderly pattern of the tiled roof—as from the actions of the figures within it.
(Ref. fms ?; 24-16)

Plate 46: Deadmans Pool: the River Esk with Arncliffe Woods in the background. This photograph is an interesting example of tone control by treatment of the negative, the reverse of which has been coated with a matt varnish giving

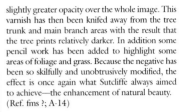

slightly greater opacity over the whole image. This varnish has then been knifed away from the tree trunk and main branch areas with the result that the tree prints relatively darker. In addition some pencil work has been added to highlight some areas of foliage and grass. Because the negative has been so skilfully and unobtrusively modified, the effect is once again what Sutcliffe always aimed to achieve—the enhancement of natural beauty.
(Ref. fms ?; A-14)

Plate 47: The interior of a Whitby jet works. Taken *c*.1890 in William Wright's works which faced onto Haggersgate, but had its display and business premises on Marine Parade. These were reputed to be the only jet works in Whitby with power-driven lathes; they were driven by gas engines (see Chapter 4 for details of the jet industry). Working conditions were not always as pleasant as the photograph shows. Matthew Snowdon, a skilled jet-worker, recalled that: 'Covered with dust from the grindstones, inhaling the grit from the stone and the fine dust from the ground jet, these men would spend ten hours a day at work, and think nothing of it. No part of jet manufacture was free from dust, but grinding was the worst of all. After being at work in the grinding shops an hour or so, you would hardly be able to distinguish one man from another, so dense was the dust.' (From *The Story of Whitby Jet* by H.P. Kendall.)

Seated round the benches from left to right are: J.E. Wilson, John William Barker, John Spence, Tom Breckon, James Moat Leck, and the boy is George Arthur Headlam. On the left wearing a hard hat is Henry Davison or Robert Headlam. Standing from left to right: John Headlam, the foreman, with his hands on the bench, John Young, John Lythe, George Robinson (second foreman), David Young, William Sutherland, and Arthur Gale.
(Ref fms 858A; 27-38)

Plate 48: Children playing what is known locally as 'jacks', a game played with a round stone or small ball and five stones. The ball was thrown into the air and the object of the game was to pick up the stones in succession before the ball hit the ground. The group is outside what was then David Storry's grocery shop at the foot of the 199 steps leading up to St Mary's Parish Church, Whitby. In the window are sweets and sticks of rock in glass jars. Sutcliffe has asked the girl facing the camera to look down at her companions. He very rarely allowed his subjects to look towards the camera, but in certain cases he made exceptions to his rule and wrote that in such photographs 'the figure is allowed to look towards the camera, for the camera may in such an instance be supposed to take the place of a friend or companion.'
(Ref. fms 302; 20-17)

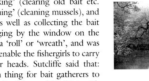

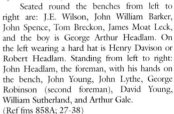

Plate 49: Titled *The Umbrella Seller.* Taken at Strickland's Yard, The Cragg, Whitby. The umbrella seller has not been identified but is said to have been an itinerant trader from Stockton-on-Tees. Mrs Esther Winspear, standing to the right of the umbrella seller, lost both her brother and father in the 1861 lifeboat disaster. The man in the doorway was Mr John Hill, a bathing machine proprietor born in about 1790. This would mean that the photograph must have been taken fairly early in Sutcliffe's career before he had fully mastered the art of handling figures so that they appeared to be posed quite naturally. The group in this photograph have been so carefully posed that they form a sort of 'tableau' of everyday life. The fishing nets hanging on the wall were known as 'shurrup nets' because of their ability to 'shurrup' (shut up) around the catch of fish. (Ref. fms ?; B-49)

Plate 50: Probably a wet-plate photograph of a thatched farmhouse in a valley. The fact that the branches of the tree to the right of the photograph have moved during the exposure proves to be an advantage, as the details of the foliage are eliminated and the eye travels into the background towards the thatched farmhouse bathed in sunlight. (Ref. 144 fms; 6-69)

Plate 51: An early wet-plate study of Rigg Mill near Whitby. The 'clouds' were worked onto the back of the negative with red opaque. An example of 'f.64' photography which produced an abundance of sharp detail. (Ref. 618 fms; 7-38)

Plate 52: Taken on Lealholm Bank, this shows a tramp with a well-known local character called Willie Wedgewood, in his 'postman's' uniform. He never was a postman, but all his life he was employed to carry messages over great distances on foot around the dales. Although he was simple-minded, he could always be relied on to deliver the message or parcel, whatever the weather, for a few pence. He collapsed on the road wearing his uniform and died at the Union Workhouse, Whitby in 1895. His obituary in the *Whitby Gazette* lamented the loss of 'the last of the local human oddities' and said: 'Nothing pleased his vanity more than to swagger about in the cast-off uniform of a postman or a soldier. He had great skill in imitating the trombones of Farndale Brass Band. He was known as the "Lealholm Express" and the "Dales Carrier". His pockets produced a medley of strange odds and ends, but nothing of value.' Sutcliffe described how the plate was taken: 'I remember once coming across two picturesque figures on the moors. They were willing to be photographed. They sat down by the roadside,

but do what I could, not a ghost of an image even at f.8 could I see on the ground glass the light was so weak, and my camera (a whole plate one) had no scale. Further down the road was a trough used for watering horses. This, if full, would reflect enough sky to focus on, and would provide a seat for the sitters, to say nothing of the help it would give them in suggesting that it was thirsty work being photographed ... There was enough water to focus by, and an exposure of sixty seconds was given, and what is more, neither of the sitters had moved a muscle.' (*Yorkshire Weekly Post,* 18 September 1909.) (Ref. fms 240; 20-10)

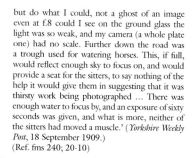

Plate 53: Sheep grazing as the sun begins to burn off the early morning mist in Eskdale. Taken at Hurricane Corner, at the top of Lealholm Bank. (Ref. fms 344; 25-37)

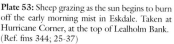

Plate 54: Titled *Dinnertime;* the ploughman is looking at his pocket-watch. Taken in Foulbriggs Field, Lealholm Hall, with Hill House Farm in the background. Charles Noel Armfield wrote of it: 'The perfection of the detail of the figures, of the plough and its tackle, of the horses and their harness, and the play of light and shade upon them are, even at first sight, so self-evident that I shall not dwell upon them, but what strikes me as so fine in the pictorial arrangement is the utter absence of all parallelism, and the fine broken wedge of dark, running from the lower left hand corner of the picture nearly up to the line of horizon, formed by the bushes, the figures and the furrows, which first of all takes the eye well into the picture and then so happily insists on "a way out"; then there is to be specially noted that most subtle effect to the right of the picture of the moist atmosphere in the ravine cutting off the one upland from the other—this is an effect very common in the moorland districts, excepting during an east wind. ... In this photograph the tone all through is perfect, and contains many lessons which artists may study with advantage.' ('Mr F.M. Sutcliffe', in *Sun Artists,* 1891.) (Ref. fms 347; 4-32)

Plate 55: Titled *Limpets. A* delightful wet-plate portrait of two barefoot Whitby girls taken by a rock on Whitby Scar, to the east of the harbour mouth, with Saltwick Nab in the background. Taken *c.*1876-80. (Ref. fms 23; 11-24)

Plate 56: An example of a group photograph taken by Sutcliffe in the course of his work as a professional photographer. (Ref. fms 422 [12 x 8 neg.]; 21-16)

Plate 57: Titled *The Flag of Distress*, this shows the brig *Mary & Agnes* being beaten by breakers on Whitby beach on 24 October 1885. She was bound for Newcastle out of London with a cargo of scrap iron, but got 'embayed', and her Master, Thomas Pearson, was unable to work off the land on either tack. With her sails blown away his ship was driven ashore. (See Chapter 7 for details of how this was taken.)
(Ref. fms 327; 10-29)

Plate 58: The Glasgow registered paddle steamer *Flying Spray* at Coffee House Corner in about 1895. Among the six cobles in the foreground is the one registered W3, which belonged to Tom Cass, the harbour pilot.
(Ref. fms ?; 7-3)

Plate 59: The ship is the *Rachel Lotinga*, a 'snow' (a variant of the brig rigged sailing ship), strikingly silhouetted at the mouth of Whitby harbour. On the left is the fluted Doric column of the lighthouse on the West Pier.
(Ref. fms 91; 10-45)

Plate 60: Titled *Black and White*. This shows a sweep and a miller sitting on a cart at the top of Flowergate, Whitby. The sweep is William Batchelor, and the miller George Hale of the Union Mill, which then stood on the West Cliff.
(Ref fms 396; B-34)

Plate 61: Bay Bank, Robin Hood's Bay. Bloomswell leads off to the left, and the road continues its one in three gradient round the double bend to cross the King's Beck and become New Road. Bay Bank was where the amateur had taken his unsuccessful photograph of a flock of sheep, which he accused Sutcliffe of spoiling (see Chapter 10).
(Ref. fms 767; C-12)

Plate 62: Jane Fordon—a Whitby girl who appears in several of Sutcliffe's studies of the fishing community—about to give Hannah Ledley a piggy-back ride. The photograph has been carefully posed, and was probably taken on Whitby Scar. The background has been deliberately thrown out of focus to concentrate attention on the figures.
(Ref. fms 250; B-48)

Plate 63: Ann and Isaac Scarth—the parents of George Scarth the besom-maker—at the door of Rock Head Cottage, Glaisdale. She is holding a huge cabbage, and he is reading the *Whitby Gazette*—Sutcliffe always liked to show some reason for the figures in his photographs to be placed as they were. On another occasion he had asked an old farmer who was posing with his wife outside their cottage if he would read a newspaper as an excuse for sitting at the doorway: 'Yes, a newspaper would do very well, but there was not one in the house. The photographer had one, however, in his pocket, which he unfolded and handed to the old farmer, to read. The group was taken. In a few days it was all over the village that Mr S., the photographer, had taken old Jimmy Longstaff reading the newspaper upside down. Jimmy thought they were laughing at him, but everyone in the village knew that Jimmy could neither read nor write, though his stocking was well filled. The photographer had focused on the lettering of the newspaper, but he had not noticed the letters were the right way up on the ground glass.' (*Amateur Photographer*, 6 March 1902.)
(Ref. fms109; B-36)

Plate 64: 'Boardie Willie'—a sandwich-board man photographed in the 1890s at Coffee House Corner, Whitby. He is thought to be George Ventress of Carter Yard, The Cragg. This is an example of Sutcliffe posing a subject for comic effect.
(Ref. 60 fms; 18-35)

Notes to the Text

Abbreviations used in the notes:
fms: Frank Meadow Sutcliffe
YWP: Frank Sutcliffe writing in his column 'Photography Notes' in the *Yorkshire Weekly Post*
Am Phot: *Amateur Photographer*
Brit Journ Phot: *British Journal of Photography*

Chapter 1: Childhood

1. fms, *Whitby Prints*, ed. Thomas H. English (Whitby, 1931), Vol. II, section P- 4.
2. Charles Noel Armfield, 'Mr F.M. Sutcliffe', *Sun Artists*, No. 8, July 1891, ed. W.A. Boord, p.55.
3. *YWP*, 6 November 1915.
4. fms, 'Factors in My Success', *The Photogram*, April 1902, p.107.
5. *Ibid.*
6. fms, 'Concerning Fog', *Am Phot*, 28 May 1903, p.433.
7. John Ruskin, 'Academy Notes 1858, New Society of Painters in Watercolours', *The Works of John Ruskin*, ed. Cook and Wedderburn (London, 1904), Vol. XIV, p.193.
8. fms, 'The Sutcliffe Exhibition in the Camera Club Rooms', *The Journal of the Camera Club*, Vol. II, November 1888, pp.151-3.
9. Thomas Sutcliffe, 'Keys to Spiritual Problems', Rev. W. Baker and Thomas Sutcliffe (London, 1870), p.176.
10. *YWP*, 30 March 1929.
11. Lake Price, *A Manual of Photographic Manipulation Treating of the Practice of the Art and its various applications to Nature* (second edition, London, 1868), pp.4-6.

Chapter 2: Early Ventures in Photography

1. *YWP*, 2 August 1924.
2. *YWP*, 12 March 1910.
3. fms, *Whitby Prints*, ed. Thomas H. English (Whitby, 1931), Vol. II, section P.4.
4. *YWP*, 12 July 1919.
5. Rev. F.C. Lambert, 'The Pictorial Work of Frank M. Sutcliffe', *The Practical Photographer*, No. 8, May 1904, pp.2-3.
6. fms, 'The Sutcliffe Exhibition in the Camera Club Rooms', *The Journal of the Camera Club*, Vol. II, November 1888, pp.151-3.
7. fms, 'Factors in My Success', *The Photogram*, April 1902, p.107.
8. *Punch* (Vol. 33), 19 September 1857, p.118.
9. *YWP*, 17 January 1914.

10. *YWP*, 18 June 1927.
11. *YWP*, 5 March 1927.
12. *YWP*, 22 May 1909.
13. *YWP*, 21 March 1908.
14. *YWP*, 7 July 1923.
15. *YWP*, 27 February 1926.
16. fms, 'Practical Jokes', *Am Phot*, 2 January 1906, p.2.
17. fms, 'Photographer to John Ruskin', *The Photographic Journal*, June 1931, pp.255-6.
18. *Ibid.*
19. No author given, 'A Lake-side Home: Brantwood', *The Art Journal*, November 1881, p.353.
20. fms, 'A Day's Sunshine at Brantwood', *Am Phot*, 9 February 1900, pp.107-8.
21. *Ibid.*
22. fms, 'When John Ruskin Trembled', *The Photographic Journal*, November 1937, pp.604-5.
23. fms, *The Photographic Journal*, June 1931, pp.255-6.
24. fms, *Am Phot*, 9 February 1900, pp.107-8.
25. *YWP*, 2 June 1928.
26. fms, *The Photographic Journal*, November 1937, pp.604-5.

Chapter 3: The Failure of a Society Photographer

1. J. Radford Thomson, *Pelton's Shilling Illustrated Guide to Tunbridge Wells* (Tunbridge Wells, 1888), p.2.
2. *Ibid.* pp.47-8.
3. fms, 'The Sutcliffe Exhibition in the Camera Club Rooms', *The Journal of the Camera Club*, Vol. II, November 1888, pp.151-3.
4. All details of local photographers taken from the *Tunbridge Wells Gazette, Tonbridge Chronicle, and Weald of Kent and Sussex Advertiser*, various dates: 19 March 1875 to 31 March 1876.
5. *Brit Journ Phot*, 12 September 1873, p.515.
6. *YWP*, 16 March 1918.
7. *YWP*, 22 June 1918.
8. fms, introduction to *Whitby Writers 1867-1949*, ed. Marion Keighley (Whitby, 1957).
9. *YWP*, 27 September 1924.

10. Robert Tate Gaskin, *The Old Seaport of Whitby* (Whitby, 1909), p.357.
11. fms, introduction to *Whitby Writers 1867-1949*, ed. Marion Keighley (Whitby, 1957).
12. Andrew Pringle, 'Whitby', *The Photographic News*, 13 October 1893, pp.643-4.
13. *Ward Lock Guide to Whitby*, c.1890, p.6.
14. Andrew Pringle, 'Whitby', *The Photographic News*, 13 October 1893, pp.643-4.
15. *Whitby Gazette*, 18 September 1886.

Chapter 4: The Trials of a Portrait Photographer

1. W. J. Warren, 'F. M. Sutcliffe of Whitby. An Appreciation and some Examples of his Work', *Am Phot*, 15 June 1900, pp.470-1.
2. *YWP*, 28 September 1918.
3. *YWP*, 29 May 1915.
4. fms, 'How to Catch Flies', *The Brit Journ Phot Almanac*, 1897, pp.734-5.
5. fms, 'Photographer to John Ruskin', *The Photographic Journal*, June 1931, pp.255-6.
6. *YWP*, 12 July 1913.
7. *YWP*, 25 January 1930.
8. *YWP*, 30 May 1908.
9. fms, 'To Parents and Guardians', *Am Phot*, 12 July 1901, pp.31-2.
10. *YWP*, 25 September 1909.
11. fms, 'The Sutcliffe Exhibition in the Camera Club Rooms', *The Journal of the Camera Club*, Vol. II, November 1888, pp.151-3.
12. fms, 'Pictorial Portraiture', *Am Phot*, 25 August 1899, p.143.
13. fms, 'Lighting the Sitter', *Photography*, 4 May 1893, pp.269-70.
14. fms, 'On Photographic Portraiture Yesterday and Today', *Am Phot*, 29 September 1899, pp.249-50.
15. *YWP*, 28 November 1908.
16. fms, 'On Photographic Portraiture Yesterday and Today', *Am Phot*, 29 September 1899, pp.249-50.
17. fms, 'Old Backgrounds', *Am Phot*, 26 December 1901.
18. fms, 'Under the Skylight,' *Photography*, 17 November 1892, pp.722-3.

19. fms, 'On Winking', *Am Phot*, 26
December 1901, p.262.
20. fms, 'Under the Skylight', *Photography*,
17 November 1892, pp.722-3.
21. *YWP*, 1 August 1908.
22. *YWP*, 14 March 1914.
23. *YWP*, 16 March 1918.
24. *Whitby Gazette*, reprinted in *Brit Journ
Phot*, 7 December 1894.
25. fms, 'Pictorial Portraiture', *Am Phot*, 25
August 1899, p.143.
26. fms, 'On Chairs', *Am Phot*, 3 August
1900, p.90.
27. fms, 'On Likeness Taking', *Am Phot*, 3
May 1901, p.355.
28. *YWP*, 23 December 1911.

Chapter 5: 'The Pictorial Boswell of Whitby'

1. Harold Hood, 'Sutcliffe of Whitby', *Brit
Journ Phot*, 5 January 1923, p.4.
2. *YWP*, 30 June 1928.
3. *YWP*, 8 March 1919.
4. *YWP*, 10 February 1912.
5. fms, 'On Out-Door Photography and on
Printing', *The Year-book of Photography
and Photographic News Almanac for
1875*, ed. G. Wharton Simpson, p.70.
6. fms, 'A Charming Sitter', Am *Phot*, 19
November 1903, p.407.
7. fms, 'Under the Skylight', *Photography*,
17 November 1892, pp.722-3.
8. *YWP*, 3 May 1913.
9. *YWP*, 26 August 1916.
10. *YWP*, 8 October 1910.
11. fms, 'On Faith', *Am Phot*, 13 November
1902, p.383.
12. *YWP*, 25 July 1908.
13. *YWP*, 18 November 1916.
14. *YWP*, 29 November 1924.
15. *YWP*, 13 October 1928.
16. *YWP*, 21 January 1922.
17. *YWP*, 7 May 1927.
18. *YWP*, 7 August 1909.
19. Lake Price, *op. cit.*, pp.4-6.
20. *YWP*, 3 April 1915.
21. *YWP*, 20 August 1910.
22. *YWP*, 3 March 1923.
23. *YWP*, 30 May 1914.
24. *YWP*, 5 August 1911.
25. *YWP*, 9 March 1912.
26. *YWP*, 28 August 1926.
27. *YWP*, 20 September 1919.
28. *YWP*, 31 March 1923.
29. *YWP*, 7 April 1923.
30. *YWP*, 14 August 1926.
31. *YWP*, 27 June 1908.
32. *YWP*, 9 March 1912.

Chapter 6: Sutcliffe's Style (i)

1. *YWP*, 28 September 1912.
2. *YWP*, 28 January 1911.
3. *YWP*, 3 February 1912.
4. *YWP*, 23 February 1924.
5. *YWP*, 11 June 1910.
6. fms, 'On Figure Photography', *Camera
Notes*, Vol. V, 1901, pp.15-16.
7. *Whitby Times*, 17 June 1887.
8. fms, 'The Sutcliffe Exhibition in the
Camera Club Rooms', *The Journal of the
Camera Club*, Vol. II, November 1888,
pp.151-3.
9. fms, letter to Harold Hood, 8 May 1930,
printed in *The Photographic Journal*,
August 1942, pp.293-4.
10. No author given, *Brit Journ Phot*, 22
October 1886, p.665.
11. Transcript of taped interview with Mr
Locker by Bill Eglon Shaw, 5 January
1968.
12. No author given, 'The Nude in Photography: With Some Studies Taken in
the Open Air', *The Studio*, Vol. I, 1893,
pp.104-6.
13. *Whitby Times*, 22 July 1887.
14. fms, 'On Figure Photography', *Camera
Notes*, Vol. V, 1901, pp.17-18.
15. *Brit Journ Phot*, 20 April 1894, p.244.
16. fms, letter to Harold Hood, 8 May 1930,
The Photographic Journal, August 1942,
pp.293-4.
17. 'The Spirit of the Times', *Photography*, 17
December 1891, p.820.

Chapter 7: Sutcliffe's Style (ii)

1. *YWP*, 27 July 1912.
2. *YWP*, 9 January 1915.
3. *YWP*, 2 May 1908.
4. *YWP*, 24 June 1911.
5. Lake Price, *op. cit.*, pp.189-90.
6. *YWP*, 19 July 1913.
7. *YWP*, 30 October 1920.
8. *YWP*, 12 December 1908.
9. fms, 'Intentions', *Am Phot*, 17 October
1905, p.314.
10. *YWP*, 14 September 1912.
11. *YWP*, 27 May 1922.
12. Rev. F.C. Lambert, 'The Pictorial Work
of Frank M. Sutcliffe', *The Practical
Photographer*, No. 8, May 1904, pp.2-3.
13. fms, 'A Note on Colour', *Am Phot*, 11
December 1902, p.472.
14. *YWP*, 27 June 1908.
15. *YWP*, 27 March 1909.
16. *YWP*, 23 March 1912.
17. *YWP*, 11 April 1914.
18. *YWP*, 28 March 1908.

19. *YWP*, 6 December 1913.
20. fms, 'Photography at the Seaside', read
at the Photographic Convention, Leeds,
1896, *Am Phot*, 24 July 1896, p.68.
21. fms, 'Concerning the Wind', *Am Phot*,
14 May 1903, pp.394-5.
22. *YWP*, 4 December 1920.
23. J.L. Hankey, 'The Frank M. Sutcliffe
Memorial Lecture', *The Photographic
Journal*, August 1942, p.286.

Chapter 8: Photography – 'Art's Youngest and
Fairest Child'

1. Attrib. to Joseph Durham, ARA, *The
Photographic Journal*, 21 February 1857.
2. *YWP*, 31 May 1913.
3. *YWP*, 30 September 1911.
4. *YWP*, 16 September 1916.
5. *YWP*, 25 December 1909.
6. *YWP*, 12 September 1925.
7. Rev. F.C. Lambert, 'The Pictorial Work
of Frank M. Sutcliffe', *The Practical
Photographer*, No. 8, May 1904, pp.2-3.
8. *YWP*, 22 August 1908.
9. fms, 'Landscape with Figures', *The
Practical Photographer*, No. 11, August
1904, p.42.
10. fms, 'The Camera in the Country', *Am
Phot*, 12 January 1909, p.39.
11. *YWP*, 15 September 1923.
12. Henry Naegely (Henry Gaëlyn), *J.F.
Millet and Rustic Art* (London, 1898),
p.59.
13. George Clausen, *Jules Bastien-Lepage as
Artist*, pp.112-13, published with *Jules
Bastien-Lepage and his Art. A Memoir*,
Andre Theuriet (London, 1892).
14. Alice Meynell, 'Newlyn', *The Art Journal*,
1889, p.98.
15. fms, 'Photography at the Seaside', *Am
Phot*, 24 July 1896, p.68.
16. Grant Allen, writing about Hastings, 'On
and Off Shore', *The Art Journal*, 1883,
pp.286-7.
17. Lillias Wasserman, 'Some Fisher Folk',
The Art Journal, 1887, p.58.
18. *YWP*, 16 December 1911.
19. *Am Phot*, 3 July 1891, p.16.
20. P. H. Emerson, *Naturalistic Photography
for Students of the Art* (London, 1889),
p.247.
21. John E. Austin, 'Holidays with the
Camera', *Am Phot* (supplement), 1891,
p.9.
22. *YWP*, 9 April 1927.
23. *Am Phot*, 20 July 1894 (supplement on
the Photographic Convention), p.41.

Chapter 9: New Movements in Photography

and Painting

1. *YWP*, 14 January 1928.
2. fms, 'A Romance of Two Worlds', *Am Phot*, 13 February 1902, p.131.
3. *YWP*, 19 February 1910.
4. fms, 'A Romance of Two Worlds,' *Am Phot*, 13 February 1902, p.131.
5. *YWP*, 12 July 1913.
6. *YWP*, 24 October 1914.
7. *YWP*, 19 September 1925.
8. W. J. Laidlay, *The Origin and First Two Years of the New English Art Club* (London, 1907), p.3.
9. Francis Bate, 'The Naturalistic School of Painting', Part I, *The Artist*, 1 March 1886, p.68.
10. P.H. Emerson, 'The Ideal Photographic Exhibition', *Am Phot*, 23 October 1885, p.462.
11. fms, 'The Worship of Technique', *Photography*, 26 July 1894, p.466.
12. Francis Bate, 'The Naturalistic School of Painting', Part VIII, *The Artist*, 1 October 1886, p.308.
13. P.H. Emerson, *Naturalistic Photography for Students of the Art* (London, 1889), p.150.
14. No author given, 'Naturalistic Focusing', *Brit Journ Phot*, 22 February 1895, p.114.
15. P.H. Emerson, 'The Present State of the Focus Question: Another View', *Am Phot*, 24 October 1890, p.289.
16. *YWP*, 11 June 1921.
17. P.H. Emerson, *Naturalistic Photography for Students of the Art* (London, 1889), p.117.
18. fms, letter to the Editors, *Am Phot*, 8 November 1889, p.303.
19. P.H. Emerson, 'Naturalistic Photography', *Brit Journ Phot*, 7 April 1893, p.212.
20. Philip H. Newman, 'Imagining and Imaging', *Am Phot*, 11 July 1890, p.30.
21. H.P. Robinson, *Picture Making By Photography* (second edition, London, 1889). Extract reprinted *Brit Journ Phot*, 16 August 1889, pp.542-3.
22. G. Davison, letter to the editor, *Brit Journ Phot*, 13 September 1889, p.611.
23. 'Wide-Angle' review of the exhibition of the Photographic Society, *The Photographic News*, 3 October 1890, p.759.

24. fms, 'How to Look at Photographs', *The Photographic News*, 29 July 1892, pp.489-90.
25. *YWP*, 4 April 1908.
26. No author given, review of the New English Art Club exhibition, *Am Phot*, 11 April 1890, p.252.
27. Reviewer not named; quoted in 'The Linked Ring', Joseph T. Keiley, *Camera Notes*, Vol. V, 1901, p.115.
28. fms, '"To Be," Manipulated, "Or Not to Be", That is the Question', *Photography*, 9 January 1896, p.18.
29. *YWP*, 26 June 1909.

Chapter 10: Whitby

1. *Whitby Gazette*, reprinted *Brit Journ Phot*, 7 December 1894.
2. fms, reported in *Am Phot*, 23 December 1892, p.461.
3. G. Davison, to the editor, *The Photographic News*, 5 October 1888, p.637.
4. No author given, review of 'The Sutcliffe Exhibition at the Camera Club', *Am Phot*, 19 October 1888, pp.249-50.
5. fms, 'To Parents and Guardians', *Am Phot*, 12 July 1901, pp.31-2.
6. fms, 'An Opportunity Lost', *Am Phot*, 14 September 1900, p.211.
7. W.J. Warren, 'F.M. Sutcliffe of Whitby. An Appreciation and some examples of his work', *Am Phot*, 15 July 1900, p.472.
8. fms, 'The Professional with Artistic Instincts', *The Practical Photographer*, March 1897, pp.68-9.
9. fms, 'How to Look at Photographs', *The Photographic News*, 29 July 1892, pp.489-90.
10. fms, 'The Five Senses', *Am Phot*, 11 December 1906, p.519.
11. No author given, review of the Photographic Society exhibition, *Brit Journ Phot*, 11 October 1889, p.665.
12. No author given, review of the Keighley exhibition, *Am Phot*, 17 January 1890, p.35.
13. fms, 'Stagnation', *Am Phot*, 28 November 1901, p.429.
14. fms, 'The Photographer's Mecca', *Am Phot*, 14 August 1906, p.139.
15. *YWP*, 24 September 1927.
16. *YWP*, 19 July 1913.
17. *YWP*, 29 August 1908.

18. *YWP*, 12 May 1923.
19. *YWP*, 5 July 1924.
20. fms, 'A Chapter on Laughter', *Am Phot*, 6 March 1902, p.189.
21. fms, 'A Fisherman's Yarn', *Am Phot*, 19 February 1903, p.146.
22. *YWP*, 26 March 1910.
23. fms, 'Snap Shots', *Photography*, 11 November 1897, p.707.
24. fms, 'My Kodak's Second Birthday', *Am Phot*, 30 March 1900, pp.256-7.
25. *YWP*, 22 July 1911.
26. *YWP*, 4 September 1909.
27. fms, 'All Work and No Play', *Am Phot*, 8 December 1899, pp.450-1.
28. fms, 'My Kodak's Second Birthday', *Am Phot*, 30 March 1900, pp.256-7.
29. fms, 'Striking a Bargain: An Old Custom Still Alive', *Am Phot*, 26 June 1902, pp.521-2.
30. fms, autobiographical note prob. *c*.1940, *Whitby Writers, op. cit.*

Chapter 11: Epilogue

1. *YWP*, 15 April 1916.
2. Irene Sutcliffe, 'Frank M. Sutcliffe, Hon. FRPS, Some Reminiscences', *The Photographic Journal*, December 1942, p.398.
3. *YWP*, 9 March 1912.
4. *YWP* 28 February 1914.
5. fms, 'The Photographer's Mecca', *Am Phot*, 14 August 1906, p.139.
6. *YWP*, 14 August 1926.
7. fms, 'Fisher Folk', *Am Phot*, 7 July 1904, p.11.
8 *YWP*, 3 May 1913.
9. *YWP*, 4 June 1921.
10. *YWP*, 2 April 1910.
11. fms, 'A Letter from Mecca', *The Photographic Journal*, August 1942, p.292, given as written in 1920, but more likely written 1905-6.
12. fms, 'On Amateurs', *Am Phot*, 1 October 1903, p.269.
13. fms, introduction to *Whitby Writers 1867-1949*, ed. Marion Keighley (Whitby, 1957).
14. *YWP*, 12 July 1913.
15. *YWP*, 21 November 1908.
16. fms, 'Art and Photography', *Photography*, 7 May 1891, p.290.

Select Bibliography

BY FRANK SUTCLIFFE

Sutcliffe first contributed a short piece to the *Year Book of Photography and Photographic News Almanac* in 1875 and went on to write a great many articles on photography. He was an 'editorial contributor' to *Photography* and wrote many leading articles in the 1890s. Between 1895 and 1913 *The Amateur Photographer* carried a large number of articles by Sutcliffe, often illustrated with his photographs. Sutcliffe also contributed to *The Practical Photographer*, *The Photogram*, *Camera Notes* and many other periodicals. From 1908 to 1930 he wrote a weekly newspaper column entitled 'Photography Notes' for *The Yorkshire Weekly Post*.

See also his introduction to *Whitby Writers* 1867-1949, edited by Marion Keighley (Whitby, 1957). Sutcliffe's autobiographical reminiscences were probably written in about 1940.

ABOUT FRANK SUTCLIFFE

Armfield, Charles Noel, 'Mr F.M. Sutcliffe,' in *Sun Artists* (edited by W.A. Boord), No. 8, July 1891, pp.55-60.

Frank, Peter, 'History and Photographs: Frank Meadow Sutcliffe of Whitby (1853-1941)', *History Workshop*, No. 2 (Autumn 1976), pp.93-5.

Hankey, J.L., 'The Frank M. Sutcliffe Memorial Lecture', *The Photographic Journal*, August 1942, pp.280-91.

Hiley, Michael, *Frank Meadow Sutcliffe*, Aperture, Millerton, New York, 1979.

Shaw, Bill Eglon, 'Sutcliffe of Whitby', *Creative Camera*, March 1968, pp.100-3.

Warren, W.J., 'F.M. Sutcliffe of Whitby. An Appreciation and Some Examples of His Work', *The Amateur Photographer*, June 15, 1900, pp.470-73.

SELECTIONS OF SUTCLIFFE'S PHOTOGRAPHS

Shaw, Bill Eglon (compiled by), *Frank Meadow Sutcliffe, Photographer. A Selection of his Work*. The Sutcliffe Gallery, Whitby, 1974

Shaw, Bill Eglon (compiled by), *Frank Meadow Sutcliffe, A Second Selection*. The Sutcliffe Gallery, Whitby, 1978

Shaw, Michael (compiled by), *Frank Meadow Sutcliffe, Photographer. A third selection*. The Sutcliffe Gallery, Whitby, 1990

Shaw, Michael (compiled by), *Frank Meadow Sutcliffe, Hon F.R.P.S. (1853-1941). A fourth selection*. The Sutcliffe Gallery, Whitby, 1998

Shaw, Michael, *Every Now and Then*, The Sutcliffe Gallery, Whitby, 2002

OTHER PHOTOGRAPHERS AND PAINTERS

Fox, Caroline and Greenacre, Francis, *Artists of the Newlyn School* 1880-1900, Newlyn Orion Galleries, 1979

Harker, Margaret, *The Linked Ring; The Secession Movement in Photography in Britain*, 1892-1910, William Heinemann, London, 1979

Phillips, Peter, *The Staithes Group*, Phillips & Sons, Nottingham, 1993

Richardson, G., *T. Watson, Photographer of Lythe, near Whitby*, Est. 1892, The Lampada Press, 1992

Robertson, Alexander, *Atkinson Grimshaw*, Phaidon Press, Oxford, 1988

Wilmerding, John, *Winslow Homer*, Praeger, New York, 1972

ABOUT THE WHITBY AREA AND THE FISHING COMMUNITY

Atkinson, Rev. J.C., *Forty Years in a Moorland Parish; Reminiscences and Researches in Danby in Cleveland*, Macmillan, London, 1891

Barker, Malcolm, *Portrait of a Lifeboat Hero; The Story of Henry Freeman of Whitby*, Smith Settle, Otley, 2000

Farnill, Barrie, *A History of Robin Hood's Bay; The Story of a Yorkshire Community*, revised edition, North York Moors National Park, 1990

Frank, Peter, *Yorkshire Fisherfolk; A social history of the Yorkshire inshore fishing community*, Phillimore, Chichester, 2002

Gaskin, John and Stamp, Cordelia, *Whitby Yards*, Cordelia Stamp, Whitby, 1990

(Horne & Son), *Horne's (Official) Guide to Whitby*, ninth edition, Horne and Son, Whitby, 1904, reprinted by Caedmon of Whitby, 1993

Howard, John, *Staithes; Chapters from the History of a Seafaring Town*, John Howard, Scarborough, 2000

Humble, A.F., *The Rowing Life Boats of Whitby*, Horne and Son, Whitby, 1974

Kendall, Hugh P., *The Story of Whitby Jet; Its Workers from Earliest Times*, Whitby Literary and Philosophical Society, 1936

Minter, Ian and Shill, Ray, *Storm Warrior; The Turbulent Life of Henry Freeman*, Heartlands Press, Birmingham, 1991

Storm, Alan, *Storm and Company*, Caedmon of Whitby, 1993

Tindale, John, *Fishing out of Whitby*, Dalesman Books, Clapham, 1987

White, Andrew, *A History of Whitby*, Phillimore, Chichester, 2004

Index

Page numbers in *italic* indicate an illustration on that text page,
as distinct from the sequence of numbered Plates.